The Written World of God

Also available from Anqa Publishing

Ibn ʿArabī: The Alchemy of Human Happiness: *fī maʿrifat kīmiyāʾ al-saʿāda*
Translated & edited by Stephen Hirtenstein

Ibn ʿArabī: Prayers for the Week – the Seven Days of the Heart:
Awrād al-usbūʿ
Translated & edited by Pablo Beneito & Stephen Hirtenstein

Ibn ʿArabī: Contemplation of the Holy Mysteries: *Mashāhid al-asrār*
Translated by Cecilia Twinch & Pablo Beneito

Ibn ʿArabī: The Universal Tree and the Four Birds: *al-Ittiḥād al-kawnī*
Translated & edited by Angela Jaffray

Ibn ʿArabī: A Prayer for Spiritual Elevation and Protection: *al-Dawr al-aʿlā*
Study, translation, transliteration & Arabic text by Suha Taji-Farouki

Ibn ʿArabī: The Four Pillars of Spiritual Transformation: *Ḥilyat al-abdāl*
Translated & edited by Stephen Hirtenstein

Ibn ʿArabī: The Secrets of Voyaging: *Kitāb al-Isfār ʿan natāʾij al-asfār*
Translated & edited by Angela Jaffray

The Unlimited Mercifier: The Spiritual Life and Thought of Ibn ʿArabī
Stephen Hirtenstein

Ibn ʿArabi and Modern Thought: The History of Taking Metaphysics Seriously
Peter Coates

Ibn al-ʿArabī and the Sufis
Binyamin Abrahamov

The Nightingale in the Garden of Love: the Poems of Üftade, by Paul Ballanfat
Translated from French by Angela Culme-Seymour

The Lamp of Mysteries: A Commentary on the Light Verse of the Quran
Translated & edited by Bilal Kuşpınar

The Teachings of a Perfect Master: An Islamic Saint for the Third Millennium
Henry Bayman

The Written World of God

The Cosmic Script and the Art of Ibn ʿArabī

by

DUNJA RAŠIĆ

ANQA PUBLISHING • OXFORD

Published by Anqa Publishing PO Box 1178
Oxford OX2 8YS, UK www.anqa.co.uk

First published 2021

A CIP catalogue record for this book is available from the British Library

ISBN 978 1 905937 68 4

Cover design by Andrew Meaden

Typesetting by Ben Jarlett

Contents

THE WRITTEN WORLD OF GOD
The Cosmic Script and the Art of Ibn ʿArabī

Acknowledgements vii
Transcription and Transliteration System viii
List of Symbols and Abbreviations ix
PART ONE The Cosmic Script
1.1. Introduction 3
1.2. The Letters and the Science of Letters 20
1.3. The Path of Reflection and the Path of Revelation 42
PART TWO The Act Of Genesis
2.1. The Breath of the All-Merciful 67
2.2. The Isolated *Alif* (ا) as the Divine Essence 86
2.3. The Creator and the Created, as Symbolized by the Cherubim Letters and the Star of *Lām-Alif* (لا) 94
2.4. Image of the Primordial Cloud and All It Contains: *Hamza* and Its Elongations 114
2.5. The Throne and the Heavenly Spheres 134
2.6. *Ẓāʾ*, *Thāʾ*, *Dhāl*, *Fāʾ*, *Bāʾ* and *Mīm*: the Six Kingdoms 184
2.7. Conquest of the Great City: the Letter *Wāw* and the Step-levels of Spiritual Development 198
List of Tables 204
List of Figures 205
Bibliography 211
Index 222

Acknowledgements

I thank all those who commented on my initial drafts. My indispensable collaborator throughout was my husband, Alexander Stahl, whose knowledge, patience and artistic talent have contributed more to this book than I could ever describe.

I am grateful to Feyzullah Yılmaz, who helped me gain access to precious manuscripts in Ibn ʿArabī's hand when all hope seemed to be lost – and to Wail Diaa Chouiha, who helped me read through the text whenever the lines got blurry.

But most of all, I owe my gratitude to the shaykh Sidi Muhammad Laid Tijani, *Perennia Verba* and Sufis of the Tijani Zawiya in Tamacine for encouraging me to make the first steps of the writing process – and to Pablo Beneito and Stephen Hirtenstein of Anqa Publishing, for successfully leading me through it. Their enthusiasm and support were wonderfully heartening.

Transcription and Transliteration System

Name	*Orthographic symbol*	*Transliteration system*
Alif	ا	ā
Bā'	ب	b
Tā'	ت	t
Thā'	ث	th
Jīm	ج	j
Ḥā'	ح	ḥ
Khā'	خ	kh
Dāl	د	d
Dāl	ذ	dh
Rā'	ر	r
Zāy	ز	z
Sīn	س	s
Shīn	ش	sh
Ṣād	ص	ṣ
Ḍād	ض	ḍ
Ṭā'	ط	ṭ
Ẓā'	ظ	ẓ
'Ayn	ع	'
Ghayn	غ	gh
Fā'	ف	f
Qāf	ق	q
Kāf	ك	k
Lām	ل	l
Mīm	م	m
Nūn	ن	n
Hā'	هـ	h
Wāw	و	w
Yā'	ي	y

List of Symbols and Abbreviations

Sifr.	*al-Futūḥāt al-Makkiyya*, Evkaf Müzesi 1845+
Fut.	*al-Futūḥāt al-Makkiyya*, Dār al-Kutub al-Ilmiyya, 2011
al-Manṣūb	*al-Futūḥāt Al-Makkiyya,* ed. ʿAbd Al-ʿAzīz Sulṭān Al-Manṣūb, 2010
FM	*al-Futūḥāt al-Makkiyya*, Beirut, n.d
fol.	folio
pl.	plural
sg.	singular
Ar.	Arabic
Eng.	English

PART ONE
THE COSMIC SCRIPT

Existence is a letter, you are its meaning.
And in creatures I have no hope – other than Him.

Ibn 'Arabī[1]

1 Ibn 'Arabī, *The Meccan Revelations* vol.2, p.127.

1

THE COSMIC SCRIPT

1.1. Introduction

Apart from God, Ibn ʿArabī believed, a man can speak, an angel can speak and a jinni can speak. However, human beings are the only ones with the potential to come to terms with the secret properties of letters. The science of letters (*ʿilm al-ḥurūf*) represents one of the central elements of Ibn ʿArabī's teachings. Until today, it also tends to be perceived as one of his most abstruse. Ibn ʿArabī identified the science of letters as familiarity with letters, the Qur'anic revelation and everything in the world of nature. To study the letters was to follow the visual signs pointing to the mysteries of existence.[2] In many ways, this book is a commentary on, and an exposition of this statement. Ibn ʿArabī's impact on Islamic intellectual history was extensive, a fact that is reflected in the continuing scholarly interest in his works. Nevertheless, a comprehensive study on his contributions to the Islamic science of letters has never been systematically undertaken. The absence of such discussions is regrettable as Ibn ʿArabī's meditations on language and letters, even when analysed on their own, apart from other elements of his teachings, offer a comprehensive insight into his notions of the world and its Creator.

In the Akbarian tradition, the world was perceived as everything other than God (*kull mā siwā Allāh*).[3] In accordance with the Islamic

2 Ibn ʿArabī's magnum opus *The Meccan Revelations* (*al-Futūḥāt al-Makkiyya*) was also intended to serve the same purpose. *Fut.*I:94; al-Manṣūb, 1/187; *FM.*I:57.

3 al-Qayṣarī, *Foundations of Islamic Mysticism*, p. 118. See also De Cillis, *Free Will and Predestination in Islamic Thought*, p. 178.

normative tradition, Ibn ʿArabī held that the world is a product of God's speech. In his works, the world is commonly compared to a book inscribed on parchment unrolled (*al-raqq al-manshūr*). While the face of this parchment was thought to contain the Most Beautiful Names of God, its lower side stands for the world of nature.[4] From this perspective, the act of genesis unfolds as ontological speech and writing. As early as the ninth century CE, grammarians of the Baghdad school believed they had found correspondences between the rules and regulations of Arabic grammar and the laws that govern the structure and nature of the universe. In the eyes of the early Arab grammarians, Arabic was a pure, flawless language, whose origins were traditionally perceived as divine. In Islamic culture, theories of the divine origins of the language were primarily based on 1) the Qurʾanic revelation and 2) the presumed qualities of Classical Arabic. The overview of arguments these theories have been based upon was compiled by al-Suyūṭī (d. 911/1505) in the fifteenth century CE:

> [Abū al-Aswad] al-Duʾalī stated that if the language was not the achievement of God, it would either have to be a product of agreement between the people or an invention of a single man. However, no one in his generation or in generations before his time has ever heard of an agreement and/or invention such as this – not even men as competent as the companions of the Prophet. Hence, language must have appeared with the appearance of the first human being in the world and it must have been created by God. (…) Abū ʿAlī al-Fārisī, God have mercy on him, said to me one day: 'it (i.e the Arabic language) comes from God' and he based his argument on the words of the Exalted One: 'He taught Adam the names, all of them.' This leaves no space for contradiction as it is possible that the interpretation of these words is 'He (i.e. God) enabled Adam to start it (the language)'. Therefore, the idea that the language comes from God, praise be to Him, leaves no place for doubts. Even if a contradiction was to occur, it would inevitably crumble with the help of this argument.[5]

4 *Fut.*I:158, 551. al-Manṣūb, 1/187; *FM.*I:101,366.

5 Quoted according to Czapkiewicz, *The Views of the Medieval Arab Philologists on Language and its Origins*, pp.26, 46. Among the early Arab grammarians, a rare opposition to the theory of the divine origins of language came from al-Sirāfī, who believed that the origins of the Arabic language are to be sought in the human soul instead. See al-Sirāfī, *Sharḥ Kitāb Sībawayh* vol.3, p. 124.

In Islamic intellectual history, grammarians, philosophers and religious scholars have been actively trying to come to terms with the properties of the Arabic language and its relation to thought and reality. Ignorant people have no clue on the importance of grammatical analyses, noted Ibn ʿArabī on the matter.[6] Seven centuries later, a similar stand was advocated by Louis Massignon. 'It is useless to examine the works of Muslim mystics,' Massignon wrote, 'unless one has studied very closely the mechanism of Arabic grammar, lexicography, morphology, syntax.'[7] In reverence for the spoken and written language, Sufis have been long known for their habit of salvaging every scrap piece of paper with the Arabic letters on it, in fear of its power being desecrated otherwise. According to Annemarie Schimmel, this custom survived in Bengali rural areas even today.[8]

Originally proposed by grammarians of the Baghdad school,[9] popular analogies between the rules and regulations of the Arabic grammar and the structure and nature of the universe subsequently led Sufis to identify nature studies as the reading of a macrocosmic book. Apart from the universe, the great book of the macrocosm, Sufi works on the science of letters equally focused on the physiognomy and nature of human beings (i.e. on the microcosm) and the text of the Qurʾanic revelation. These were the main research objects of the Islamic science of letters, which are traditionally referred to as the three great books. Sufis like al-Tirmidhī (d. 279/892) maintained the belief that familiarity with the content of the three great books could be achieved through familiarity with the letters of the Arabic alphabet. 'Contained in the

6 *Fut.*I:165; al-Manṣūb, 1/334; *FM.*I:106.

7 Massignon, *The Passion of Al-Hallāj* vol.3, p. 79.

8 Schimmel, *Calligraphy and Islamic Culture*, p. 190. See also Ritter, *The Ocean of the Soul*, p. 307.

9 Prior to the mid-ninth century, leading experts in Arabic grammar studies were chiefly conducting their analyses in Basra and Kufa. As a result, the Arabic grammar tradition speaks of the rival schools of Basra and Kufa. However, from the mid-ninth century, notable grammarians gradually started moving to Baghdad, the capital of the ʿAbbasid Empire. The Kufan grammarian Thaʿlab (d. 291/904) and his rival, the Basran grammarian al-Mubarrad (d. 285/898) both lived and worked in Baghdad – and it was here that their students and successors developed the normative, prescriptive grammar system that is sometimes referred to as the Baghdad school of grammar. Due to the predominance of Basran elements in the post-ninth century development of Arabic grammar, scholars like Carter identify the Baghdadian school as the continuation of the Basran school of grammar. According to Carter, all opposing elements to the Basran system have been traditionally identified as something 'Kufan'. However, later studies clearly indicate that the Baghdad school of grammar assimilated elements from both scholarly traditions. See Bernards, *Establishing a Reputation: The Reception of Sībawayh's Book*, p. 9 and Carter, 'Ṣarf et khilāf, contribution à l'histoire de la grammaire arabe', pp. 299–304.

letters,' noted al-Tirmidhī, 'is the complete knowledge of the primal beginnings, God's attributes and names. They also contain knowledge of His regulating the world which covers from the creation of Adam to the day of the appointed time.'[10] Nothing exists before being named. When God created Adam in His own form and taught him the names of all things in existence, He also endowed him with the potential to master the science of letters. Following the temptations of Satan, the descendants of Adam lost their inherent familiarity with letters. As a result, proficiency in reading the ontological language of the three great books required special training and divine mercy to support it. Masters of this art were thought to be able to use letters to cure illnesses, converse with animals, conquer death and return to the pure, primordial state of being. This was the final stage of enlightenment and the ultimate goal of the science of letters.[11]

While the present study seeks to provide an insight into the long-standing, traditional appreciation of letters in medieval Islam, a comprehensive study on the science of letters would require familiarity with all things in existence. The present study is not as ambitious, and its research scope is mostly limited to the surviving works of Ibn ʿArabī and several eminent Akbarians: Ṣadr al-Dīn al-Qūnawī (d. 673/1274), Muʾayyid al-Dīn al-Jandī (d. 700/1300), ʿAbd al-Razzāq al-Qāshānī (d.736/1335), Dawūd al-Qayṣarī (d.751/1350) and ʿAbdī b. Muḥammad al-Būsnawī (Bosnevi, d. 1054/1644). In broad terms, the present study examines Ibn ʿArabī's science of letters as a distinct hermeneutical approach to the sacredness of the Arabic language. It considers how the universe came to be, for which purpose it was created and the hierarchical structure it was endowed with. It is an old story told anew: through the letters of the Arabic alphabet and the meanings attributed to them. Alternatively, the story could have been told by focusing on numbers instead. However, letters were chosen on the basis of Ibn ʿArabī's belief that 'the meaning of letters fully encompasses the absolute existence: God and the world, or more

---

10 Al-Tirmidhī, *The Concept of Sainthood in Early Islamic Mysticism*, p. 224. For Ibn ʿArabī's stand on the matter see *Fut.*I:172; al-Manṣūb, 1/345; *FM.*I:111.

11 'At the final stage of his enlightenment', noted Faḍl Allāh Astarābādī on the science of letters, 'he received knowledge concerning the most basic, simple elements of form, the primary ontological letters (*ḥurūf*) of which every visible form is composed, just as written words are composed of the letters of the alphabet.' Mir-Kasimov, *Christian Apocalyptic Texts in Islamic Messianic Discourse*, p. 17. See also al-Sulamī, *Sharḥ maʿānī al-ḥurūf*, pp. 372–5.

specifically, He who imposes the law and those upon whom the law is imposed'.[12]

In specific terms, the present study is concerned with the major research objectives, field of inquiry and the changing fortunes of the science of letters in Islamic intellectual history prior to the late fourteenth century CE. At this point, Ibn ʿArabī was yet to be generally known as the Greatest Shaykh – and the science of letters was yet to be established as the most eminent of sciences under the patronage of the Timurid, Safavid, Mughal and Ottoman rulers.[13] In an attempt to come to terms with Ibn ʿArabī's contributions to the Islamic science of letters, the present study pivots on two sets of research objects: textual evidence and the visual arts. In addition to Ibn ʿArabī's magnum opus *The Meccan Revelations* (*al-Futūḥāt al-Makkiyya*) and *Bezels of Wisdom* (*Fuṣūṣ al-ḥikam*), the present study examines the textual evidence from several other short treatises dealing with the topic – with a special emphasis on *The Book of Alif* (*Kitāb al-Alif*), *The Book of the Letter Bā'* (*Kitāb al-Bā'*), *The Book of Mīm, Wāw and Nūn* (*Kitāb al-Mīm wa-l-Wāw wa-l-Nūn*) and *The Book of Majesty* (*Kitāb al-Jalāla*). Apart from the mutual topic, the aforementioned works share a general assumption that the properties of each letter are determined by its 1) shape, 2) place of articulation and 3) the spirit that governs it. In most cases, Ibn ʿArabī uses the word spirit (*rūḥ*) as a synonym for the meaning of letters. However, this term can also stand for the power they contain.

In his works, Ibn ʿArabī differentiates between three types of letters: written, spoken and summoned[14]. When a letter is written, its spirit remains passive and silent. Of its own accord, it will take no action whatsoever against the writer and reader of the text that contains it. The existence of these spirits is tightly connected to the fate of a written text. However, once a letter has been spoken, its spirit rises into the air, and people connect with it by means of hearing. While the spirits of a written letter can be easily altered and eliminated with the destruction of a written text, spirits of the spoken letters are more resilient in nature.[15] These spirits merge with one another as sentences are being formed and tend to stay in the air long after the speech has

12 Ibn ʿArabī, *The Meccan Revelations* vol.2, p. 108.

13 For the subsequent development of the Islamic science of letters, see Melvin-Koushki. 'Early Modern Islamicate Empire', pp. 357–9; Mir-Kasimov, 'The Ḥurūfī Moses', p. 22; and Bashir, *Messianic Hopes and Visions*, pp. 3–109.

14 *Fut.*I:288; al-Manṣūb, 1/555; *FM.*I:190

15 *Fut.*I:288–290; al-Manṣūb, 1/556; *FM.*I:190.

ended. Eventually, the spirits of spoken letters ascend and return to the Creator. However, if spoken words were poisonous or bitter, their spirits might return to haunt the speaker. Ibn ʿArabī believed that an audience is usually safe from the negative effects of the spoken letters. In this aspect, his teachings evoke the general stand of the Arabic grammar tradition that it is up to listeners to decide on the meaning of a sentence. Unless he invests his personal energy to fuel the negative vibrations of a spoken letter, a listener will remain unaffected by it. In contrast, the summoned letters (*al-ḥurūf al-mustaḥḍara*) have a permanent effect and hold the power to influence a listener irrespective of his will and actions. Spirits of the summoned letters get to be manifested when the act of writing is followed by the act of speaking and imbued with the spiritual concentration (*ḥimma*) of a summoner. In this case, speaking and writing serve to help one's imagination to form a clear image of the letter he intends to summon. Provided that the spiritual concentration is strong enough, the summoned letters will pass from the imagination of a summoner to the imaginal world (*barzakh*) to do the bidding of their master. In rare cases, however, the act of reading from the Qurʾan was also thought to be sufficient to invoke the spirits of the letters. In their shape and effect, the summoned letters were thought to be stable. Alternations in pronunciation and handwriting have no effect on the summoned letters, and their properties are solely determined by the spirits that govern them.[16] According to Ibn ʿArabī, few people were proficient in summoning a single spirit of a single letter – and fewer still were capable of summoning multiple letters at once. The summoning process was thought to be a dangerous, 'repugnant knowledge, both intellectually and according to the (Islamic religious) law'.[17] For in spite of the fact that the summoned letters have been attributed with a variety of pragmatic features, Ibn ʿArabī primarily associated them with the dark arts. While his works contain an abundance of information on the meaning of letters, relatively little has been said on the summoning process and the perceived functions of the spirits of letters. As a result, the present study mostly deals with the spoken and written letters of the Arabic alphabet. While Ibn ʿArabī's analyses of phonology and the spirits (i.e. meanings) he attributed to each letter of the Arabic alphabet are easily accessible from the contemporary editions of his works, his inquiries into the orthographical structures of letters are closely related to the properties of his handwriting and calligraphy.

16 *Fut.*I:290; al-Manṣūb, 1/556; *FM.*I:191.

17 *Fut.*I:289; al-Manṣūb, 1/556; *FM.*I:191.

In his *Art of Islam*, Titus Burckhardt maintained that 'it can be said without fear of exaggeration that nothing has typified the aesthetic sense of the Muslim peoples as much as the Arabic script'.[18] While the term 'calligraphy' comes from the Greek words for beauty (*kallos*) and writing (*graphein*), Ibn ʿArabī's meditations on the topic extend well beyond the properties of elegant handwriting. In Sufi circles, calligraphy was perceived as a technical science which involved the production of letters in accordance with the strictly defined geometrical ratios, strokes and angles – each of which is imbued with symbolic meanings. Firm in the belief that proficiency in calligraphy can lead to familiarity with the meaning of letters, Ibn ʿArabī analysed the orthographic forms of letters with geometric precision. By means of calligraphy, his notions of the ideal shapes and the meanings of letters are directly put into practice. In order to come to terms with Ibn ʿArabī's meditations on the orthographic structures and the symbolic values he attributed to them, special attention will be given to the twenty-seven holographs and the several dozens of surviving autographs in Ibn ʿArabī's own hand. The properties of Ibn ʿArabī's calligraphy will be analysed in accordance with the criteria provided by the major Sufi thinkers and the aesthetical concepts originating from the Andalusian tradition. However, the present study also deals with the cryptographic scripts Ibn ʿArabī developed, together with their putative keys and relationship to the 'standard' letters of the Arabic alphabet.

The defining parameters of the present study – the science of letters, pre-modern cosmology and the interpretations of the rules and regulations of Arabic grammar in Sufi literature – present us with many challenges, both conceptually and methodologically. Most of these challenges spring from the fact that Ibn ʿArabī perceived the science of letters as a mystery forbidden to be disclosed in books. 'It is a noble science in itself,' Ibn ʿArabī recorded, 'though it is quite rare to practise it without being affected by it. It is thus preferable not to seek it since it is with this science that, in eternity, God privileged his saints.'[19] As a result, the relevant passages from Ibn ʿArabī's works are intentionally vague and seemingly full of contradictions. Faced with a similar obstacle as he was attempting to conduct a research on Ibn ʿArabī's cosmology, William Chittick noted how easy it would be to have Ibn ʿArabī say whatever one wants him to say. In Ibn ʿArabī's teachings, Chittick observed, everyone seems to be able to find what

18 Burckhardt, *Art of Islam: Language and Meaning*, p. 52.
19 Ibn ʿArabī, *The Meccan Revelations* vol.2, p. 123.

he wants alongside a proper quote to support his view.[20] On his side, al-Nābulusī (d. 1143/1731) argued that this is how it is supposed to be. In his commentary on Ibn ʿArabī's *Bezels of Wisdom*, al-Nābulusī noted that, when it comes to Ibn ʿArabī's works, there is no such thing as a single 'correct' interpretation. In this aspect, Ibn ʿArabī's works can be compared to the opposing views different Muslims have on God. 'The God in whom one must have faith is One,' al-Nābulusī explained. 'However, His appearance differs in [the writings] of the people of the doctrine, people of discursive reasoning and people of the witnessing states (*aḥwāl*).'[21] Differences in interpretations were believed to occur due to different capacities of the people conducting them. This can lead to dogmatic clashes between the people in spite of the fact that the God they worship is one and the same.[22] Conducted in October 2012, *Establishing Ibn ʿArabī's Heritage Project* research identified eighty-four written works which were, without any possible doubt, composed by Ibn ʿArabī.[23] Over the course of centuries, these were the subject of countless different interpretations. The present study on the Islamic science of letters is yet another product of the continuing scholarly interest in Ibn ʿArabī's works. As such, it does not presume to be a definitive study: what it offers is the first systematic overview of the topic. Paradoxes that could not be resolved through the course of the present study and the seemingly contradictory parts of Ibn ʿArabī's teachings are enumerated next to one another. Some of them, like the practical usage of the talismans and Ibn ʿArabī's notions of the hierarchy and articulation of the letters *bāʾ* and *hāʾ* are tasks for studies to come.

Apart from obfuscations, data exposition was another major problem of the present study. The Islamic science of letters traditionally associates the sequence of the letters of the Arabic alphabet with the order in which the universe came into existence. Data exposition of the present study was originally set to be modelled on this sequence – as presented in the surviving works of Ibn ʿArabī:

> The number of letters, by the agency of the Breath, is twenty-eight: no more, no less. The first is the Intellect and this is the Pen, as stated by the Prophet: 'The first thing that God created

20 Chittick, *The Self-Disclosure of God*, p. 9.

21 al-Nābulusī, *Sharḥ Jawāhir al-nuṣūṣ* vol.1, p. 3.

22 Lane, *Abd al-Ghani al-Nabulusi's Commentary*, p. 42.

23 Clark and Hirtenstein, 'Establishing Ibn ʿArabī's Heritage', pp. 1–32.

> was the Intellect' – or in another report: 'The first thing that God created was the Pen' reads a certain hadith. The first thing that God created from the Breath, the Mist, was receptive to the first created things in the universe in the following order: the Intellect, and this is the Pen [i.e. *hamza*], then the Soul and this is the Tablet [*hā'*], then the Universal Nature [*'ayn*], then the Dust [*ḥā'*], then the Universal Body [*ghayn*], then the Form [*khā'*], then the Throne [*qāf*], then the Pedestal [*kāf*], then the Starless Sphere [*jīm*], then the Sphere of the Fixed Stars [*shīn*], then the first heaven [*yā'*], then the second [*ḍād*], then the third [*lām*], fourth [*nūn*], fifth [*rā'*], sixth [*ṭā'*] and the seventh heaven [*dāl*] – and then the Orbit of Fire [*tā'*], Air [*zāy*], Water [*sīn*] and Earth [*ṣād*], then the minerals [*ẓā'*], then the plants [*thā'*], then the animals [*dhāl*], then the angels [*fā'*], then the jinn [*bā'*], then the human beings [*mīm*] and then the step-levels of spiritual elevation [*wāw*].[24]

The introductory chapter on research objectives and history of the science of letters was thus set to be followed by twenty-nine chapters: one chapter for each letter of the alphabet. These were to analyse the phases of the genesis as it evolved, starting with *alif*, the letter that is not a letter, and ending with the letter *wāw*. However, the surviving works of Ibn 'Arabī do not treat the letters equally. While some letters are barely mentioned, letters like *alif*, *bā'* and *yā'* were dedicated a whole book each. This is not necessarily an implication of the importance of each letter: Ibn 'Arabī never presumed to have divulged all the secrets of the science of letters. Such a task would have been beyond his powers. By his own admittance, he had no knowledge of the orbit period of the letter *nūn*. The secret nature of the letter *jīm* in relation to celestial orbits was another mystery he unsuccessfully tried to resolve.[25] Ibn 'Arabī's research interests and familiarity with the meaning of specific letters are reflected in the amount of writings he dedicated to each of them. 'In each letter there is a fountain of insight different from any other, a fresh flavour different from any other and a pleasant taste different from any other,' noted Abū Sa'īd al-Kharrāz (d. ca. 286/899) on the meaning of letters.[26]

24 *Fut.*IV:36; al-Manṣūb, 4/154–5; *FM.*II:395.
25 *Fut.*III:172; al-Manṣūb, 5/13-4; *FM.*II:115.
26 al-Sulamī, *Sharḥ ma'ānī al-ḥurūf*, pp. 372–5.

Irrespective of its prominence in the surviving works of Ibn ʿArabī, within the scope of the present study, each letter of the Arabic alphabet will be allowed to tell its story – for as the early Sufi proverb goes, 'there is no letter that does not worship God in the Arabic language in its own way'.[27] Similar notions appear to have been widespread among Sufis – but in spite of this fact, clear division of research units and a well-built narrative structure are atypical for Sufi works on the science of letters. In this aspect, the surviving works of Ibn ʿArabī are no exception. Overlapping content, the complexity of the research object and the systematic lack of data exposition in Ibn ʿArabī's works set a major challenge for all future studies dealing with the topic. For example, the story of a relationship between the Creator and the created could be told through the analysis of Ibn ʿArabī's writings on the letters *bā'*, *mīm*, *lām-alif* and/or the disjoined letters *alif-lām-mīm*. While the concept they refer to is the same, each of these letters offers a new angle to the story. In spite of this fact – or precisely because of it – data exposition of the present study required several compromises to be able to adhere to the contemporary standards of academic writing. In order to avoid redundancy, letters whose meanings are similar were occasionally analysed together, within a single chapter of the present study. *Lām-alif*, which Ibn ʿArabī treated as the twenty-eighth or twenty-ninth letter of the alphabet, was analysed as the second letter of the present study instead. In this case, a narrative based on the order of the alphabet was abandoned in favour of greater clarity of data exposition. In all other cases, data exposition follows Ibn ʿArabī's sequence of letters. In addition, several chapters of the present study contain sub-chapters dealing with Ibn ʿArabī's interpretations of the letters in different words and sentences. While letters of the Latin alphabet typically appear as individual glyphs in the text, the Arabic letters connect with one another to form an organic band (Fig. 1).

Since the rules of orthography demand that most Arabic letters are connected with a preceding and a following letter, the shape of each letter can be subjected to changes in different words and sentences. The orthographic forms of letters are chiefly determined by the position they occupy in a word. Apart from their isolated, independent form, the Arabic letters have three further forms: initial, medial and final (Table 1). These forms were thought to be crucial for determining the meaning of a letter. The Islamic science of letters traditionally held that

27 Nwiya, *Exégèse coranique et langage mystique*, p. 165.

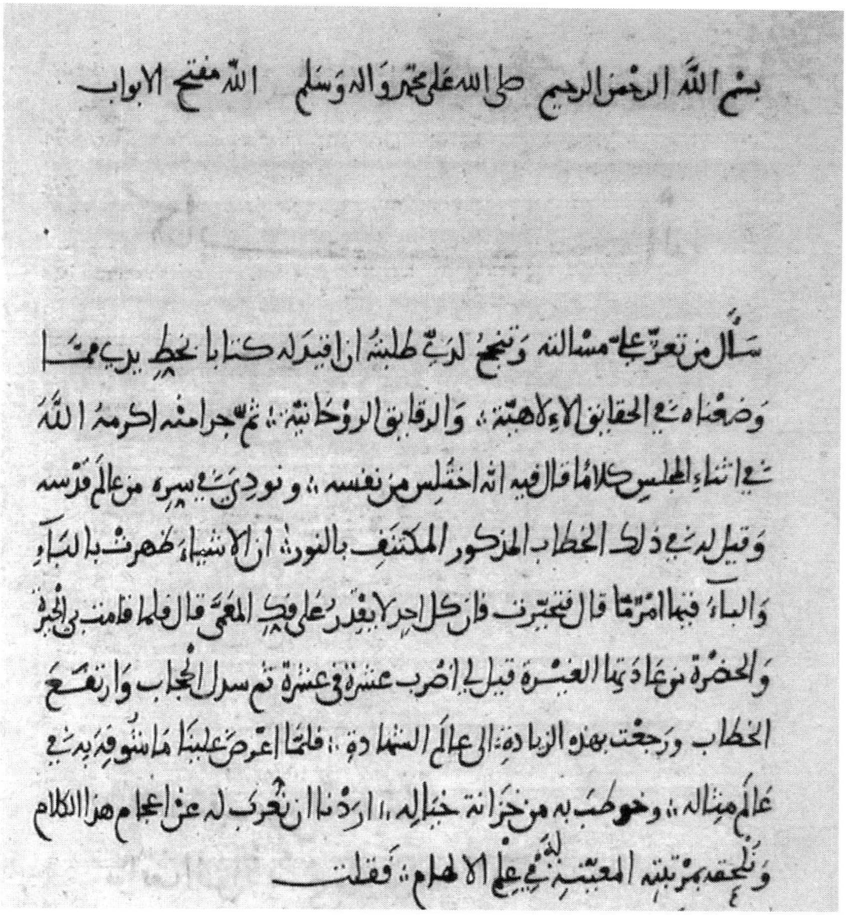
بسم الله الرحمن الرحيم صلى الله على محمد وآله وسلم الله مفتح الابواب

Fig. 1 In the Master's hand: the opening paragraph of Ibn ʿArabī's Book of the Letter Bāʾ

isolated letters are superior to complex words and sentences.[28] As a result, Ibn ʿArabī's research was mostly limited to the isolated forms of letters – and unless specified otherwise, all analyses conducted within the scope of the present study pivot on the isolated forms as well. Not only did Ibn ʿArabī believe that the meaning of letters is determined by their position, he also held that the meaning of each letter can vary from one word to another. Properties of the letter *qāf* in the imperative mood of the verb 'protect' (*qi!*) were thus thought to be lost in imperative

28 Juan Cole attributed this fact to the Neoplatonic influences that emphasized 'the goodness of the One'. Cole, 'The World as Text: Cosmologies of Shaykh Ahmad al-Ahsa'i', p. 149.

Table 1 The Arabic script in the common hijāʾī order

Letter	Isolated Form	Final Form	Medial Form	Initial Form	Ibn ʿArabī's Cryptograph
Alif	ا	ـا	ـا	ا	
Bāʾ	ب	ـب	ـبـ	بـ	
Tāʾ	ت	ـت	ـتـ	تـ	
Thāʾ	ث	ـث	ـثـ	ثـ	
Jīm	ج	ـج	ـجـ	جـ	
Ḥāʾ	ح	ـح	ـحـ	حـ	
Khāʾ	خ	ـخ	ـخـ	خـ	
Dāl	د	ـد	ـد	د	
Dhāl	ذ	ـذ	ـذ	ذ	
Rāʾ	ر	ـر	ـر	ر	
Zāy	ز	ـز	ـز	ز	
Sīn	س	ـس	ـسـ	سـ	
Shīn	ش	ـش	ـشـ	شـ	
Ṣād	ص	ـص	ـصـ	صـ	
Ḍād	ض	ـض	ـضـ	ضـ	
Ṭāʾ	ط	ـط	ـطـ	طـ	

Letter	Isolated Form	Final Form	Medial Form	Initial Form	Ibn 'Arabī's Cryptograph
Ẓā'	ظ	ـظ	ـظـ	ظـ	 [1]
'Ayn	ع	ـع	ـعـ	عـ	
Ghayn	غ	ـغ	ـغـ	غـ	
Fā'	ف	ـف	ـفـ	فـ	
Qāf	ق	ـق	ـقـ	قـ	
Kāf	ك	ـك	ـكـ	كـ	
Lām	ل	ـل	ـلـ	لـ	
Mīm	م	ـم	ـمـ	مـ	
Nūn	ن	ـن	ـنـ	نـ	
Hā'	ه	ـه	ـهـ	هـ	
Wāw	و	ـو	ـو	و	
Yā'	ي	ـي	ـيـ	يـ	
Lām-alif	لا	ـلا	ـلا	لا	

1 The holograph of Ibn 'Arabī's *The Book of Theophanies* (*Kitāb al-Tajalliyāt*) does not contain cryptographs for the letters *ṭā'* and *ẓā'*. The cryptographic form of the letter *ṭā'* can only be found in Ibn 'Arabī's *Book of the Fabulous Gryphon* (*'Anqā' mughrib*). Based on the fact that cryptographs for *'ayn* and *ghayn* and *ṣād* and *ḍād*, the neighbouring letters whose shapes are similar, are the same in The Book of the Fabulous Gryphon,  is almost certainly the cryptograph Ibn 'Arabī used for the letter *ẓā'*. However, this cannot be determined with absolute certainty. Later manuscripts contain three different versions of this cryptograph: ,  and .

forms of other verbs. In this aspect, Ibn ʿArabī's notion of letters can be compared to chemical elements and the great variety of substances they form. 'Letters are like natural medicines – no, they are like all things which have a special usage when used on their own and a special usage when used in combinations,' noted Ibn ʿArabī on the matter.[29] When applicable, contrasting interpretations of individual letters in different words and sentences are enumerated next to one another in a chapter dealing with the letter in question.

In order to minimize the possibility of misinterpretation, central to the approach of the present study was, whenever possible, to let Ibn ʿArabī speak for himself. Ibn ʿArabī recommended this approach in the second chapter of *The Meccan Revelations*:

> No scholar can declare wrong an interpretation that is supported by words [i.e. a quote]. However, it is not necessary to uphold the interpretation or to put it into practice, except in the case of the interpreter himself and those who follow his authority.[30]

The second possible approach to Ibn ʿArabī's writings on the science of letters was also proposed by the author himself: 'Verify for yourself what we cited and have it clarified,' Ibn ʿArabī suggested, 'and there will appear to you strange wonders that will bewilder the intellect with the splendour of their beauty.'[31] Alongside divine mysteries of eternity, imagination and timelessness, the science of letters reveals its secrets only by means of revelation. A revelation received by one prophet could be easily granted to another. While the notion of divine revelation (*kashf*) has been extensively researched in the fields of history of philosophy and religious studies, Ibn ʿArabī was sceptical regarding the possibility of conducting a successful research on divine mysteries by means of the rational mind. He primarily perceived *kashf* as knowledge granted by God to those who are pure of heart. Such knowledge is as hard to convey by means of everyday speech as 'the taste of honey, bitterness of aloe, the pleasure of sexual intercourse, love, passion, desire and the like – for these are the things that cannot be comprehended by the one who is incapable of them nor by the one who did not experience them'.[32] When it comes to the science of

29 *Fut.*IV:79, al-Manṣūb, 5/547; *FM.*II:300.
30 Chittick, *Ibn ʿArabi, Heir to the Prophets*, p. 125.
31 *Fut.*I:89; al-Manṣūb, 1/181; *FM.*I:54.
32 *Fut.*I:54; al-Manṣūb, 1/123-4; *FM.*I:31.

letters, it is therefore appropriate to say that he who has no *kashf* has no knowledge. Faced with a limited potential of the spoken and written language, Sufis turned to symbols and analogies to instruct those who were yet to experience the spark of revelation. In his attempts to express the ineffable, Ibn ʿArabī also found it convenient to rely on the visual arts. What could not be expressed in words thus found its expression in diagrams and calligraphy. In the twenty-seven surviving holographs of Ibn ʿArabī's works, thirty diagrams have been preserved. These diagrams are the visual grammar of Ibn ʿArabī's works. He believed them to be necessary so that a seeker, by the means of imagination, can gain nearness to knowledge which cannot be obtained by the rational faculty.

> The disciple will represent in himself the spiritual meaning (*maʿnā*) in materialized form, thus facilitating its explicit expression by having it integrated in his imagination. The one who considers [the spiritual meaning in materialized form] will then aspire to complete his consideration and get to know the totality of its spiritual meanings. This is due to the fact that sensation (*al-ḥiss*), once it's poured into the mold of form and figure (*qālab al-ṣūra wa al-shakl*), is taken with the spiritual reality. The disciple finds pleasure in it, it provides him with delight - and this leads him to realize what manifests to him the figure and what is materialized to him by this form[33].

With the rising popularity of Ibn ʿArabī's works, from the fourteenth century CE, Sufis began to demonstrate an increasing tendency to rely on the visual arts to make their works more accessible to the general public. As a result, the artistic value of Sufi manuscripts increased, with scholars becoming increasingly proficient in the (re) production of elaborate diagrams. Not only were diagrams a central feature of Ibn ʿArabī's method of exposition of the science of letters and other mysteries divine – as such, they also served as a foundation for the data exposition of the present study. Following the introductory chapter on the field of inquiry and origins of the science of letters, Ibn ʿArabī's diagrams are analysed alongside segments of the universe they were said to represent. For the sake of further clarity, several noteworthy illuminations from the later manuscripts are also included.

33 Ibn ʿArabī, *Inshāʾ al-dawāʾir*, p. 6.

Through his diagrams, Ibn ʿArabī was determined to help adepts with reduced capacities (*al-afhām al-qāṣira*) to come to terms with the higher spiritual realities. By relying on the visual arts, it was my intention to present Ibn ʿArabī's teachings in an innovative and easily approachable way – just as Ibn ʿArabī himself intended to do in the thirteenth century CE.

In the first part of the present study, we will identify research objectives of the Islamic science of letters and determine which of them were thought to be susceptible to rational analyses. This was intended as a foundation for *The Act of Genesis*, the second part of the present study, which examines the properties and symbolism attached to each of the twenty-eight letters of the Arabic alphabet. In the eyes of Ibn ʿArabī, any attempt at conducting a research on the science of letters was a brazen, highly improper thing to do – for he believed that it is not up to scholars to interpret the revelations they did not receive for themselves.[34] However, this is something we will have to live with. Being powerless to induce the arrival of a revelation, we shall approach the topic in the only way we can: meticulously and rationally. Research units that belong to the domain of revealed knowledge and were, as such, thought to be unsusceptible to the intellectual capacities of the mind, are to be systematically presented in the wider historical and cultural context of Islamic intellectual history. Without the protection God grants to His messengers, this approach represents a calculated risk. For, according to Ibn ʿArabī, the possible consequences for any misstep are madness, misery and slander in this life – with the fires of hell awaiting in the next. But even though the philosophers from Ibn ʿArabī's *Contemplations of the Holy Mysteries* were said to be sentenced to hell for engaging in rational interpretations of divine mysteries, in Islam it is also said that 'God loves the artisan who seeks perfection in his craft'.[35]

---

34 *Fut.*III:36; al-Manṣūb, 4/425; *FM.*II:56.

35 Akkach, *Cosmology and Architecture*, p. 50.

Introduction

Divinity, adieu!
These metaphysics of magicians,
And necromantic books are heavenly;
Lines, circles, scenes, letters, and characters;
Ay, these are those that Faustus most desires.
Oh, what a world of profit and delight,
Of power, of honour, of omnipotence,
Is promis'd to the studious artizan!'

Christopher Marlowe[36]

36 Marlowe, *The Tragical History of Doctor Faustus*, p.4.

1.2. The Letters and The Science of Letters

From the eighth century CE onwards, the letters of the Arabic alphabet were the primary research object of the Islamic science of letters. According to the legend circulating among the people of Ḥīra, three men assembled in the city of Anbār to develop the Arabic script from Syriac. Their names were Murra, Jidla and Aslam b. Sidra. While Ibn ʿAbbās believed them to be of Bawlān background, other legends linked them with the tribe of Ṭayyī and the Bedouin communities encamped with ʿAdnān b. ʿUdd.[37] Medieval narratives of the three men of Anbār had an impact on later theories of the origins of the Arabic script. Among the eminent contemporary proponents of these theories was Jean Starcky, who believed that the Arabic alphabet was developed from the Syriac court script of the Lakhmid kings of Ḥīra.[38] However, today it is generally believed that the origins of the Arabic alphabet are to be sought in the Phoenician script instead. 'Among the family of scripts descending from the Phoenician alphabet,' Gruendler wrote, 'Arabic seems to be the most remote from its ancestor.'[39]

From the fourth century CE, when the earliest archaeological finds have been placed, rectilinear Phoenician characters have been gradually transformed into loops and curves to form the twenty-eight letters of the Arabic alphabet. In the Arabic grammar tradition, any set of phonemes, together with its orthographic symbols, is referred to as *ḥurūf* (sg. *ḥarf*). The science of letters owes its name to this term, which is generally defined as the minimum structure a single word could be made of. However, the pioneering works of the Arabic grammar tradition also identified *ḥarf* as one of the three main elements of speech in Arabic. As such, this term came to be perceived as any element of speech that is neither noun nor verb.[40] Covering a wide range of prepositions, pronouns, adverbs and conjunctions, the term *ḥarf,* as such, can be translated as 'particle'. However, this term also stood for each of the seven sessions in which the Qurʾan was revealed to

37 For an overview of legends circulating among medieval scholars of the origins of Arabic script, see Ibn Nadīm, *Kitāb al-Fihrist* vol.1, p.6, and al-Baladhuri, *The Origins of the Islamic State* vol.2, p.270.

38 Similar theories were popular among the Muslim writers of the late eighth and early ninth centuries. Starcky, *Petra et la Nabatène*, p.932–4.

39 Gruendler, *The Development of the Arabic Script*, p.1.

40 Ibn al-Sarrāj, *Kitāb al-Uṣūl fī al-naḥw* vol.1, pp. 40–1.

Muhammad.[41] Within the scope of the present study, we shall deal with the first and the most common meaning of this term: the interpretation of *ḥurūf* as the letters of the Arabic alphabet and the building blocks of the universe. This was the primary use of this term in the Islamic science of letters as well.

In the late fourteenth century CE, Ibn Khaldūn (d. 808/1406) attributed the pioneering works on the science of letters to Aḥmad b. ʿAli al-Būnī (d. 622/1225) and Ibn ʿArabī.[42] On his side, Ibn ʿArabī made no such claims and al-Būnī associated the origins of this science with the writings of Hermes and Aristotle.[43] Late Timurid and early Safavid era authors like Faḍl Allāh al-Astarābādī (d. 796/1394), Ibn Turka Iṣfahānī (d. 835/1432) and Sharaf al-Dīn ʿAlī Yazdī (d. 858/1454), whose works took Ibn ʿArabī's theories to an unprecedented level, also perceived the science of letters as a legacy of Solomon the Wise and his Greek disciples, Pythagoras and Plato.[44] Similar theories still continue to find their supporters today. For example, Matthew Melvin-Koushki identified the science of letters as the primary means of Islamicizing Hellenic heritage of the late antiquity in the thirteenth century CE. 'That is to say, the reinterpretation of first the Torah and then the Qurʾan in Neopythagorean-Gnostic mode rendered the Hebrew or Arabic letters of scripture cosmogonic and their totality the matrix of creation.'[45] However, the emergence of similar notions in Islamic culture can be traced back to eighth-century Iraq and the teachings of al-Mughīra b. Saʿīd (d. 120/737). A rumoured sorcerer, revolutionary and self-proclaimed prophet, al-Mughīra was among the first to rely on the letters of the Arabic alphabet to convey his idea of God:

> He is a man of light, with a crown of light on his head. He has the body and limbs of a man. His body has an inside, within which is a heart, whence wisdom flows. His limbs have the shape of the letters of the alphabet. The *mīm* represents the head; the *sīn* the teeth; the *ṣād* and *ḍād* the two eyes; the *ʿayn* and *ghayn* the two ears; as for the *hāʾ*, he said, you will see in it a Great Power, and

41 Al-Nassir, *Sībawayh the Phonologist*, p. 21. See also Mālik b. Anas, *al-Muwatta* vol.1, p. 201.

42 Ibn Khaldūn, *al-Muqaddima* vol.3, p. 171.

43 Fahd, 'La magie comme 'source' de la sagesse, l'apres l'œuvre d'al-Bunī', p. 6.

44 Salvatore, *The Wiley Blackwell History of Islam*, pp. 353–76.

45 Melvin-Koushki, 'Introduction: De-orienting the Study of Islamicate Occultism', p. 92.

he implied that it was in the place of the genitalia and that he had seen it; the *alif* was in the place of the foot.[46]

Through the power of letters, al-Mughīra claimed to have brought seventeen people back from the dead. Apart from gnostic cosmology, his teachings were influenced by the polytheistic religions of Mesopotamia and a great variety of Manichaean, Jewish and Syriac-Christian sources. Following his unsuccessful rebellion against the Umayyad regime, al-Mughīra was captured and put to death in 737 CE. Under the collective name of al-Mughīriyya, his followers were among the many Shiʿi groups to take up arms against the Umayyad dynasty in the eighth century CE. Persecuted, marginalized and internally divided, what these groups had in common was the unquestionable loyalty to ʿAlī b. Abī Ṭālib (d. 41/661), the fourth caliph of Islam, and his descendants.

A focal medium of expression for their teachings was *jafr*: a genre of esoteric, apocalyptic literature, whose primary goal was to advocate the legitimacy of ʿAlī as the rightful heir of the Prophet and boost the morality of adepts. According to Ḥājjī Khalīfa (d. 1086/1675), *jafr* was 'the summary knowledge (of that which is written) on the tablet of fate and destiny, which contains all that has been and all that which will be, totally and partially'.[47] Among the most influential examples of this genre were *The Book of Jafr* (*Kitāb al-Jafr*), an anonymous work attributed to ʿAlī b. Abī Ṭālib, and *The Book of Fatima* (*Muṣḥaf Fāṭima*). Passing down through the line of imams, these works were believed to contain secrets of the past, present and future, including the names of messengers of God and all kings and imams to come.[48] This genre relied on the letters of the Arabic alphabet as phonetic and phenomenological signs with a potential to unlock the secrets of revelation, universe and all in it – to the point where the science of letters came to be perceived as a branch of *jafr*.[49]

Among Shiʿis, the origins of the science of letters were traditionally associated with ʿAlī b. Abī Ṭālib. The caliph was reported to have learned about the secret properties of letters from the Prophet

46 Quoted according to Wasserstrom, *The Moving Finger Writes*, p. 16. For a detailed overview of al-Mughīra's teachings, see Tucker, 'Rebels and Gnostics: al-Mughīra Ibn Saʿīd and the Mughīriyya', p. 38.

47 Lambton, *The State and Government in Medieval Islam*, p. 227.

48 See Modarressi, *Tradition and Survival*, pp. 4–5, 18–9, and Melvin-Koushki, *The Occult Philosophy of Ṣā'in al-Dīn Turka Isfahanī*, p. 171.

49 Fahd, T., 'Djafr', EI2. Consulted online 06 May 2020.

Muhammad. The Shiʿi normative tradition identified the Prophet as the first person to have come to terms with the properties of the seventy-two letters of the Supreme Name of God. These letters were thought to be imbued with miraculous powers. Unlike the early prophets of Islam, who were believed to have been familiar with several letters each, Muhammad was the first to discover the properties of all seventy-two.[50] This knowledge he subsequently shared with ʿAlī. On his deathbed, the Prophet also taught ʿAlī that just as every verse of the Qurʾan has its literal (*ẓāhir*) and allegorical meaning (*bāṭin*), so does each and every letter of the Arabic alphabet. Al-Sulamī referred to these meaning dimensions as *ḥadd* (horizon, definition) and *maṭlaʿ* (allegory, the point of ascent) of letters. 'What further substantiates the teachings about the letters,' al-Sulamī wrote, '... is that the Messenger of God said:

> Learn the alphabet and its interpretation! Woe unto the scholar who ignores its interpretation! The people said: O Messenger of God, what is it about the alphabet?
>
> He replied: All marvels that exist are within it.[51]

When it comes to the science of letters, metaphysical and orthographic properties of the letter *bāʾ* and the ninety-nine names of God were among the focal points of research among the early Shiʿi brotherhoods. The surviving records of their teachings also indicate a strong interest in the symbolism of the disjoined or 'isolated' letters (*al-ḥurūf al-muqaṭṭaʿāt*).[52] Also known as the sura openers (*fawātiḥ as-ṣuwar*), these are the combinations of up to five letters which can be found in the Qurʾan, at the beginning of the twenty-nine different suras (Table 2).

Even today, the original meaning of the disjoined letters remains unknown. With no real consensus on their meaning and purpose, the disjoined letters have been pragmatically interpreted in Islamic cultural tradition as mnemonic devices, means of ordering the suras and/or initials of the original text editors of the Qurʾan. However, they were concurrently perceived as symbols of 1) the divine origins of the world, 2) spiritual dimension of the alphabet and/or 3) the world of spirits. As such, these letters were thought to be imbued with power

50 Ayoub, *Redemptive Suffering*, pp. 62–3.

51 al-Sulamī, *Sharḥ maʿānī al-ḥurūf*, pp. 370–1.

52 Melvin-Koushki, *The Occult Philosophy of Ṣāʾin al-Dīn Turka Isfahanī*, p. 172.

Table 2 The Disjoined Letters

Sura	The Sura Openers
al-Baqara	*Alif – Lām – Mīm*
Āl ʿImrān	*Alif – Lām – Mīm*
al-Aʿrāf	*Alif – Lām – Mīm – Ṣād*
Yūnus	*Alif – Lām – Rāʾ*
Hūd	*Alif – Lām – Rāʾ*
Yūsuf	*Alif – Lām – Rāʾ*
ar-Raʿd	*Alif – Lām – Mīm – Rāʾ*
Ibrāhīm	*Alif – Lām – Rāʾ*
al-Ḥijr	*Alif – Lām – Rāʾ*
Maryam	*Kāf – Hāʾ – Yāʾ – ʿAyn – Ṣād*
Ṭāʾ Hāʾ	*Ṭāʾ – Hāʾ*
ash-Shuʿarāʾ	*Ṭāʾ – Sīn – Mīm*
an-Naml	*Ṭāʾ – Sīn*
al-Qaṣaṣ	*Ṭāʾ – Sīn – Mīm*
al-ʿAnkabūt	*Alif – Lām – Mīm*
ar-Rūm	*Alif – Lām – Mīm*
Luqmān	*Alif – Lām – Mīm*
as-Sajdah	*Alif – Lām – Mīm*
Yāʾ Sīn	*Yāʾ – Sīn*
Ṣād	*Ṣād*
Ghāfir	*Ḥāʾ – Mīm*
Fuṣṣilat	*Ḥāʾ – Mīm*
ash-Shūrā	*Ḥāʾ – Mīm – ʿAyn – Sīn – Qāf*
az-Zukhruf	*Ḥāʾ – Mīm*
al-Dukhān	*Ḥāʾ – Mīm*
al-Jāthiya	*Ḥāʾ – Mīm*
al-Aḥqāf	*Ḥāʾ – Mīm*
Qāf	*Qāf*
al-Qalam	*Nūn*

to reveal divine mysteries to the worthy and obscure the vision of the unworthy.[53]

Nevertheless, the primary use of the science of letters in early Shiʿi literature was mostly limited to divination. The major divination techniques included 1) gematria (*ḥisāb al-jummal*), 2) divination from the Qurʾanic verses (*khawaṣṣ al-qurʾān*) and 3) *ʿilm al-awfāq*, where predictions have been based on the correlations between astrological conjunctions and letters.[54] As a result, the science of letters gradually came to be associated with practical magic. Having been ascribed magical properties, letters have been used in traditional medicine and folk magic to imbue talismans, amulets and magic squares with special powers.

With the rising prominence of the Arabic alphabet in folk magic and high occultism, by the fourteenth century CE the science of letters also came to be known as *sīmiyāʾ*: letter magic. By this time, its Shiʿi origins had been thoroughly obscured. Writing in the mid-fourteenth century, Ibn Khaldūn attributed the first works on the science of letters to 'the extremists among the Sufis', al-Būnī and Ibn ʿArabī, who wished to remove the veil of sense-perception, perform miracles and manipulate the four elements of the material world. But rather than having it catalogued under Sufi beliefs and practices, Ibn Khaldūn identified the science of letters as a branch of *siḥr* instead.[55] Kubilay Akman and Donna Brown translated *siḥr* as 'Qurʾanic theurgy' and interpreted it as all contemplations based on the science of letters, their relationship to the ninety-nine names of God and allegorical interpretations of the Qurʾan.[56] However, in Islamic culture, the term *siḥr* could apply to anything wondrous: subtle, elegant poetry, the healing properties of plants, and the invocation of celestial spirits and/or the most beautiful names of God could be equally covered by this term.[57] On his side, however, Ibn Khaldūn set forth the notion of *siḥr* as one of the forbidden, occult sciences 'showing how human souls may become prepared to exercise an influence upon the world of elements,

53 For a detailed overview of the most influential interpretations of the disjoined letters in medieval Islam, see Melvin-Koushki, *The Occult Philosophy of Ṣāʾin al-Dīn Turka Isfahanī*, pp. 172–3; Petersen, *Interpreting Islam in China: Pilgrimage, Scripture and Language in the Han Kitab* and Akkach, *Ibn ʿArabī's Cosmology and the Sufi Concept of Space and Time*, p. 97.

54 Hamdan, 'Ghazali and the Science of *Ḥurūf*', p. 191.

55 Ibn Khaldūn, *al-Muqaddima* vol.3, p. 171–2.

56 Akman and Brown, 'Ahmad Al-Buni and His Esoteric Model', p. 52.

57 Fahd, 'Siḥr', *EI2* vol.9, pp. 567–71.

with or without the aid of celestial beings'.[58] Having classified it as a branch of *siḥr,* Ibn Khaldūn analysed the science of letters alongside alchemy, astrology and other occult sciences. Although short-sighted, Ibn Khaldūn's classification was not entirely unfounded.

Overlapping fields of inquiries were a universal problem in the history of Islamic culture. *Taṣnīf al-ʿulūm*, a popular scientific genre dealing with the classification of sciences,[59] documents several dozens of disciplines which relied on the letters of the Arabic alphabet to decipher (and manipulate) reality. Among them were the mainstream Islamic theology (*kalām*), philosophy (*falsafa*) and mysticism (*taṣawwuf*) – as well as alchemy (*ʿilm al-kīmiyāʾ*), astrology (*ʿilm al-nujūm*), bibliomancy (*ʿilm al-faʾl*) and the Qurʾanic spell magic (*ʿilm al-ruqā*). However, the major works of this genre rarely discussed specific properties of various occult sciences, apart from emphasizing the fact that their use was forbidden by Islamic religious law. This makes it difficult to separate one discipline from another and identify distinct properties of *sīmiyāʾ* in high occultism and folk culture alike. Strictly speaking, however, certain properties of the science of letters match the Islamic (and Western) definition of the occult sciences. In Islamic culture, the notion of elitism has been commonly associated with the occult sciences. Analyses conducted by Melvin-Koushki also indicate a strong tendency among medieval scholars to catalogue the occult sciences as natural sciences (*al-ʿulūm al-ṭabīʿī*) in general. In *Epistles of the Brethren of Purity* (*Rasāʾil Ikhwān al-Ṣafāʾ*), it was therefore envisaged that one's education should ideally begin with the basic knowledge of mathematics and progress through familiarity with logic, physics and metaphysics. The studies were set to conclude with occult sciences, which required proficiency in all aforementioned disciplines to be mastered.[60] Medieval scholars associated occult sciences (*al-ʿulūm al-gharība*) with all disciplines and practices which were generally perceived as unusual, difficult to master and set to bend the human soul and reality to the will of the practitioner – a fact that was emphasized by the term itself (i.e. *gharīb* – occult, strange, extraordinary). Among certain groups of scholars, sharp intellect and

58 Ibn Khaldūn, *al-Muqaddima* vol.3, p.156.

59 *Taṣnīf al-ʿulūm* genre became popular in the Arab world *c.*750–800 CE. For surveys of this genre, see Bakar, *Classification of Knowledge*, p.43–6, 121–145, 203–218; Heck, 'The Hierarchy of Knowledge', pp.27–54, and Stearns, 'Writing Natural Science', pp. 923–951.

60 Melvin-Koushki, 'Introduction: De-orienting the Study of Islamicate Occultism', p. 289.

erudition were deemed insufficient to achieve the mastery of the science of letters. For example, in the early Shiʿi brotherhoods familiarity with the letters was originally reserved for imams, the heirs and successors of ʿAlī. In this aspect, the science of letters also matches the Western concept of the occult. Derived from the Latin word *occultus*, the term occult implies something that is secret, hidden and concealed – but not from everyone. In the mid-ninth century CE, Sufi thinkers expanded the circle of people who could potentially master the science of letters to each and every person who is pure of heart. As a result, Ibn ʿArabī identified the science of letters as 'the knowledge of [God's] friends' by means of which beings come into existence. It was 'the secret science, privilege of the initiated and those pure of heart, prophets and saints'.[61] In his works, the science of letters is indistinguishable from cosmology, ontology and hermeneutics. Ibn ʿArabī's approach was not unique: in Islamic culture, the science of letters has been equally associated with alchemy, astrology, astronomy, metaphysics, religious studies, physics, chemistry and mathematics. For this reason, Ibn ʿArabī was not wrong to label it as 'the universal science' (*al-ʿilm al-kullī*)[62] – nor was Ibn Khaldūn completely mistaken to classify it as an occult science. However, Ibn Khaldūn made two mistakes. First, the emergence of the science of letters in Islamic culture predates the works of al-Būnī and Ibn ʿArabī by at least four centuries. In spite of their contributions to the Islamic science of letters, their works were a product of the centuries-long appreciation of letters in medieval Islam. As a matter of fact, the science of letters made its way into Sufi literature as early as the ninth century CE. With the growing influence of Sufism, the science of letters was set to enter mainstream Islam as well.

According to al-Ghazālī (d. 505/1111), early Sufis abided by the belief that insights obtained by means of revelation should never be put into writing.[63] This prohibition also covered the basic premises of the science of letters. Among the first Sufis to circumvent the prohibition were Sahl al-Tustarī (d. 283/896), Abū Saʿīd al-Kharrāz (d. 286/899), Manṣūr al-Ḥallāj (d. 309/922) and Ibn Masarra (d. 319/931). Having acquired familiarity with the Shiʿi works on Qurʾanic hermeneutics and the symbolism of letters, Sufi thinkers adopted, expanded and refined

61 Ibn ʿArabī, *Kitāb al-Mīm*, fol. 14.

62 Ibn ʿArabī maintained that the science of letters is the most universal and the most Islamic of all sciences. His arguments were later popularized by Shams al-Dīn Āmulī (d. 753/1352). See Melvin-Koushki, 'Astrology, Lettrism, Geomancy: The Occult-Scientific Methods of Post-Mongol Islamicate Imperialism', p. 143.

63 Chittick, *Ibn ʿArabi, Heir to the Prophets*, p. 2.

them. This process was partially based on the innovative analyses they conducted. However, the development of the science of letters in the ninth and tenth centuries CE has been also determined by the increasing tendency of Sufis to rely on Hellenistic philosophy.

The influx of Hellenistic philosophy into Sufi literature intensified in the mid-tenth century CE, when the rising popularity of *The Epistles of the Brethren of Purity* inspired Ibn Masarra, Aḥmad al-Nasafī (d. ca. 331/943) and al-Sijistanī (d. post 361/971) to combine Qur'anic hermeneutics with Neoplatonism and Neopythagoreanism.[64] The newly-introduced Hellenistic elements in the Islamic science of letters were identified by Pierre Lory as 1) the perception of language as a means to deify human beings and achieve happiness in the afterlife and 2) the practical application of the Neopythagorean number theories to affirm the Islamic notion of the oneness of God (*tawḥīd*).[65] In the early eleventh century, Ḥamīd al-Dīn al-Kirmānī's (d. 411/1021) treatises introduced these teachings to North Africa and Muslim Spain, and it was here that they reached a new stage of refinement in the works of al-Būnī and Ibn ʿArabī. In the late twelfth and early thirteenth centuries, the science of letters thus provided Sufis with an opportunity to integrate 1) Pythagorean theories on the relationship between numbers and letters with 2) the Aristotelian and Stoic teachings on the composition and mixing of the four elements and natures and 3) the Neoplatonic categories, hierarchies and theories concerning the progression and movement of celestial bodies.[66] Writing on Sufi letter mysticism, Michael Ebstein differentiated between two types of the science of letters: 1) type α, the classical Sufi approach dealing with Qur'anic hermeneutics, and 2) type β, which perceives the letters of the alphabet as the primordial building blocks of the universe. According to Ebstein, the main difference between the two springs from the fact that even though the classical approach acknowledged that the letters are sacred, it lacked the cosmogonic and cosmological dimension of type β. Ebstein identified Ibn ʿArabī as a representative of type α – in contrast to al-Tustarī, whom he perceived as one of the

64 Daftary, *Ismaili History and Literary Traditions*, pp. 7–8.

65 Lory, *La science des lettres en Islam*, pp. 65–74.

66 For Neoplatonic influences in the science of letters, see Taylor, *In the Vicinity of the Righteous: Ziyara and the Veneration of Muslim Saints in Late Medieval Egypt*, p. 12; Saleh, *Licit Magic: The Touch and Sight of Islamic Talismanic Scrolls*, p. 45 and Schimmel, *Mystical Dimensions of Islam*, p. 263.

major representatives of type β.[67] However, in the works of Ibn ʿArabī, hermeneutical analyses of the Qurʾan and the cosmological aspects of the science of letters are equally covered. As a matter of fact, Ebstein was also among those who noticed that Ibn ʿArabī shared al-Tustarī's concept of speech as a medium of the creative will of God (*irāda*).[68] As a result, it is impossible to make a distinction between type α and type β Sufism on the basis of the surviving works of Ibn ʿArabī – nor do these works allow us to ascertain whether he was directly inspired by al-Tustarī.

The scarcity of direct quotes in Ibn ʿArabī's works makes it difficult to determine which scholarly works he consulted in order to develop his teachings. On his side, Ibn ʿArabī claimed that his works were primarily based on personal experiences and divine revelations. His claims subsequently led Binyamin Abrahamov to suggest that the impact of other Sufi teachers on Ibn ʿArabī's works was limited to the field of ethics. When it comes to philosophical and mystical aspects of his teachings, Abrahamov tended to agree with Chittick that Ibn ʿArabī has no real predecessors.[69] In light of the fact that Ibn ʿArabī was ready to admit that his teachings on the letters follow in the footsteps of Ibn Masarra and others, such observations appear to be exaggerated. In *The Meccan Revelations,* Ibn ʿArabī praises Abū Ṭālib al-Makkī (d. 386/998) as one of the few Sufi masters to realize that the letters of the Arabic alphabet, just like human beings, can receive divine revelations and form communities (*umam*), with prophets and obligations of their own. Possibly inspired by al-Makkī, Ibn ʿArabī divided these letters into the letters of the world of *Mulk* (*ʿālam al-mulk*), *Malakūt* (*ʿālam al-malakūt*) and *Jabarūt* (*ʿālam al-jabarūt*).[70] In a similar way, Ibn ʿArabī's notion of the universe as a book might have been (in)directly inspired by Ibn Masarra, while his terminology might or might not have been based on the works of al-Ḥallāj.[71] As indicated by Takeshita, esoteric interpretations of the Qurʾan and the notions of the world akin to those promoted in Ibn ʿArabī's works can be found in many Sufi

67 Ebstein and Sviri, 'The So-Called Risālat al-ḥurūf (Epistle of Letters) Ascribed to Sahl al-Tuṣtāri and Letter Mysticism in al-Andalus', pp. 230–1.

68 Ibid, p. 216.

69 See Abrahamov, *Ibn al-ʿArabi and the Sufis*, p. 102, and Chittick, *Ibn ʿArabi, Heir to the Prophets*, p. 2.

70 *Fut.*I:95; al-Manṣūb, 1/190; *FM.*I:58. Al-Makkī's views on the topic can be consulted at Yazaki, *Islamic Mysticism and Abu Talib al-Makki*, pp. 105–7. Properties of this division in Ibn ʿArabī's works will be explained later on.

71 López-Anguita. 'Ibn ʿArabī's Metaphysics in the Context of Andalusian Mysticism', p. 8.

circles and several schools of theology.[72] In this regard, Ibn ʿArabī's works are typical representatives of thirteenth-century Sufism, which successfully united 1) Qur'anic hermeneutics with 2) Hellenistic philosophy and 3) Islamic occultism.

Before we proceed with an in-depth analysis of Ibn ʿArabī's writings on the science of letters, it is, however, important to make a distinction between high occultism, folk magic and the rarefied theories of Ibn ʿArabī. The failure to do so was Ibn Khaldūn's second mistake. On his side, Ibn ʿArabī acknowledged that the letters of the Arabic alphabet could be used to predict the future and return to the pure, primordial state of being. In *The Meccan Revelations*, he points out Ibn Barrajān's (d. 536/1141) prophecy that Saladin was destined to conquer Jerusalem in 1187 CE as an example of a successful divination by means of letters. Ibn Barrajān made this prophecy by applying several numerological calculations on the first five verses of the Sura *al-Rūm*. In his *Book of the Fabulous Gryphon*, Ibn ʿArabī notably relied on a similar method to predict the arrival of the Seal.[73] Like al-Mughīra, he believed that the mastery of letters can be used to revive the dead – a fact that led him to associate the science of letters with Jesus, the prophet reported to have resurrected the dead and breathed life into figurines made of clay.[74] In addition, Ibn ʿArabī argued that the recitation of the disjoined letters can be used to induce mystical visions.[75]

Writing on the practical uses of the science of letters, Ibn Khaldūn pointed out that the Sufis relied on the letters of the Arabic alphabet to cure illnesses and 'bring down the spirituality of spheres and tying it down with the help of pictures and numerical proportions'.[76] A common method to achieve this goal was to use the letters to make talismans, which Ibn Khaldūn described as ferments of the four elements: fire, water, air and earth. While fiery letters were thought to increase sensuality, watery letters have been used to repel

72 Takeshita, 'Ibn ʿArabī's Theory of the Perfect Human and its Place in the History of Islamic Thought', pp. 18–21.

73 'An appearance [of the Seal of the Saints] shall arise after the passing of *khā'* of the alphabet (after 600H), his birth after the passing of the *ṣād* and the *thā'* (60+500H) after the birth of his developmental form (*mīlād al-inshā'*)', Elmore, *Islamic Sainthood*, p. 531. See also Goldziher, 'Ibn Barrağān', pp. 544–6, and *Fut.*I:97–8; al-Manṣūb, 1/193–4; *FM.*I: 59–60.

74 *Fut.*I:255–6; al-Manṣūb, 1/509, *FM.*I:167–8.

75 *Fut.*I:100; al-Manṣūb, 1/196–7; *FM.*I:61.

76 Ibn Khaldūn, *al-Muqaddima* vol.3, p. 75.

fever.[77] Similar tendencies have been documented in high occultism and folklore, with letters serving as a focal component in the art of making talismans (*ʿilm al-ṭalāsim*). Ibn ʿArabī's meditations on the summoned letters and the illuminated holograph of his *Book of Theophanies* indicate that he was, at least to some degree, familiar with these talismans – a fact that appears to have been a source of shame and discomfort for Ibn Sawdakīn (d. 646/1248), al-Jīlī (d. ca. 832/1428) and the later interpreters of his works. Nevertheless, on the authority of Jaʿfar al-Ṣādiq (d. 148/765) and his pupil Jābir (d. ca. 199/815), Ibn ʿArabī identified talismans as instruments for transferring spiritual powers from one plane of existence to another.

> The disciple of Jaʿfar Ṣādiq, peace be upon him, said, 'I asked my master and mentor why is talisman referred to as "talisman". The imam replied: "Because of its overreaching [influence]."' This means that each talisman gives its full power to the one who relies on it. I described this phenomenon in *The Book of Temples* (*Kitāb al-Hayākil*), which we will now refer to, God willing. Each talisman springs from the domain of the Absolute Being which has no relations to embodied beings due to its relation with the First [i.e. God] that admits no second. This was elaborated in *The Book of Letters* (*Kitāb al-ḥurūf*), which is a part of *The Meccan Revelations*. Let us refer to it, God willing.[78]

Ibn ʿArabī identified talismans as embodiments of the spiritual properties of the disjoined letters. According to Porter, the most common combination of the disjoined letters on Islamic talismans was *kāf-hā'-yā'-ʿayn-ṣād*, which appears at the beginning of the Sura *Maryam*.[79] However, the only surviving talisman in Ibn ʿArabī's hand refers to the disjoined letters *alif-lām-mīm* (Fig. 2).

When combined, these letters stand for the world of *Malakūt* (*alif*), *Jabarūt* (*lām*) and *Mulk* (*mīm*). A similar opinion was advocated by al-Sulamī and Manṣūr al-Ḥallāj:

> Al-Ḥallāj said that the entirety of letters is kingdom (*mulk*) and that the king of the kingdom is *alif*. *Lām* is its outer form (*ṣūra*)

77 Ibid, pp. 145, 172.

78 Ibn ʿArabī, *Kitāb al-Tajalliyāt*, fol. 31.

79 Porter, 'Stones to bring Rain? Magical Inscriptions in Linear Kufic on Rock Crystal Amulet-Seals', pp. 144–9.

Fig. 2 Ibn ʿArabī's talisman for harnessing the spiritual power of the disjoined letters alif-lām-mīm

> and *alif* is the soul (*rūḥ*) of *lām*. The knowledge of *lām* is the essence of *alif* and the knowledge of *mīm* is the essence of *lām*. *Lām* is the soul and light of *mīm*. *Alif* is manifested with respect to the hidden *mīm*, while *mīm* is linked to the manifested *lām*.[80]

Ibn ʿArabī taught that the disjoined letters *alif-lām-mīm* are a symbol of God (*alif*) and His relation to the world He created (*lām, mīm*). The disjoined letter *alif* was used in Ibn ʿArabī's works as a symbol of transcendence (*tanzīh*) and inaccessibility of the Divine being[81]. In the world of letters, *alif* was akin to a ruling caliph in

---

80 al-Sulamī, *Sharḥ maʿānī al-ḥurūf*, pp. 372–5. In his interpretation of the quoted passage, Böwering observed that while *alif* stands for God, *lām* represents the divine gifts (*al-ālā'*) and *mīm* is the universe. Böwering, 'Sulamī's Treatise on the Science of the Letters (*ʿilm al-ḥurūf*)', p. 354.

81 *Fut.*I:100; al-Manṣūb, 1/198; *FM.*I:61. In this aspect, its symbolism is close in meaning to the isolated form of *alif*, which will be analysed in a separate chapter of the present study.

human society. At the same time however, *alif* was associated with the *ḥadīth qudsī*, 'our Lord descends down to the sky of this world',[82] and the unbroken unity between the Creator and the created. Ibn ʿArabī identified the orthographic form of the disjoined letter *alif* with the so-called Straight Path (*al-ṣīrāṭ al-mustaqīm*) which leads to the state of unity with God.[83] When standing next to *alif, lām* was perceived as a symbol of the creative power which brought the world to existence. The disjoined letter *lām* was thought to represent the creation of the world in six days, from Sunday to Friday – or alternatively, the archangel Gabriel as the bringer of revelations. As for *mīm*, which is the last letter of the combination, it came to be associated with the Prophet Muhammad as a model of human excellence.[84] In addition to the talisman which was set to capture the power of the disjoined letters *alif-lām-mīm*, Ibn ʿArabī's works speak of the thirteen different talismans that could be used to increase the rational capacities and imagination of an individual. Echoes of similar beliefs and practices can be traced in the second chapter of *The Meccan Revelations,* which divides the letters of the Arabic alphabet into four step-levels:

1. Divine letters: *alif, zāy, lām*
2. Human letters: *nūn, ṣād, ḍād*
3. Jinn letters: *ʿayn, ghayn, sīn, shīn*
4. Angelic letters: *bāʾ, tāʾ, thāʾ, jīm, ḥāʾ, khāʾ, dāl, dhāl, rāʾ, ṭāʾ, ẓāʾ, fāʾ, qāf, kāf, mīm, hāʾ, wāw, yāʾ, hamza*

Each of the step-levels was thought to be guarded by four angels and endowed with a different nature: hot, cold, wet and/or dry (Table 3). While divine, human and the first pair of jinn letters were thought to be hot and dry, *sīn* and *shīn* were deemed to be cold and dry letters. With the exception of *hāʾ* and *hamza*, whose nature was cold

82 *Ṣaḥīḥ al-Bukhārī* #1094.

83 *Fut.*I:100; al-Manṣūb, 1/197; *FM.*I:61. The term *al-ṣīrāṭ al-mustaqīm* refers to the seventh verse of the Sura *al-Fātiḥa*: 'Show us the straight path, the path of those You bestowed favour upon, not anger upon, and not of those who go astray.' (Q.1:7)

84 Bosnevi's commentary on Bezels of Wisdom offers a different point of view. He believed that *lām* stands for the world that was yet to be created. The hooked end of its orthographic form (ل) represents the letter *nūn*, the universal symbol of manifested existence, and *mīm* is the Perfect Human. Bosnevi, *Sharh Fuṣūṣ al-ḥikam* vol.1, p.202.

and wet, and *ḥā'* and *khā'* (which were believed to be cold and dry), Ibn ʿArabī attributed the angelic letters with a hot and dry nature.[85]

Table 3 The Four Natures of the Letters

Hot	Cold	Dry	Moist
alif	*bā'*	*jīm*	*dāl*
hā'	*wāw*	*zāy*	*ḥā'*
ṭā'	*yā'*	*kāf*	*lām*
mīm	*nūn*	*sīn*	*ʿayn*
fā'	*ṣād*	*qāf*	*rā'*
shīn	*tā'*	*thā'*	*khā'*
dhāl	*ḍād*	*ẓā'*	*ghayn*

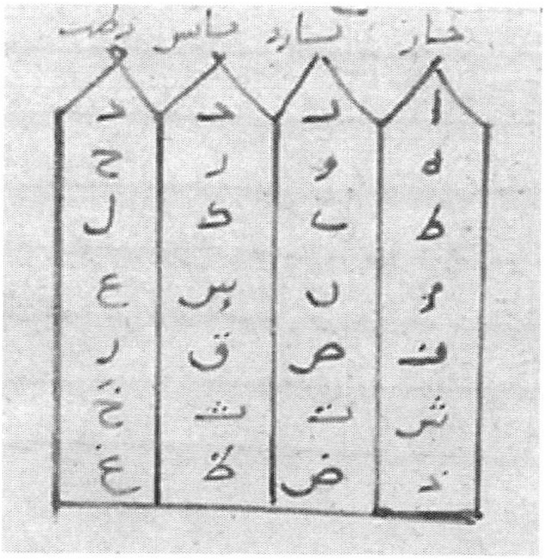

Ibn ʿArabī's works refer to the aforementioned natures as 'Mothers'. With the turning of the heavenly spheres (*aflāk*), the four Mothers get mixed up together to create fire, water, air and earth. While hot and dry natures unite to create fire, the union of hot and cold natures was thought to result in the emergence of air. The mixture of cold and wet would then create water, and the product of the union between cold and dry natures was the element of earth.[86] Ibn ʿArabī compared the transmutation of the Mothers into organic matter to the permutation of phonemes into language. 'Letters are the material for words,' he wrote, 'just as water, earth, fire, and air build the formation of our bodies.'[87] 'When these elements are brought out, i.e. water, fire, air and earth, He makes them transform one into another and so fire returns to air, and air to fire, just as the letter *tā'* is transformed to *ṭā'* and the *sīn* to *ṣād'*.[88] However, Ibn ʿArabī's understanding of the exact nature of

85 It should be noted, however, that alif was not perceived as a 'real' letter of the Arabic alphabet. As such, it was not limited to any step-level and/or nature in particular. In addition, Ibn ʿArabī pointed out that mystics know of two more step-levels: the step-level of the letter *nūn* ('we do not know Him except through us and He is the object of devotion') and the step-level of *alif* and *wāw* ('*alif* belongs to Him, *wāw* means you. There is nothing in existence but God and you', *Fut.* I:93; al-Manṣūb, 1/187; *FM.*I: 57). These step-levels will be analyzed in separate chapters of the present study.

86 *Fut.*I:90–91; al-Manṣūb, 1/184; *FM.*I:55. See also *Fut.*I:218–9; al-Manṣūb, 1/411–2; *FM.*I:142–3.

87 *Fut.*I:132; al-Manṣūb, 1/285; *FM.*I:85.

88 *Fut.*I:92; al-Manṣūb, 1/185; *FM.*I:56.

this process remains unclear. The relevant passages from *The Meccan Revelations* are vague – and as a result, it is also close to impossible to determine which criteria he referred to in order to divide the letters into four step-levels. Another difficulty lies in determining the nature of the relationship between the four elements and the letters of the Arabic alphabet –how did it come to be that the element of *hamza* is fire, while the letter *qāf* is both fire and water? Some letters like *hā'* were even described as being of the greater element of earth and the lesser element of air.[89]. In this aspect, the text of *The Meccan Revelations* demonstrates the same lack of clarity that was identified as the main problem of the Aristotelian theory of matter: for it is unclear how substances are constructed from opposites like hot and cold, moist and dry so that they do not disintegrate.[90] 'It would be necessary to write a full book to cite and explain this further,' Ibn 'Arabī remarked.[91] He never did.

Ibn 'Arabī was quick to notice how tables of correspondence between the four elements, four Mothers and the letters of the Arabic alphabet vary from one scholarly work to another. In contrast to Ibn 'Arabī's teachings, which are presented in Table 4, alternative divisions by Ibn Sawdakīn and al-Būnī are illustrated in Table 5 and Table 6. On his side, Ibn 'Arabī pondered whether discrepancies between the different works of science can be taken as an indicator of a general tendency among scholars to lead the uninitiated astray.[92] Ultimately however, there was no general consensus in the Islamic science of letters on the matter.

The closest Ibn 'Arabī comes to an explanation of the relationship between the four elements, four Mothers and the letters of the Arabic alphabet is asserting that the letters do not have the power to bring forth coldness, warmth, dryness and wetness when invoked 'just because they are letters but because of their shapes'.[93] The real reason behind the intentional vagueness of his remarks is revealed several pages later, where he identifies the topic in question as an insight into God's knowledge of the world before it was created. The basic

89 This was the basis of Ibn 'Arabī's division of letters on the pure and mixed letters of the Arabic alphabet. While a pure letter emerges from a single element, the mixed letters consist of two or more elements. See *Fut.*I:106–19; al-Manṣūb, 1/208; *FM.*I:66–75.

90 Freudenthal, 'The Problem of Cohesion between Alchemy and Natural Philosophy: from Unctuous Moisture to Phlogiston', p. 107.

91 *Fut.*I:87; al-Manṣūb, 1/178, *FM.*I:53.

92 Ibn 'Arabī, *The Meccan Revelations* vol.2, p. 124.

93 *Fut.*I:289; al-Manṣūb, 1/557; *FM.*I:190.

prerequisite of every rational analysis, Ibn ʿArabī believed, is an object of research. What never existed, cannot be known – and the same goes for the nature of all things before they were created. 'This is a strange mystery and difficult complexity which is forbidden to be revealed' – and it would be pointless to attempt to circumvent this prohibition 'since the intellect could not take it'.[94] Having admitted that he only came to catch a glimpse of this secret, Ibn ʿArabī maintained that it is sufficient to say that the Creator wanted the four Mothers united as a part of His plan to create the world with the four elements as its foundation.[95] Further clarification on Ibn ʿArabī's stand on the matter can be found in his *Book of Mīm, Wāw and Nūn*:

> I speak here, in the manner of Ibn Masarra al-Jabalī and the likes of him, of the secrets of the letters, rather than dealing with their practical uses – for to speak of the practical uses of [these] things usually exposes the person to accusations and denunciations (…). Denunciations are usually provoked because it is necessary for those who attempt these things [letter magic] to be familiar with the composition in question: its forms, times, scripts (*aqlām*) and so on. Even if the slightest aspect of the whole operation is off, it will all come to nothing – which will then lead the operator to blame it on the operation itself and say: 'I have tried out what he said and nothing came of it!' For this reason, it is preferable for those who follow our path to maintain a total silence when it comes to applied sciences (*al-ʿulūm al ʿamaliyya*). It is forbidden to go into detail about these matters in a way that is fully comprehensible to the elite and the masses alike – for this would enable the ones who are corrupt, in spite of their unworthiness, to use them for personal advantage. For this reason, I only made certain allusions in my books for the sake of my companions, since I am confident that no one else will understand what I am alluding to. By leaving everyone else in confusion, I am not concerned that I might be denounced since, praise God, my religion is sound![96]

The complexity and refinement of Ibn ʿArabī's theories is the first point of difference between his works and thirteenth-century folklore.

94 *Fut.*I:91; al-Manṣūb, 1/184; *FM.*I:55–6.
95 *Fut.*I:91–92; al-Manṣūb, 1/184; *FM.*I:55–6.
96 Ibn ʿArabī, *K. al-Mīm*, fol.17.

Table 4 Correspondences between the four elements and the letters of the Arabic alphabet

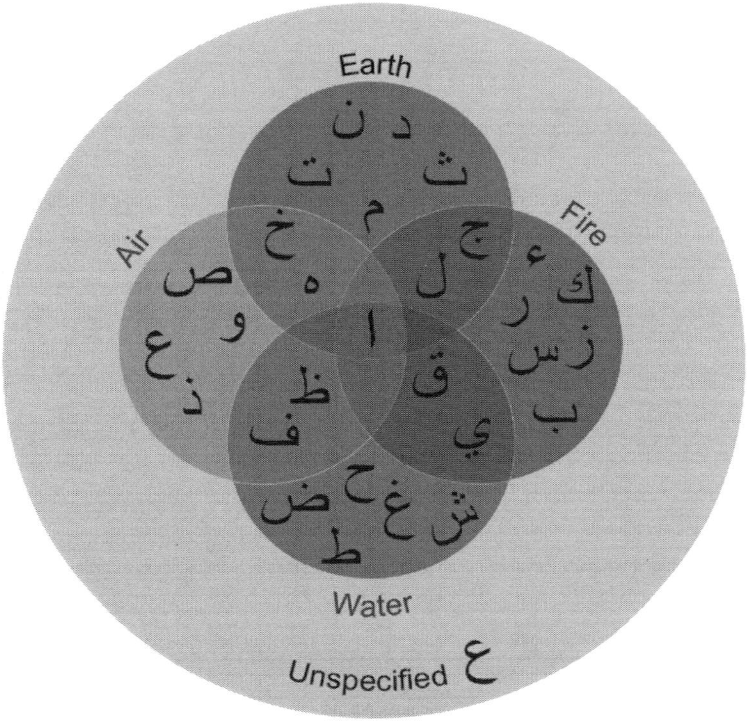

Table 5 Ibn Sawdakīn's table of correspondences between the four elements and the letters of the Arabic alphabet

Fire	Water	Air	Earth
ا	د	ج	ب
ه	ح	ز	و
ط	ل	ك	ي
م	ع	ص	ن
ف	ر	ق	ض
س	خ	ث	ت
ذ	ش	غ	ظ

Table 6 Al-Būnī's table of correspondences between the four elements and the letters of the Arabic alphabet

Fire	Water	Air	Earth
ا	ج	ب	د
ه	ز	و	ح
ط	ك	ي	ل
م	س	ن	ع
ف	ق	ص	ر
ش	ث	ت	خ
ذ	ظ	ض	غ

However, similar analyses can be found in Islamic high occultism. When it comes to the science of letters, the works of thirteenth-century occultists were of comparable quality to Sufi literature.[97] The major point of difference between the two is, however, reflected in their approach to the practical use of letters. While he associated the properties of the letters with the four elements, lunar mansions and certain numerical values – just like the leading occultists of his time – Ibn ʿArabī's works were not intended to serve as occult manuals. In the eyes of Ibn ʿArabī, the science of letters was never one of the occult sciences to begin with. He therefore refused to acknowledge that human beings could master the secret properties of letters by means of hard work and devotion. Piety, purity of heart and the help of supernatural beings had a limited role in Islamic high occultism. To achieve the desired result, all one needed was the right recipe.[98] In contrast, at first sight, Ibn ʿArabī's works appear to be strictly theoretical. This is the main point of difference between his works and the writings of the leading occultists of his time. With the exception of a single talisman and the two examples of divination by means of letters, one of which was made by Ibn ʿArabī himself, a practitioner of letter magic would find little to work with in the surviving works of Ibn ʿArabī. As a result, Nallino dismissed his writing style as 'icy', 'theoretical' and 'bizarre of features'.[99] However, this was due to the fact that the science of letters was deemed to be dangerous, unpredictable and, in most cases, an unattainable goal for masters of the natural sciences. If one would attempt to study it without obedience to God, 'He makes him wretched'.[100] Not all people are suited to be teachers and practitioners. 'Knowledge of divine matters,' noted Ibn ʿArabī, 'despite its nobility, is not required from the majority of people. Verily, a single person with this knowledge is enough for a region, like a doctor – one is enough.'[101]

97 For cultural tendencies in thirteenth-century Islamic occultism, see Idel, 'Kabbalah and Elites in Thirteenth-Century Spain', p. 5–19, Gardiner, *Esotericism in a Manuscript Culture: Aḥmad al-Būnī and His Readers through the Mamlūk Period*, p. 26 and Martin, *Theurgy in the Medieval Islamic World*, p. 11.

98 Prior to the mid-fourteenth century, the science of letters was commonly identified with occult science and natural philosophy (*al-ʿilm al-ṭabīʿī*). While Ibn Khaldūn appears to have been aware of these tendencies, he still went on to classify Ibn ʿArabī's works with occult sciences. Ibn Khaldūn, *al-Muqqadima* vol.3, pp. 146–176. On the science of the letters in the Islamic high occultism in general, see Canteins, 'The Hidden Sciences in Islam', p. 449.

99 Nallino, 'Il poema mistico arabo d'Ibn al-Fārid', p. 23.

100 *Fut.*III:180; al-Manṣūb, 5/29; *FM.*II:121.

101 *Fut.*I:91; al-Manṣūb, 1/134; *FM.*I:35–6.

For the vast majority of people, Ibn ʿArabī believed, it is quite enough to read and recite sacred texts. It takes time and courage to come to terms with the hidden truths they contain, with great risks being attached to the process.

> Plunge into the ocean of the inaccessible Qur'an, if you are strong of breath - or limit yourself to studying its literal meaning from the books of the Qur'anic commentaries and refrain from the plunge otherwise, lest you be destroyed as the ocean of the Qur'an is profound indeed.[102]

> He, the Exalted One, said: 'We did not leave out anything out of the Book - and this is the mighty Qur'an. Nothing false comes from it in front or from behind'. Muhammad, praise be upon him, was verified through the Qur'an by possessing the All-encompassing word. Every knowledge of the prophets and the angels and every language known: the Qur'an embraces all that knowledge and elucidates it for the people of the Qur'an by the means of revelation.[103]

Ibn ʿArabī believed that no scripture matches the excellence of the Qurʾan, though they are all the speech of God. 'It (the Qurʾan) is the articulation of the universe, the statement of every speaker and the Divine names which God taught Adam.'[104] The content of the Qurʾanic revelation is divided into 114 suras. These were intended as highlights for the meaning of the text. On the cosmological level, the suras were thought to correspond to the First Intellect, the heavenly spheres and other levels of existence. On the linguistic level, Ibn ʿArabī believed, one should seek correspondences between the suras, the Most Beautiful Names of God and, ultimately, the letters of the Arabic alphabet. The letters of the Qurʾan, 320,015 in number, were thought to serve as guides for helping us (re)learn how to read and interpret the meaning of the three great books. Compared to an ocean without shore, the text of the Qurʾanic revelation was also deemed to be dangerous – as was the ontological language of the two other great books of the science of letters. To read the Qurʾan, whose language was thought to be the most accessible of the three, was sufficient to make one a man of God. But

102 *Fut.*I:119; al-Manṣūb, 1/227, *FM.*I:76.
103 *Fut.*III:120; al-Manṣūb, 4/564; *FM.*II:107.
104 *Fut.*IV:91; al-Manṣūb, 6/258; *FM.*II:492.

to understand its content, memorize it and put it to practice – 'well,' as Ibn ʿArabī said, 'this is Light upon Light upon Light!'[105] When it comes to the properties of letters, even certain prophets have only been entrusted only with a message to convey, with no real understanding of the legacy they were to leave for the generations to come.

> Divinity is too holy, too transcendent for It to be perceived and for anyone to share in Its rank – for you are the vessel and I am I (*anta l-inā' wa anā anā*). Do not seek Me within yourself, for that brings hardship and distress, nor outside yourself, for that is endless. But don't give up searching for Me, or you will be wretched. Search for Me until you meet Me, and ascend onwards thereby – but proceed honourably, with courteous demeanour in your search.[106]

Had He wished for mankind to remain ignorant of the science of letters, the Creator would have likely refrained Himself from revealing it to Adam. Sufis believed that familiarity with the letters was incorporated in the human body, the second great book of the science of letters, and transmitted down the line of prophets. Nevertheless, Ibn ʿArabī felt that it is as if the whole existence was clothed by God in the robe of ignorance. As a result, the need of the self for knowledge was thought to be greater than the need of body for food. For those who were willing to advance on the path of knowledge, Ibn ʿArabī's works were intended to serve as an invitation and a warning alike.

---

105 *Fut.*II:101; al-Manṣūb, 2/559; *FM.*I:440.

106 *Fut.*I:84. al-Manṣūb, 1/173–4; *FM.*I:51.

Knowledge is more eminent than love.

Ibn ʿArabī [105]

105 Chittick. *Ibn ʿArabi, Heir to the Prophets*, p. 27.

1.3. The Path of Reflection and the Path of Revelation

'Ignorance is death' reads a line from *The Meccan Revelations*[106] - for Ibn ʿArabī believed that it is among the greatest sins to fear the book.[107] Upon embarking on the search for knowledge, each person has two paths at their disposal. The first possibility would be to turn to ourselves and rely on the capacities of the rational mind. This was the path of reflection, rational observation and intellectual demonstration. The surviving works of Ibn ʿArabī usually refer to the rational mind as *ʿaql*. He believed that *ʿaql* presides over the soul and its essence: for it was within the power of the mind to wrestle the soul from the rule of Law or set it on the right path again.[108] However, as Ibn ʿArabī pointed out, the term *ʿaql* was derived from the same root as *ʿiqāl*, which is the Arabic word for shackles. This was not a coincidence – when it comes to the Arabic language, Ibn ʿArabī believed in none. He interpreted the root of this term as an implication that, in spite of its power over the soul, the human mind has a limited perception. As a result, rational knowledge was deemed to be relative. Ibn ʿArabī identified rational knowledge as every conclusion that was 1) drawn from self-evident circumstances and/or 2) established on a proof that appears to be self-evident. Depending on the intellectual capacities of an individual, such conclusions can be more or less worthy. The quality of rational knowledge is furthermore determined by one's choice of methodology. When it comes to methodology, 'some of it is sound, some of it is corrupt'.[109]

Fig. 3a One goal, two paths and a single starting point: a sketch from the margins of The Meccan Revelations

In contrast, revealed knowledge has no scales to be weighed on. Although the source of revelations is always the same (i.e. God, His vast knowledge and His spirits), revealed knowledge is not limited

106 *Fut.*I:266; al-Manṣūb, 3/277; *FM.*I:558.

107 Ibn ʿArabī writes: 'Fear of the Book is the worst of my sins for the Book rules over *wujūd* and us". Quoted according to Chittick. *The Self-Disclosure of God*, p. 25.

108 *Fut.*II:264; al-Manṣūb, 3/275; *FM.*I:557.

109 *Fut.*I:54; al-Manṣūb, 1/123; *FM.*I:31.

in spectrum. As such, revelations do not necessarily address divine matters. While a religious scholar might be blessed with a revelation concerning Shariʿa law, revealed knowledge could also take the form of a poetic meter in the case of a grammarian, or come as an insight in the nature of archetypes (*maʿanī*) if the recipient is a logician.[110] Al-Qayṣarī compared a spark of revelation to the lifting of a veil that suddenly brings us face to face with the dazzling beauty of a woman.[111] Once it awakens within the human heart, a spark of revelation typically results in the increase of faith. While Ibn ʿArabī explicitly defined faith as a self-evident knowledge, free from limits of the mind, he also associated it with deep feelings of security, inner certainty and gratitude. Imbued with faith, knowledge by means of revelation was thought to be permanent and immune to the self-doubts of a recipient. As a result, revelations were thought to result in certainty, knowledge and happiness. However, this is not to say that revealed knowledge and rational investigation cannot lead to identical conclusions (Figs. 3a and 3b). To reach his goal, Ibn ʿArabī pointed out, a rider could mount any horse – but the goal and the rider are always one and the same.

> The one who sees with two eyes [i.e. is blessed with divine revelation] takes the path of happiness that is not preceded by misery. It is an easy, pure road, just like a clean garment. Meanwhile the other path, even though it also ends in happiness, is filled with difficulties and savage beasts. The two roads are adjacent. They emanate from the same source and end at the same destination, and I have envisioned them and drawn them as such.[112]

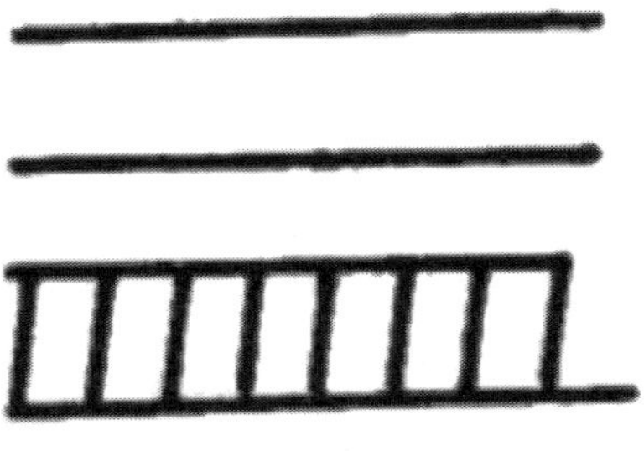

a) The Path of Revelation

b) The Path of Reflection

Fig. 3b The Path of Reflection and the Path of Revelation

110 *Fut.*I:253; al-Manṣūb, 1/505; *FM.*I:166.

111 al-Qayṣarī, *Foundations of Islamic Mysticism*, p. 144.

112 *Sifr* 26: fol.83b. *Fut.*VI:181–2; al-Manṣūb, 9/311; *FM.*III:418.

In Fig. 3b, the upper portion of the diagram represents the path of revelation. No obstacles are depicted on it – this was the straight path to knowledge and happiness. Knowledge of God by the means of revelation thus came to be perceived as the most precious gift of the Almighty to mankind.[113] However, the downside of this path is that a seeker cannot influence the time of arrival and the nature of a revelation he will receive. The progress he makes, if any, is beyond his control. To pray for a specific revelation or make demands on God was believed to be of little use. In his *Bezels of Wisdom*, Ibn ʿArabī reflects on the case of ʿUzayr, who was eventually threatened by God that he will lose his status of a messenger unless he stops praying for knowledge he was never meant to receive. In the case of divine messengers, the content of revelations they receive was thought to be tailored to the needs of communities they were sent to. However, Ibn ʿArabī believed that it was not due to cruelty that ʿUzayr was denied the knowledge he sought.[114] In his works, one's lack of interest in divine matters could be interpreted as a special form of divine mercy. Ignorant, pious people usually remain safe in their ignorance from provoking the divine wrath by engaging in inaccurate interpretations of divine mysteries.

> However, once they indulge in interpretations, they cease to be perceived as common men and obtain a certain rank among rational thinkers and interpreters. They will then be judged according to the quality of their interpretation and God will hold them accountable for it. They may hit the target – or miss the point altogether when it comes to that which was lacking in the literal, obvious meaning of what the Lawgiver (i.e. the Prophet Muhammad) brought us.[115]

Ibn ʿArabī held that the witnesses of divine revelations (*shuhadāʾ*) are the only people who can speak of divine mysteries with authority. In his works, they are commonly referred to as 'People of the Presence' and 'The Close Ones' due to their closeness with God. Some of them, but not all of them, eventually get to be appointed as prophets. But whereas all a) prophets (*nabiyūn*) are without fail b) righteous (*sāliḥūn*), c) truthful (*ṣiddīq*) d) witnesses (*shuhadāʾ*) of divine revelations, not all recipients of revelation are suited to serve

113 *Fut.*II:549–50; al-Manṣūb, 4/253; *FM.*I:756.

114 *Fut.*III:96-7; al-Manṣūb, 4/444–5; *FM.*II:64

115 *Fut.*I:59; al-Manṣūb, 1/130; *FM.*I:34.

as prophets. This was depicted in the fourteenth book of *The Meccan Revelations* (Fig. 4). The representatives of the four categories depicted in Fig. 4 share common traits; with each of them being a true believer, the possessor of knowledge, close to God.[116] However, this doesn't mean that they are equal in rank.

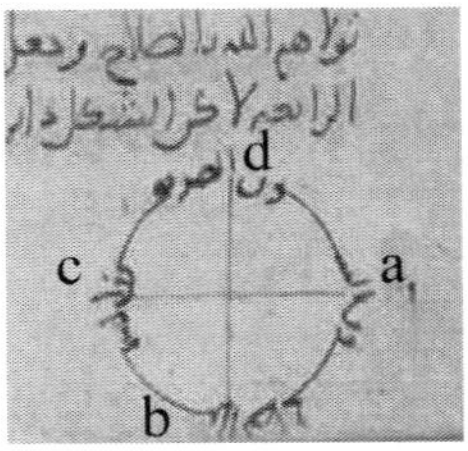

Fig. 4 The four categories of Closeness

As in life, so in death – as depicted in Ibn ʿArabī's diagram of the Dune of Vision (Fig. 5). This diagram depicts the Dune of Vision (*kathīb al-ruʾya*), which is a) a dune of withe musk (*kathīb min al-misk al-abyaḍ*) at the summit of the paradise in the garden of Eden (*jannat ʿadn*). It also contains Ibn ʿArabī's depiction of the chairs, thrones and seats of the Close Ones. These are positioned in accordance with the degree occupied by the inhabitants of the garden of Eden, who will be able to see God on the Judgement Day. The diagram depicts the inhabitants of the paradise being divided into four communities (*ṭawāʾif*): believers, saints, messengers and prophets.[117] However, even among the prophets, some were thought to be ranked above others. Ibn ʿArabī argued that there is no escaping the fact that every human has a hierarchical level, someone greater, lesser or equal. Beyond this limit, one cannot go.

A similar opinion was advocated by al-Sulāmī:

> He [i.e. the Creator] made engravings of letters in the innermost beings of mystics, aspirants and penitents. Each one of them turns in his innermost being to a particular letter, becomes familiar with it and feels at ease with it – according to the degree of his state. When mystics fully achieve the station of knowledge, when they feel at ease before their object of research and stand upright in His presence on the carpet of power, close to Him and in conversation with Him, they transcend the secret meanings of the letters. Thus they become fully acquainted with the various

116 *Sifr* 19: fol.111.
117 *Sifr* 28: fol.94.

> aspects of wisdom that God has entrusted to each of the letters. Then all creatures, whether they are human beings, jinn, beasts of prey, birds or animals, become familiar and at ease with them. They speak with mystics and mystics understand them and, vice versa, mystics speak to them and are understood by them. This is a mighty station. Seekers become aware of letters as utterances of the divine proclamation while penitents merely become familiar with listening to their articulation without reaching the understanding mystics and seekers possess.[118]

There are certain mysteries and transcendent realities that transcend the rational mind.[119] If one were to receive a revelation beyond his capacity to comprehend it, such a man would be bound to perish. Among the Sufis, it has thus been narrated how Jesus the prophet once encountered an ascetic. Emaciated and weak, for seventy years the ascetic prayed to receive a single thing: a single atom of God's love. Nonetheless, his request was refused repeatedly. Moved by pity, Jesus prayed to God in his stead – and for a long time, his prayers remained unanswered. One day however, God addressed Jesus and instructed him to visit the ascetic once again. He found him in front of a cave: unresponsive, with mouth agape, his gaze was fixed on the sky. God said to Jesus:

> He was asking for an atom's weight of Our love, but We knew that he was too weak to carry it. Thus We granted him a seventieth part of an atom which left him awestruck as he is – and what would be his condition if We granted him more![120]

With insanity and unconsciousness as alternatives, Ibn ʿArabī believed that it is sometimes better to look at a word and see only a vowel, with no hint of the deeper meanings it contains. 'God is the measurer who appoints the predetermined measure and makes you acquire the capacity to do what is predetermined,' reads the opening chapter of *The Meccan Revelations.*[121] However, Ibn ʿArabī later went on to ascertain that the main veil between the knowledge and a seeker is not a divine whim but *khuluq*. In his works, this term stands for the

---

118 al-Sulamī, *Sharḥ maʿānī al-ḥurūf*, p. 372–5.
119 Elmore, *Islamic Sainthood,* p. 242.
120 al-Bauniyyah, *The Principles of Sufism*, pp. 130–1.
121 *Fut.*I:15; al-Manṣūb, 1/69; *FM.*I:1.

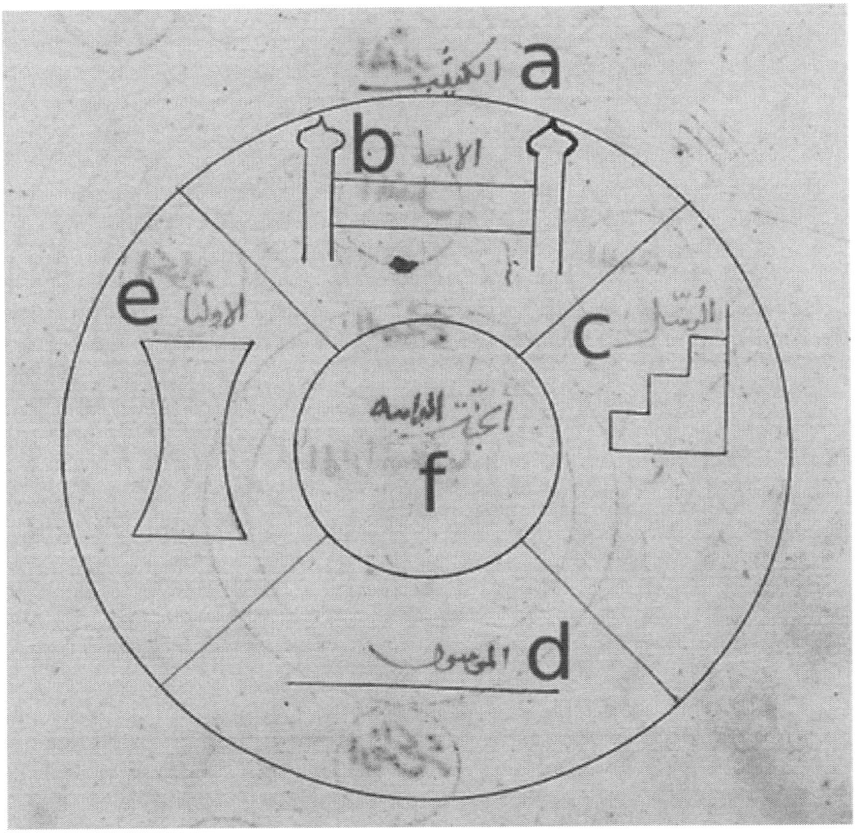

Fig. 5 Different ranks of the inhabitants of paradise: b) Prophets, c) Messengers, d) Believers and e) Saints. Ibn Arabī associated this vision with a) the Dunes of Musk and f) the Paradise of Eden, which is the highest of the seven heavenly gardens in Islam.

character and appearance in general. *Khuluq* represents the physical constitution, moral character and the inner life of a person.[122] This is the human nature in the broadest sense – and our nature is our destiny. Each person's destiny was believed to be predetermined. Once it has been woven in the human chest, fate dictates the amount of knowledge we will be able to receive and process. By fate, we are bound for heaven or hell.[123] Ibn ʿArabī perceived destiny as one of the most exalted divine secrets. Except by means of revelation, it was generally thought to be impossible to know one's fate in advance, and human beings were usually left in the dark when it comes to their rank in the

122 Winkel, *Interactions* vol.2, p.28.
123 *Fut.*I:15. al-Manṣūb, 1/69; *FM.*I:1. See also De Cillis. *Free Will and Predestination in Islamic Thought*, p.172, 189.

universe. The true Friends of God, he believed, know better than to attempt to find out on their own what fate has in store of them – 'since the True doesn't come closer to someone who disobeys Him with his disobedience, and the seeker of this knowledge has already disobeyed Him in his search'.[124]

To a degree, one's *khuluq* could be refined by engaging in religious studies and the acts of piety. The same degree of control each person holds over his personal fate. 'The offspring of Adam ascend with their each and every breath,' noted Ibn ʿArabī on the matter.[125] With the exception of humans and jinn, most living beings were denied the opportunity of inner growth. Having created heaven and earth, reads the eleventh verse of the Sura *Fuṣṣilat*, God asked them to come to Him *willingly or unwillingly* (Q.41:11). Although he was familiar with the quote, Ibn ʿArabī held that, in this case, refusal was out of the question. Like angels, the heaven and the earth were thought to be created in absolute obedience to the divine will. In contrast, Ibn ʿArabī believed that human beings and jinn were given the freedom to make a choice of their own. If they wished, they could choose not to worship God. The choice to turn to or from knowledge and obedience to God puts the fate of each human being into his own hands. For this reason, messengers and revelations have been sent to different communities and individuals. Unlike God, an individual usually lacks knowledge of his inner capacities and the outcome of the choices he makes. Nevertheless, self-development and knowledge of the divine mysteries remain a possibility.

> If you did not have the potential to receive perfection, it would be incorrect to admonish you and letting you know about the perfection would be vain and useless. So blame only yourself if you do not receive that to which you have been called![126]

When it comes to the predetermination of human fate, Ibn ʿArabī did not approve of a passive attitude towards life and knowledge. God does not need us – we exist for our own sake, not His.[127] Upon determining the personal capacities of each man, God also granted

124 *Fut.*III:96–97; al-Manṣūb, 4/445; *FM.*II:64.
125 *Fut.*I:392; al-Manṣūb, 2/56; *FM.*I:259.
126 Quoted according to Chittick, 'Microcosm, Macrocosm and the Perfect Man in the View of Ibn al-ʿArabī', p. 10.
127 *Fut.*I:247; al-Manṣūb, 1/495; *FM.*I:247.

them the possibility of self-determination. According to Ibn ʿArabī, a mere desire for self-development is already a strong indicator that the person in question is not intended for hell. He believed that there is no cruelty in God – for His mercy takes precedence over His wrath.[128] If one was not meant for something, he probably wouldn't yearn for it either.

In the opening chapter of *The Meccan Revelations*, Ibn ʿArabī narrates the story of the two Sufi scholars, Abū Yazīd al-Bisṭāmī (d. ca. 261/875) and Junayd (d. 298/910). He describes them as men whose knowledge exceeded intellectual demonstrations and the works of natural scientists (i.e. occultists). Upon being asked how to achieve the high level of self-refinement and knowledge they possessed, Junayd was reported to have answered: 'By sitting under these stairs for 30 years!' And Abū Yazīd al-Bisṭāmī said: 'You take your knowledge dead from the dead, but we take ours from the living God who never dies.'[129] These spiritual practices, which chiefly focused on 'remembrance' of God, subsequently came to be known as *dhikr*. One of the main goals of this practice was to empty the heart from thinking. As all revelations take place in the heart, it was of utmost importance for it to be pure. This was the primary condition for self-improvement and the arrival of divine revelations. Ibn ʿArabī identified the heart as the seat of intelligence and the most noble organ of the human body. As such, the heart was also believed to be the spring of the life force. Provided that the heart is pure, revelation 'waxes like the Sun and Moon over it'.[130] A common way to purify the heart was to engage in *dhikr* and follow the path of the great masters and dedicate yourself to retreat and invocation. In other words, Ibn ʿArabī defined *dhikr* as an act of remembering the Divine:

> 'The one who is prepared and engages change to spiritual retreats and the constant remembrance of the Divine in *dhikr*, by emptying the site - your heart – from reflective thinking and sitting helplessly, dependent, with nothing in hand at the door of your Cherisher – at that moment God will be gracious to you and provide you with some knowledge of Him !"'[131]

128 *Ṣaḥīḥ al-Bukhārī*, 3022. See also *Fut.*I:255; al-Manṣūb, 1/509; *FM.*I:167.
129 *Fut.*I:54; al-Manṣūb, 1/123, 574; *FM.*I:31.
130 Elmore, *Islamic Sainthood,* p. 231.
131 *Fut.*I:54–5; al-Manṣūb, 1/123; *FM.*I:31.

Dhikr is the only thing, Ibn ʿArabī believed, that God asks in return for the gift of life and knowledge. Although the scope of revelations each person could receive is predetermined, preparedness to receive the spark was perceived as a crucial component for initiating the process.

On his side, Ibn ʿArabī received the spark of revelation that brought him understanding of the letters in 1201 CE. In the city of Bougie (Bijāya), during the month of Ramadan, a vision saw him joined in marriage with all letters and stars.[132] One year later, during his pilgrimage to Mecca, he had a vision of a Youth who gave him further instructions in the Islamic science of letters. This encounter subsequently inspired him to write *The Meccan Revelations*, where he refers to his teacher as the Youth (*al-fatā*) and *al-imām al-mubīn* – a term that was interpreted by Chodkiewicz as the Qur'anic reference to the First Intellect and the knowledge of the Perfect Human. According to Chodkiewicz, the term *al-imām al-mubīn* serves to imply that nothing was omitted from Ibn ʿArabī's works.[133] However, this is not what Ibn ʿArabī presumed.

> This book [*The Meccan Revelations*], despite its length, vastness and the multitude of its sections and chapters is not enough for us to exhaustively deal with a single thought we have on this path, let alone with the path itself! However, I have not failed to convey any of the basics you will depend on along this path.[134]

> If I was to begin the discourse on the mysteries of letters and their realities, the hand would grow weary, the pen would wear down, the oil from the lamp would dry up and any sheet of paper and tablet would become too narrow. If it were a parchment outspread [that I used], it would be like the one described in His words: if the oceans were ink for the words of my Lord, the sea would be consumed before His words are exhausted – and we were to bring the same amount of that in addition! He said: 'If every tree on earth would turn to pens and the ocean into ink and seven more oceans after, the words of God would never be exhausted.'[135]

---

132 Ibn ʿArabī, *Kitāb al-Bā'*, p. 23.
133 Chodkiewicz, *An Ocean Without Shore*, p. 29.
134 *Fut.*IV:17; al-Manṣūb, 6/118; *FM.*II:382.
135 *Fut.*I:94; al-Manṣūb, 1/187–8; *FM.*I:57.

The quoted excerpt refers to the Sura *al-Kahf*: *If the sea were ink for the words of my Lord, it would certainly run out before the words of my Lord are exhausted* (Q.18:109). In this context, it was used to illustrate Ibn ʿArabī's struggles to cope with the surge of revelations. The quoted verse can also serve as an explanation for the systematic lack of data exposition in Ibn ʿArabī's works.

While Ibn ʿArabī's refined system of heavenly spheres and the step-levels of spiritual accomplishments prompted Schimmel to describe him as 'a genius of systematization',[136] Netton praised 'the very systematic way in which he expressed his ideas'.[137] Similar observations on Ibn ʿArabī's 'intricate ontological structure (…) that brings together a wealth of philosophical, theological, scientific, linguistic, metaphysical and mystical knowledge, weaving them together into a cohesive, multidimensional whole' were made by Samer Akkach as well.[138] This was, however, far from Ibn ʿArabī's own view. In his efforts to faithfully commit to paper the content of the revelations he received, Ibn ʿArabī was not overly concerned with systematization. 'In all that I have written,' he claimed, 'I never had a set object like other authors nor a particular way of composing. Flashes of divine inspiration used to come upon me, threatening to burn me up. I could only keep my mind off them by setting down what I could. If my works assume any form of composition, that form was never intended.'[139] Having interrupted his work on a certain topic, he could pick it up several hundreds of pages later – and the surviving manuscripts of his works are full of empty spaces where diagrams were supposed to be added later on. Ibn ʿArabī's works also demonstrate a tendency to abandon unfinished discussions with remarks such as 'this amount will suffice; the chapter has grown too long' and a spark of revelation could equally lead him to put down one book in order to begin his work on another.[140] Upon abandoning a research topic, he sometimes laments that he cannot stop to explain: his free will played no part in the writing process. Such was the power of the revelations he received, that he would occasionally throw away his notebook and

136 Schimmel, *Mystical Dimensions*, p. 263

137 Netton, *Allāh Transcendent*, p. 269.

138 Akkach, *Cosmology and Architecture in Pre-modern Islam*, p. 24.

139 Affifi, 'The Works of Ibn 'Arabī', pp. 112–3. See also *Fut.*I:96; al-Manṣūb, 1/192; *FM.*I:59.

140 Ibn ʿArabī claimed he was forced to neglect *The Book of the Fabulous Gryphon* and several other works upon receiving the divine order to focus on *The Meccan Revelations*. See *Fut.*I:153; al-Manṣūb, 1/317; *FM.*I:98.

storm out of the room, unwilling to record a thing – only to return to the writing process sometime later. A typical description of a divine revelation was preserved in Ibn ʿArabī's *The Settings of the Stars* (*Mawāqīʿ al-nujūm*).

Fig. 6 Ibn ʿArabī's illustrations of one of the tablets of revelation he received. It was said to have appeared on a patch of emerald-green silk.

> I had no idea what to write next. I waited for the revelation to continue with such expectancy that I became disturbed and almost at death's door. A luminous tablet (Fig. 6) was then placed in front of me. It contained radiant green lines on which was stated: 'This is a chapter of subtle description and most rare unveiling and the discourse regarding the chapter …' I copied [what I saw] right to the end and then the tablet was withdrawn.[141]

In order to cope with the surge of revelations, Ibn ʿArabī stated that he relied on close friends to read him the notes he had written so that he could 'correct what might have fallen short in the notebook due to the speed of the pen'.[142] While other authors were free to make the final decision regarding the content of their works, Ibn ʿArabī maintained that he was nothing but a transmitter of divine revelations. He claimed that he only ever recorded what he was ordered to record. No book could contain the full content of the knowledge he received. For this reason, he spoke only when he was allowed to speak and ceased writing upon being ordered to stop. As a result, there is no systematic exposition of his teachings. Nonetheless, his tone is far from apologetic:

141 Quoted according to Addas, *Quest for the Red Sulphur*, p. 65.
142 *Fut.*I:113; al-Manṣūb, 1/219; *FM.*I:71.

The True is the One from whom we get knowledge, by isolating the heart from intellectualization and preparing the hearts to receive the influx [of revelations]. He is the One Who reveals the foundations of each matter, without summarizations and perplexity![143]

Ibn ʿArabī insisted that his writing style was not the result of an intention to obfuscate revealed knowledge. When God wished him to pay more attention to vocalization than to focus on the order of narration, he felt obliged to obey. With the notable exception of *Book of the Fabulous Gryphon,* Ibn ʿArabī didn't rely on cryptographs to conceal the information from the uninitiated. As a matter of fact, the putative key for interpreting his cryptographs was openly disclosed by Ibn ʿArabī at the end of his *Book of Theophanies* (Table 7, line 1).[144] Another, more detailed set of cryptographs survived in the holograph of Ibn ʿArabī's *Book of the Fabulous Gryphon* (Table 7, line 2). Apart from these, Gerald Elmore identified five other versions of this script in later-date manuscripts of Ibn ʿArabī's works.[145]

Table 7 The cryptographic script from Ibn ʿArabī's Book of Theophanies and its cryptographs have only the initial form and do not connect to one another in writing

ا ب ت ث ج ح خ د ذ ر ز س ش ص ض ط ظ ع غ ف ق ك ل م ن ه و لا ى

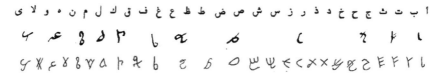

Verily, We gave the Scripture to Moses, and We made a series of messengers to come after him. And We gave the clear proofs (al-bayyināt) to Jesus, son of Mary, and We supported him with the Spirit of Holiness (rūḥ al-qudus) (Q.2:87; cf., also v.253). *And when the angels said: 'O Mary! God gives you Glad-tidings of a Word from Him (kalimah min-hu), whose name is the Messiah (al-Masīḥ), Jesus, son of Mary, high-honoured (wajīh) in This world and the Hereafter, and one of those who are brought near [to God] (al-muqarrabūn)* [Q.3:45]. *He will speak to men in the*

143 *Fut.*I:92; al-Manṣūb, 1/186; *FM.*I:56.

144 Ibn ʿArabī, MS Veliyuddin 1759, fol.80.

145 These variations, which are likely to be attributed to scribal omissions, can be consulted in Elmore, *Islamic Sainthood in the Fullness of Time*, pp. 574–583.

Fig. 7 The only surviving piece of writing in cryptographic script in Ibn ʿArabī's hand with translation by G Elmore

cradle and in his maturity, and he is of the Righteous (al-ṣāliḥūn) [v.46]. ... *And We [sic] will teach him the Scripture and Wisdom (al-kitāb wa-l-ḥikma), and the Torah and the Gospel* [v.48], *to be a Messenger (rasūl) to the Children of Israel, [saying:] come to you with a Sign (āya) from your Lord: I will create for you out*

> *of clay as the likeness of a bird; then I will breathe into it and it will become a bird, by God's leave. And I will heal the blind and the leper, and bring the dead to life, by God's leave. And I will inform you of what things you eat, and what you store up in your houses* (v.49). *When God said: 'O Jesus, I am taking you and causing you to ascend to Me, and I will purify you of those who do not believe and make those who follow you to be above those who disbelieve until the day of Resurrection'* (v.55). *Verily, the likeness of Jesus with God (mathāl 'Īsa 'inda Llāh) is as the likeness of Adam: He created him of earth, then said unto him "Be!", and he was.* (v.59)[146]

Ibn 'Arabī was not a professional calligrapher, and his works do not rely on calligraphy as a medium of artistic expression. It is, however, likely that he underwent a certain scribal training as he was supposed to assume the position of a secretary for the Almohad governor of Seville.[147] As with diagrams, efficiency and precision were his primary concerns when it came to writing. But while he preferred to illuminate his manuscripts on his own, even at the cost of never finishing the diagrams he had in mind, Ibn 'Arabī proved to be willing to rely on scribes to cope with the surge of revelations:

> The Real ordered me to write a commentary on them [the spiritual states of Abū Yazīd al-Bisṭāmī] while I was sleeping at the port of Sabta in the land of Maghrib. Thus I hastily got up before dawn and dictated the work to two copyists who were with me and they wrote it down. Before the sun had risen, two notebooks had been filled out.[148]

In general, he referred to calligraphy as 'the shape of letters'. The science of letters, Ibn 'Arabī explained, is concerned with the length and breadth of letters. While the length of letters determines their meaning and dictates their activity in the world of spirits, the breadth of letters was thought to impact their activities in the world of bodies. Such reasoning is hardly surprising since he identified *Mulk*,

146 Elmore, *Islamic Sainthood*, pp. 574–575.

147 Addas, *Quest for the Red Sulphur*, p. 31.

148 Ibn 'Arabī, *Fihrist* no. 43, MS Yusuf Ağa, fol. 190.

the corporeal world of Islamic cosmology, and the angelic realm of *Malakūt* as the breadth (*ʿarḍ*) and length (*ṭūl*) of the cosmos.[149]

Ibn ʿArabī's interpretations of the orthographic form of each letter will be addressed separately, within the second part of the present study. For the time being, a general overview of his handwriting will suffice. Extensive analyses conducted by Venetia Porter demonstrated that the predominant script in Islamic occult literature was linear Kufic and, to a lesser degree, *naskh.* These two scripts decorate the vast majority of talismans as well.[150] On his side, however, Ibn ʿArabī tended to rely on the Maghribi script. Octave Houdas identified three main types of the Maghribi script: Qayrawānī, Fāsī and Andalusī, which was predominantly used by Ibn ʿArabī.[151] All three types were traditionally written with sharp pens that produced lines of same thickness. This gave Ibn ʿArabī full control over the length and breadth of letters in his works. Having left Andalusia at the age of thirty-five, Ibn ʿArabī spent the rest of his life in the Arab East – where he appears to have developed a tendency to modify diacritical marks and the final forms of his letters in order to have them resemble the Mashriqi style of writing. The reasons that pushed him to undertake these modifications mostly remain unknown. In the year 1201 CE, he claimed to have had a vision of the most beautiful bird in the world, which advised him to undertake a journey and spread his teachings to the East. Apart from his desire to appeal to the Mashriqi audience, changes in Ibn ʿArabī's handwriting could be equally attributed to his tendency to experiment with different brushes in his old age.[152]

Stephen Hirtenstein also noted Ibn ʿArabī's tendency to use an odd number of lines (in most cases seventeen lines per manuscript page) since 'God is odd (*witr*) and loves the odd'[153]. While Ibn ʿArabī was no stranger to *yabs*, the rigid, dry handwriting style of book scribes, his texts are mostly written in the soft, cursive handwriting of administrative workers (*līn*) – with letters that are typically rounded and leaning to the right. He also claimed never to have produced a draft copy of a book – all of his texts were allegedly composed in his best hand (*mubayyaḍa*). However, Hirtenstein discovered two examples of

149 *Fut.*I:257; al-Manṣūb, 1/510; *FM.*I:169.

150 Porter, 'The use of Arabic Script in Magic,' pp. 132–5.

151 Houdas, 'Recueil de letters arabes manuscrites Alger', pp. 108–12. See also Gacek, 'Arabic scripts and their characteristics as seen through the eyes of Mameluk authors', pp. 144–9.

152 Ibn ʿArabī received this revelation in Marrakesh, in the year 597H.

153 Hirtenstein, 'In the Master's Hand', pp. 87–9.

Ibn ʿArabī's 'rough' hand (*musawwada*) as well: *The Book of God's Servants* (*Kitāb al-ʿAbādila*) and a copy of an abridged *tafsir* by Abū al-ʿAbbās al-Mahdawī. In general, Ibn ʿArabī seems to have cared less for data exposition than for handwriting. While orthography had its symbolism which had to be adhered to, data exposition was thought to be meaningless. In the same way as he believed that the higher powers led him through each step of the writing process, Ibn ʿArabī placed his faith in God to bestow understanding on the chosen readers of his works.[154] He believed that the people of God generally do not wait long for revelations to appear. Like the Prophet Muhammad, who was an illiterate man himself, not all men of God were highly educated.[155]

The more pious the person is, the more he 'persists in remembering his God in the spiritual retreat, free from all thoughts', the less likely he will be forced to preoccupy himself with preparatory sciences such as arithmetic, geometry, astronomy and medicine. While some seekers were said to have had knowledge revealed to them by means of spiritual exercises such as *dhikr*, others were known to have obtained it through rational analysis. Rather than waiting for a revelation to occur, a scholar could choose to rely on his intellectual capacities instead.[156] Nevertheless, few things were thought to be as dangerous as the rational analyses of all things divine. On his side, Ibn ʿArabī acknowledged that, in certain cases, divine mercy extends to protect researchers from making mistakes in their intellectual pursuits. The fact that divine providence would intervene was, however, not to be taken for granted. And while limiting ourselves to literal, word-for-word transmissions and reading of the sacred text would keep us safe from God's wrath, Ibn ʿArabī warned that each scholar will be called to account for the misinterpretations he communicates to the general

154 Voices and figures from Ibn ʿArabī's visions were later to be denounced as evil spirits by Ibn Taymiyya. See Ibn Taymiyya, *Majmūʿ fatāwā Shaykh al-Islām Aḥmad ibn Taymiyya*, p. 511, and Knysh, *Ibn Arabi in the later Islamic Tradition*, pp. 87–106.

155 This process is essentially similar to the spark of revelation. Ibn ʿArabī maintained that he didn't intentionally obfuscate certain parts of his works. Instead, he blamed the failure to understand his teachings (which were, as such, also the product of the divine revelation) on the limited rational capacities of his readers. However, one revelation easily reveals the hidden meanings of another. *Fut.*I:78; al-Manṣūb, 1/165; *FM.*I:47.

156 In Islamic culture, rational knowledge and revealed knowledge are sometimes referred to as knowledge by means of the eye, and knowledge by means of the heart. This reference was based on the Sura *al-Anʿām*, which states that 'whomsoever God wishes to guide, He expands his chest for Islam – and whomsoever He wishes to lead astray, He makes his chest narrow, tight, as if he were climbing to the sky' (Q.6:125). While one was thought to have limited power to open the heart on his own, opening the eye was subjected to the human will.

public. In this regard, the quoted excerpt from *The Contemplations of the Holy Mysteries* (*Mashāhid al-asrār*) hints at Ibn ʿArabī's belief that the road to hell is paved with good intentions. In this work, Ibn ʿArabī recounts his vision of the seven groups of scholars who were brought forth to face the divine judgement and were sentenced to the fires of hell. The first among them were philosophers, the men who put their faith in the rational mind to guide them towards God.

> Then came the call: 'Where are the rationalists with their pretensions?' The philosophers were brought forth with their followers and made to enter the pavilion. They were asked:
>
> 'What have you applied your intellect to?'
>
> 'To that which pleases you,' they replied.
>
> He asked: 'How do you know [what pleases Me]? By means of the rational mind or by following and adhering [to the prophets]?
>
> They replied: 'Through intellect alone.'
>
> He said: 'You have failed to understand, you did not succeed and you passed your own sentence. O, fire, pass judgement upon them!'
>
> I heard their cries from the fire. 'Who is punishing them?' I asked. He told me:
>
> 'Their intellect, for this is what they worshipped. No one questioned them except for themselves - and no one punished them except for themselves.[157]

This was the fate of spiritualists, natural scientists, materialists (*al-dahriyya*) and the Muʾtazila as well. In *The Contemplations of the Holy Mysteries,* the passions that led them astray are represented by the letter *mīm*. In a subtle word play, Ibn ʿArabī explains that rather than putting their faith in God (*maʿa-Hu*) to protect them from delusions

---

157 Ibn ʿArabī, *Kitāb Mashāhid al-asrār*, p. 226.

of the mind, philosophers were led astray by them (*ma'a-hum*).[158] The letter *mīm* thus came to be used as a symbol of what their hearts were preoccupied with: logic, spirits and/or material things. An impure heart, filled with longings other than for God, is thus passed over for the revelation it has never yearned for – and *mīm* becomes its doom. 'Do not enter a place except through Me and do not seek anything but Me,' reads a line from *The Contemplations of the Holy Mysteries*.[159]

However, even the wisest among the Sufis were occasionally tempted to find that the divine love and presence are not enough. By his own admission, Ibn 'Arabī also used to be overly focused on analytical proofs and sound demonstrations. Later on, he went on to assert that simple piety is a safer way to soothe curiosity. However, blind obedience to the authority of the *'ulamā'* offers no security from the hellfire, either. Not only was Ibn 'Arabī sceptical regarding the capability of the vast majority of religious scholars to prove themselves worthy of a revelation – he also accused the *'ulamā'*, in their ignorance, of leading the masses astray.[160] He therefore advised each person to analyse all teachings concerning God and determine for himself on which basis is each of them to be evaluated. If one finds himself attracted to a certain teaching and is subsequently unable to find a direct opposition to it in the Shari'a, he is not required to renounce it on the basis of the opinion of others. However, the safest way to proceed in order to avoid divine wrath was 1) to adopt a modest attitude which prevents one from transmitting false interpretations of divine revelations and 2) only rely on intellectual pursuits in the field of religious studies to resolve daily problems as they occur.[161] As for those who neglect their studies and fail to confront shaykhs whose teachings contradict the Qur'an, for them, there is no excuse before God. Ibn 'Arabī recommended studies of the Islamic religious law as one of the means to open and purify the heart. In addition, philosophy was believed to be beneficial in helping us conquer the snares of ego:

---

158 This observation was first made by Pablo Beneito in his translation of Ibn 'Arabī's *Kitāb Mashāhid al-asrār.* The final letter *mīm* of the word *ma'a-hum* thus came to be interpreted as any selfish, human longing clouding the Divine presence in one's heart. See Ibn 'Arabī, *Contemplations of the Holy Mysteries*, p. 103.

159 Ibid.

160 When it comes to education, how much knowledge is enough? Although a very educated man himself, in response to this question, Ibn 'Arabī quoted the hadith which reads 'whoever preserves for my community forty hadith of which they stand in need, God shall put him down as learned and knowing'. Ibn 'Arabī, *Divine Sayings*, p. 5.

161 'The smallest step on the path is submission to what you do not know and the highest step is certainty in validity.' *Fut.*I:124; al-Manṣūb, 1/236; *FM.*I:79.

> The fact that he [a philosopher] has no religion does not mean that everything he says is false. This ability to differentiate truth from falsehood is perception by means of reason. It relies on the primary rational faculty that every person has.[162]

By limiting himself to the teachings of a single school or shaykh, a person puts himself in danger 'of having the greater good escape him'.[163] But while common people were advised to seek knowledge indiscriminately, a sage knows his priorities. Ibn ʿArabī discarded all studies that do not bring a man closer to God as distractions we undertake to keep ourselves busy. There is no benefit of any rational, 'external' knowledge, unless our salvation depends on it.[164]

Analyses of the letters of the Arabic alphabet certainly match the criteria. Like Shariʿa, the science of letters was thought to have a potential to open the hearts of those who seek it. Ibn ʿArabī held that it is close to impossible for an individual to study the letters of the Arabic alphabet without being changed in the process. (Un)successful inquiries in the Islamic science of letters thus become an existential journey. In most cases, familiarity with the letters begins with rational inquiries and ends up with revealed knowledge. From the late ninth century CE, grammarians like Ibn al-Sarrāj (d. 316/929) had been actively relying on orthography and grammar to purify the soul and secure peace and prosperity in this world and the hereafter. However, when it comes to the science of letters, Ibn ʿArabī argued that professional grammarians have little to say on the matter. 'The master of a written form and phase' he may be, a grammarian is not a sage. His familiarity with the orthographic forms of letters does not equal the mastery of the science of letters either. When a grammarian attests that he sees 'Zayd', his thoughts rarely go beyond phonology, syntax and the corporeal form of a man in question.[165] The people of God, blessed with a revelation, were however capable of seeing 1) how spirits preside over letters and planets and 2) how God sends these spirits to do their bidding

162 *Fut.*I:56–57; al-Manṣūb, 1/127; *FM.*I:32.

163 Ibn ʿArabī, *Fuṣūṣ al-ḥikam*, p. 113. 'Do not attach yourself to any particular creed exclusively so that you disbelieve in all the rest; otherwise you will lose much good, nay you will fail to recognize the real truth of the matter. Let your soul be capable of embracing all forms of belief. God, the omnipresent and omnipotent, is not limited by any creed'. See *Tarjumān al-ashwāq*, p. 6.

164 Elmore, *Islamic Sainthood,* pp. 240–42.

165 *Fut.*II:378; al-Manṣūb, 3/489–9; *FM.*I:636. See also *Fut.*IV:76; al-Manṣūb, 6/238; *FM.*II:421–2.

upon being summoned by an expert in the science of letters. Similar insights were usually denied to professional grammarians. As a result, grammatical analyses do not take into consideration the spirits that govern individual words and letters.

Ibn ʿArabī compared the relationship between an orthographic form and the meaning of a letter to the relationship between a man and the clothes he wears. The orthographic forms of letters were thought to serve as outward containers (*ẓarf*) for the spirits that rule them. Ibn ʿArabī therefore referred to grammarians who were ignorant of the meaning of letters as 'outward scholars'.[166] In addition, he asserted that even a limited familiarity with orthographic structures transcends the vast majority of grammatical analyses. 'Whom God teaches the outward, literal meanings of letters like *alif, lām* and *mīm*, the role of a caliph (*khalīfa*) is suitable for him.'[167] In theory, however, orthography and phonetics were thought to be susceptible to rational analyses. Gifted grammarians were thus capable of comprehending the properties of the human vocal tract and the orthographic forms of letters without the intervention of a divine providence. On his side, however, Ibn ʿArabī was more inclined towards researching the spirits. The properties of the spirits of the letters were thought to belong to the domain of revealed knowledge.

However, this is not to say that Ibn ʿArabī's works are devoid of grammatical analyses in general. When it comes to orthography, phonetics and grammatical functions of letters serving as prepositions and particles, Ibn ʿArabī's works draw from the writings of the leading grammarians of his time. For example, he groups together the consonants *bāʾ*, *mīm* and *wāw* as labials, just as any thirteenth-century grammarian would. However, he also extends his analyses to identify the aforementioned letters as the letters of the lower world of *Mulk*, whose elements are fire and earth. The orthographic shape of letters also played a role in determining their properties. As a matter of fact, Ibn ʿArabī believed that the shape of a letter determines the properties of its spirit – and not the other way around. Some letters of the Arabic alphabet appear to be composed of several others. 'For example, the shape of the letter *rāʾ* and *zāy*, is half of the letter *nūn*, and *wāw* is half of the letter *qāf*. *Kāf* is four-fifths of the letter *ṭāʾ* and four-sixths of the letter *ẓāʾ*. The letter *dāl* is one-fifth of the letter *ṭāʾ*, while *yāʾ* consists of two curves. *Lām* exceeds *alif* by *nūn* and it also exceeds *nūn* by

166 *Fut.*I:97; al-Manṣūb, 1/193; *FM.*I:59.
167 *Fut.*IV:275; al-Manṣūb, 6/614; *FM.*II:555.

alif.'[168] In light of the fact that the shape of the letter *lām* (ل), with its long body and hooked end, evokes the shape of *alif* (ا) and *nūn* (ن) brought together, their properties could be taken into account in Ibn ʿArabī's analyses of *lām*. Letters whose shapes resemble one another, like *bāʾ* (ب), *thāʾ* (ث) and *tāʾ* (ت) were thought to be ruled by similar spirits as well (Fig. 8). On the contrary, *mīm* (م) and *wāw* (و), whose circular shapes evoke the image of celestial spheres, were believed to be entirely different in character from *nūn*, the ultimate symbol of the material world.[169] Although they shared several research topics with Sufis, the limited scope of grammatical analyses sets them apart from the Sufi works on the science of letters. 'What is wanted and sought for by the ones who verify for themselves [the Sufis],' Ibn ʿArabī recorded, 'is not a physical form of speech and writing – no, what is wanted are the meanings which this writing or speech has comprised and embraced!'[170] To be familiar with the inner meaning of letters, or how God sees them, was to understand the process of the creation of the universe. *The Act of Genesis*, as the second part of the present study, analyses this process with regard to the orthographic features and symbolism of the letters of the Arabic alphabet.

Fig. 8 Ibn ʿArabī experimenting with the orthographic forms that resemble one another in the margins of the Book of Mīm

168 *Fut.*I:128; al-Manṣūb, 1/240; *FM.*I:81.

169 Ibn ʿArabī, *K. al-Mīm*, fol.17. The properties of the aforementioned letters will be analyzed in detail in the special sub-chapters dedicated to them.

170 Whereas Ibn ʿArabī acknowledged the existence of the correspondence between a letter and its meaning, he maintained that most people gain familiarity with certain concepts by the means of the letters. However, the meaning of the letters themselves is only revealed to messengers and prophets. Attempting to study the meanings of letters without obedience to God would result only in misery. *Fut.*III:180; al-Manṣūb, 5/29; *FM.*II:121.

PART TWO
THE ACT OF GENESIS

These times now are not like times gone by. This is because today is closer to the Hereafter.

Ibn ʻArabī[1]

1 Ibn ʻArabī, *Kitāb al-Isfār,* p. 47.

2

THE ACT OF GENESIS

2.1. The Breath of the All-Merciful

In the beginning, there was only God. One, unique, He is as He always has been before the letters of limitation. At that time, all living beings, our world and the letters and numbers alike existed only in divine knowledge. They were but 'skeletons who were waiting in potentiality'[2] for the divine command to step into the material domain of existence. In Ibn ʿArabī's works, God is described as omnipotent. He had no need of servants – and yet, the cause of all things was linked by Corbin to the primordial sadness of the One who had no one to know Him and no one to name Him.[3] However, Ibn ʿArabī pointed out that it would be equally true to say that God was filled with love instead. The later interpreters of Ibn ʿArabī's works held that the act of genesis unfolds from the state of the absolute abundance of the Divine being (*karb*). Maria De Cillis drew a parallel between the Avicennian concept of absolute perfection and the Akbarian notion of God's absolute abundance which 'compels' Him to create the world. According to De Cillis, Avicenna perceived the act of genesis as 'a natural necessity being enacted by God's purposeless will and His Self-knowledge as the Cause of causes. In very similar terms, for the Shaykh al-Akbar, it is from the divine Superabundance, 'the bursting fullness [of the essential realities in the undifferentiated Essence]' that the need for the cosmos arises. It is from the divine perfect plenitude 'that [God] breathed forth

2 Winkel, *Youth: The Figurative Made Literal*, p. 11.
3 Corbin, *Creative Imagination in the Sufism of Ibn ʿArabi*, p. 184.

[the primordial creative Word *kun*]'.[4] Ibn ʿArabī compared the state of absolute abundance to lungs filled with air. If we were to try to hold it back, the pain would be unbearable. Ultimately, the air bursts out. God utters a sigh and this breath was life itself. By means of breath, the love He felt found its expression – and thus was, or so Ibn ʿArabī believed, the world breathed out (*mutanaffas*) into existence. In his works, the act of genesis is commonly referred to as the Breath of the All-Merciful (*al-nafas al-raḥmānī*):

> In reality, nature is nothing but the Breath of the All-Merciful. All forms of the world become manifest in the latter, ranging from the highest to the lowest in the virtue of the spreading of the Breath through the material substance in the world of physical bodies.[5]

Ibn ʿArabī believed that the act of breathing equals the act of speaking. 'Speech is the Breath of the All-Merciful, and His very being, intelligent and clear.'[6] From the quality of this speech, the universe emerged. The creative word of God was a common motive in the pyramid texts and religions of ancient Mesopotamia. Arthur Jeffrey traced similar beliefs in the great variety of Zoroastrian, Orphic, Mandaean and Samaritan texts as well.[7] However, Samuel Kramer held that these teachings primarily owed their prominence in the Arab Middle East to the works of Sumerian scholars. In the Sumerian myth of creation, the creative word which brought the universe into existence is referred to as *gu*. It was believed to have been uttered by Enlil, the god of Heaven and the Netherworld – presumably in Classical Sumerian.[8] On the assumption that the creative word of God served as an expression of divine knowledge and intention to create the world and its inhabitants, Ibn ʿArabī argued that His choice of words could not have been a coincidence. In accordance with the Islamic normative tradition, he believed that the world is a product of God's

---

4 De Cillis, *Free Will and Predestination in Islamic Thought*, p. 178.

5 Ibn ʿArabī, *Fuṣūṣ*, p. 219.

6 *Fut.*III:281; al-Manṣūb, 5/204; *FM.*II:181.

7 Jeffrey, *Ibn al-ʿArabī's Shajarat al-Kawn*, p. 53.

8 Albright suggests that the word *gu* could mean 'voice' and/or 'thunder', which is one of the attributes of the god Enlil. This word is the equivalent of the biblical *ḳōl Yahweh*, the voice of Yahweh. See Albright, 'The Supposed Babylonian Derivation of the Logos', p. 144 and Kramer, *From the Poetry of Sumer: Creation, Glorification, Adoration*, p. 44.

speech in Arabic. 'From the spoken letters the world of spirits comes into being and from the written letters the sensory world comes into being and from the summoned letters the world of the intellect in the imagination comes into being.'[9] Having set out to create the world, God utters a simple command: 'Be!' (*kun!*). It was through *kun*, Ibn ʿArabī believed, that we came to be from emptiness – 'praise God who brought out things from the empty void and its empty void'.[10] *The Tree of Being* (*Shajarat al-kawn*), an apocryphal text attributed to Ibn ʿArabī, describes the creative word *kun* as the root of the World Tree whose outer bark is *Mulk*, the material world. *Jabarūt*, the imaginal world of Islamic cosmology, is the sap of this tree whose marrow is the angelic realm of *Malakūt*.[11] Faḍl Allāh Astarābādī held that the word *kun* has twenty-eight meanings. These meanings manifest as the twenty-eight sounds corresponding to the twenty-eight letters of the Arabic alphabet.[12] According to Ibn ʿArabī, different meanings cannot be joined together unless they are deposited in letters. By combining letters into words, God was thought to have created the world. In other words, the act of genesis can be compared to forming a sentence.

Ibn ʿArabī believed that all living beings are products of combinations of letters. The possible number of combinations of the twenty-eight letters was thought to be unlimited – as is the ultimate number of living beings and other forms of existence. In this regard, Ibn ʿArabī's teachings were likely inspired by the Sura *Luqmān*: *If all the trees in the world were pens and the seven seas were to supply the ink, the words of God would never run out. Indeed, Allah is Exalted in Might and Wise* (Q.31:27). Ontologically, every form of existence is a divine word. 'The world, all of it, are the words of God in existence.'[13] While words are composed of letters, letters owe their existence to fluctuations of the divine breath. With a gentle exhale, *alif*, *bā'*, *jīm*, *dāl*, *dhāl*, *rā'*, *zāy*, *ḍād*, *ṭā'*, *ẓā'*, *ʿayn*, *ghayn*, *qāf*, *lām*, *mīm*, *nūn*, *wāw*, *yā'*, the eighteen voiced letters (*ḥurūf al-majhūr*) of the Arabic alphabet step into existence. Occasionally interrupting the gentle flow of the Breath, stronger exhalations brought forth the ten voiceless letters (*ḥurūf al-mahmūsa*): *ḥā'*, *khā'*, *hā'*, *kāf*, *shīn*, *sīn*, *tā'*, *ṣād*, *thā'* and

9 *Fut.*III:183; al-Manṣūb, 5/34; *FM.*II:123.

10 *Fut.*III:366; al-Manṣūb, 5/571; *FM.*II:310.

11 Alibhai, *The Shajarat al-Kawn attributed to Ibn Arabi*, p. 27.

12 Meanings also correspond to 'names' God thought to Adam – thus granting him the potential to master the science of the letters. (Q.2:31).

13 *Fut.*I:551; al-Manṣūb, 2/341; *FM.*I:366.

fā'.[14] Fluctuations in the flow of the divine breath were also thought to have resulted in the emergence of *Mulk*, *Malakūt* and *Jabarūt*. In the works of Ibn 'Arabī, the three worlds are represented by the short vowels *fatḥa* (َ), *kasra* (ِ) and *ḍamma* (ُ). The Arabic word for vowel, *ḥaraka*, can also signify a movement. In the Arabic grammar tradition, letters carrying a vowel are thus described as being set in motion (*mutaḥarrak*). This inspired Ibn 'Arabī to identify vowels as contingent modifications of the divine breath which resulted in the creation of the spiritual, imaginal and corporeal worlds. The Arabic language has three vowels: /a/, /i/ and /u/. Each of these vowels can be either short or long. Prior to the ninth century CE, short vowels were usually marked with a variety of coloured dots (Fig. 9). This vocalization system is traditionally attributed to Abū al-Aswad al-Du'alī (d. ca. 69/688).

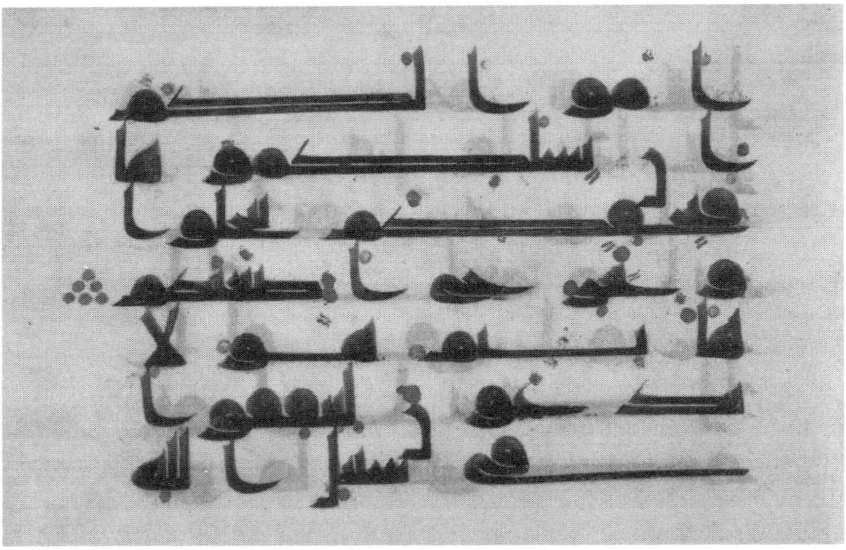

Fig. 9 The archaic vocalization system attributed to 'Abū al-'Aswad al-Du'alī

The contemporary vocalization marks, which were introduced by Khalīl b. Aḥmad (d. 175/791), typically appear above or below the consonants (Fig. 10). Even today, they still tend to be written with finer pens as this makes it easier for calligraphers to maintain the separation of vowels from the main body of the text.

14 'Words are based on letters,' Ibn 'Arabī noted, 'while letters are based on air and air is based on the breath of the All-Merciful. Names emerge visibly in the worlds and the Jesus knowledge ends up in them.' *Fut.*I:257; al-.Manṣūb,1/509; *FM.*I:168.

Fig. 10 Short vowels

Long vowels /ā/, /ī/ and /ū/ in Arabic are represented by the combination of short vowels and the letters *alif, yā'* and *wāw* (Fig. 11). Ibn 'Arabī referred to long vowels as the 'lengthening' of letters. In his works, long vowels are associated with revealed knowledge (ā) and its transmitters (ī, ū). While the long vowel /ā/ stands for God, who is the source of all knowledge, angelic messengers like Gabriel were represented by the long vowel /ū/. As for /ī/, it came to be perceived as a symbol of human messengers, lawmakers and prophets. However, the three long vowels were also used as the symbols of rational analyses and revealed knowledge. Among the noteworthy examples of this symbolism is Ibn 'Arabī's interpretation of the verb *jā'*, to arrive (جاء). In this verb, the long vowel /ā/ stands for a researcher who reached a certain (valid) conclusion on divine matters through nature studies. This vowel also serves to imply that the researcher's familiarity with the world, which was the primary research object of a man in question, preceded his knowledge of God. In contrast, other seekers gain insights into the nature of the world by means of revelation. In this case, the knowledge of God precedes one's familiarity with the world of nature. Ibn 'Arabī compared this process to elongated pronunciation – as if one would intentionally twist the verb *jā'* in everyday speech by pronouncing it as *'jāāāā''* (جاااء).[15]

Like other Semitic languages, Arabic is a consonantal script. It is based on a root system, with three or four consonants forming a semantic context. For example, the root *fā'-'ayn-lām* conveys the idea of action. Three short vowels, *fatḥa, kasra* and *ḍamma*, transform this root into the active verb *fa'ala*, 'he did' (فَعَلَ) and its passive form *fu'ila*, 'it is done' (فُعِلَ). For this reason, Ibn 'Arabī defined

15 *Fut.*IV:77; al-Manṣūb, 6/239; *FM.*II:422.

/ū/	/ī/	/ā/
بُو	بِي	بَا
Sound: bu	*Sound: bi*	*Sound: ba*

Fig. 11 The long vowels in Arabic

Rasm:
The skeleton of the script. It is made of long vowels and consonants.

I'jām:
Diacritical Marks

Tashkīl:
Short vowels and shadda

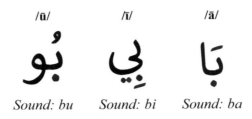

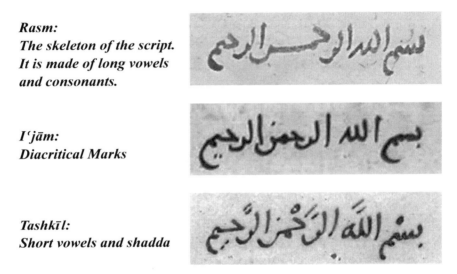

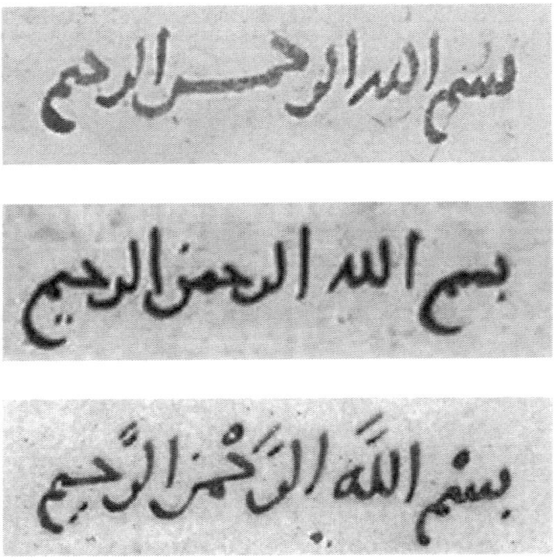

Fig. 12 Three Basmalas in Ibn 'Arabī's hand

short vowels as 'the little letters', by means of which spoken words are distinguished from one another.[16] In most cases, however, Arabic texts are not fully vowelized. This is to be attributed to fact that the rules of orthography specify that each text must contain long vowels and consonants in order to be considered legible. In contrast, short vowels are optional. With the notable exception of the Qur'an, the full vocalization thus only appears in learning books, classical poetry and religious treatises. As a result, the active verb *fa'ala* and *fu'ila* would look entirely the same in writing (فعل) – and it would be up to reader to decide on the correct pronunciation on the basis of context. Any line of text that contains neither short vowels nor diacritical marks can be identified as *rasm*. Thomas Milo suggested that this term be translated

16 *Fut.*I:132; al-Manṣūb, 1/285; *FM.*I:84.

as 'archigrapheme'.[17] The Arabic grammar tradition acknowledges the existence of eighteen different archigraphemes. They are used in combination with diacritical marks to build the twenty-eight letters of the alphabet (Table 8).

In the history of Arabic grammar studies, diacritical marks have been collectively referred to as *iʿjām*. This term was developed from the verbal noun *ʿajama* – i.e., 'to be rid of ambiguity via dotting'. When added to the body of an archigrapheme, diacritical marks serve to establish the difference between letters like *bāʾ* and *tāʾ*, *ṭāʾ* and *ẓāʾ*. For this reason, Ibn ʿArabī identified *iʿjām* as 'a face [of a letter] by means of which one letter is recognized' and distinguished from another.[18] In *The Meccan Revelations,* he distinguishes between diacritical marks that are written above and below the letters. As for letters that carry no diacritical marks, Ibn ʿArabī classified them as unpointed, dry letters. 'The unpointed letter is the one you recognize by looking at it – or, alternatively, by transmitting its special qualities.'[19] In the Arabic language, the rules of orthography specify that each text must contain two elements in order to be considered legible: *rasm* and *iʿjām*. As a result, the surviving works of Ibn ʿArabī contain few short vowels and diacritical marks. In many cases, Hirtenstein noted, these were added by later scribes, which made Ibn ʿArabī's texts readable in a certain way – thus also making it harder to determine what he originally wanted to say.[20] However, it is also important to take into account that Ibn ʿArabī compared unvowelled texts to empty forms, dead bodies awaiting to be animated by the Breath of the All-Merciful. In theory – if not in practice – Ibn ʿArabī strongly advocated the use of *tashkīl.* In the Arabic grammar tradition, this term is used for the phonetic vocalization of the Arabic script and the set of graphemes that mark it: short vowels and a gemination mark (*shadda*). Ibn ʿArabī identified *shadda* as a symbol of the creation that was created in the image of the Creator. God is beautiful, Ibn ʿArabī believed – and so is the world He created[21]. In his works, *rasm* was used as a symbol for living beings that are waiting in potentiality for a vowel, the Breath of the All-Merciful, to carry them over from nonexistence to existence. Ibn ʿArabī compared the structure of organic bodies, which were thought

17 Milo, *Authentic Arabic: A Case Study. Right-to-Left Font Structure, Font Design, and Typography*, pp. 49–61.

18 *Fut.*I:131; al-Manṣūb, 1/244; *FM.*I:83.

19 Ibid.

20 Hirtenstein, 'In the Master's Hand', p. 79.

21 *Fut.*II:550; al-Manṣūb, 4/253; *FM.*I:756.

Table 8 The archigraphemes and the letters of the Arabic alphabet

Archigrapheme	rasm		‘i‘jaam		**Letters**
ا	- - - - - - - - - - - - - - - -			►	ا
ٮ	ٮ	+	ٜ (one dot below)	- - - - ►	ب (bā’)
	ٮ	+	¨ (two dots above)	- - - - ►	ت (tā’)
	ٮ	+	∴ (three dots above)	- - - - ►	ث (thā’)
ں	ں	+	· (one dot above)	- - - - ►	ن (nūn)
ى	ى	+	.. (two dots below)	- - - - ►	ي (yā’)
ح	ح	+	· (one dot)	- - - - ►	ج (jīm)
	- - - - - - - - - - - - - - - -			►	ح (ḥā’)
	ح	+	· (one dot above)	- - - - ►	خ (khā’)
د	- - - - - - - - - - - - - - - -			►	د (dāl)
	د	+	· (one dot above)	- - - - ►	ذ (dhāl)
ر	- - - - - - - - - - - - - - - -			►	ر (rā’)
	ر	+	· (one dot above)	- - - - ►	ز (zāy)
س	- - - - - - - - - - - - - - - -			►	س (sīn)
	س	+	∴ (three dots above)	- - - - ►	ش (shīn)
ص	- - - - - - - - - - - - - - - -			►	ص (ṣād)
	ص	+	· (one dot)	- - - - ►	ض (ḍād)
ط	- - - - - - - - - - - - - - - -			►	ط (ṭā’)
	ط	+	· (one dot)	- - - - ►	ظ (ẓā’)
ع	- - - - - - - - - - - - - - - -			►	ع (‘ayn)
	ع	+	· (one dot above)	- - - - ►	غ (ghayn)
ڡ	ڡ	+	· (one dot above)	- - - - ►	ف (fā’)
ٯ	ٯ	+	¨ (two dots above)	- - - - ►	ق (qāf)
ك	- - - - - - - - - - - - - - - -			►	ك (kāf)
ل	- - - - - - - - - - - - - - - -			►	ل (lām)
م	- - - - - - - - - - - - - - - -			►	م (mīm)
ه	- - - - - - - - - - - - - - - -			►	ه (hā’)
و	- - - - - - - - - - - - - - - -			►	و (wāw)

to be made of the four elements, with the presumed role of vowels in the building of words. Without the vowels, Ibn ʿArabī believed, speech would be impossible. In a similar way, life cannot be imagined without the Breath.

> When I fashioned him and blew into him some of my spirit, which is the inrush of the vowels moving and the letters being voiced. Once they have been fashioned, the letters emerge as another configuration. This configuration is then referred to as a 'word' – just like a single person among us is referred to as a 'human being'. (…). Consonants belong to words – just like water, earth, fire and air build the physical configuration of our bodies. Then He blows His spirit into someone with the command to 'Be!' – and thus one becomes a human being.[22]

Ultimately, all beings are the final forms of divine words. While Ibn ʿArabī compared vowels to the life-giving spirit, consonants were thought to correspond to (in)organic matter. From this perspective, consonants can be viewed as a lifeless body awaiting the spirit, i.e. the vowel, to revive it. The spirit merges with air to create a jinn, merges with light to create an angel and merges with clay to create a human being[23]. When vowels merge with consonants, words are endowed with meaning. In particular, Ibn ʿArabī held that letters become meaningful upon exiting the mouth. When pronounced, a personal name like Zayd causes an image of a man to appear in our mind. The meaning of a word thus creates a mental image – and Ibn ʿArabī believed that the creative word *kun* has a similar effect on the universe.

> When a person intends to manifest a word in its entity, then, while making manifest the entities of letters in his breath he intends to manifest designated letters and he does not manifest any others. Some are heard as joined to others and a word arrives newly to the hearing. The word is the relation of the joining of those letters. It is nothing superadded to the letters, only the relation of only the relation of their coming together. This fact of coming together bestows a form that the letters could not bestow without the relation that brings them together. Such is the composition

22 *Fut.*I:132; al-Manṣūb, 1/285; *FM.*I:84–5.

23 *Fut.*I:132; al-Manṣūb, 1/285; *FM.*I:85.

of the entities of the cosmos – which is compound from the noncompound things within it.[24]

Created by means of letters, different parts of the universe were thought to have retained the properties of letters which brought them into existence. The origins of the universe thus came to be reflected in its structure. There are twenty-eight lunar mansions, Ibn ʿArabī believed, because there are twenty-eight letters of the alphabet – and not the other way around.[25] In Islamic culture, twenty-eight was perceived as the perfect number. It stands for the twenty-eight letters of the Arabic alphabet, twenty-eight stars of the zodiac constellations and the number of vertebrae in the backbone – among other things. In the human life cycle, the twenty-eighth year of life marked the beginning of adulthood.[26] The act of genesis was believed to have taken place in twenty-eight stages, starting with the First Intellect, which was brought into existence with the arrival of the letter *hamza*. The process continues with the emergence of the Preserved Tablet (symbolized by *hāʾ*), the Universal Nature (*ʿayn*), Primordial Matter (*ḥāʾ*) and the Universal Body (*ghayn*). The original Form, from which all individual forms of existence are formed (*khāʾ*), the heavenly Throne (*qaf*) and its Pedestal (*kāf*) were the next to be created. From here on, the Breath continues with the creation of the celestial spheres. These were the Starless Sphere (*jīm*), the Sphere of the Fixed Stars (*shīn*) and the seven heavens (symbolized by the letters *yāʾ*, *dād*, *lām*, *nūn*, *rāʾ*, *ṭāʾ* and *dāl* respectively), the Orbit of Fire (*tāʾ*), the Orbit of Air (*zāy*), the Orbit of Water (*sīn*) and Earth (*ṣād*). Minerals (*ẓāʾ*), plants (*thāʾ*), animals (*dhāl*), angels (*fāʾ*), jinn (*bāʾ*) and humans (*mīm*) were created next. The last ones to be created were the step-levels of spiritual ascent (*marātib*). In the works of Ibn ʿArabī, this term stands for the hierarchy of the world and the spiritual ascent which is the end goal (*ghāya*) of every being in existence. As such, the step-levels are symbolized and brought into existence by the letter *wāw*.[27] Beginning with *hamza* and ending with *wāw*, the sequence of the letters which brought forth the universe corresponds to the order of the Arabic alphabet.

---

24 Quoted according to Chittick. *The Self-Disclosure of God*, p. 116.

25 *Fut.*IV:103; al-Manṣūb, 7/283–4; *FM.*II:440.

26 Bashir, *Fazlallah Astarabadi and the Hurufis*, p. 53. See also Bosnevi, *Sharḥ Fuṣūṣ* vol.2, pp. 264–264.

27 On the step-levels of spiritual ascension, see Sviri, 'KUN – the Existence-Bestowing Word in Islamic Mysticism', pp. 16–7.

Table 9 The Act of Genesis and its stages

Letter	***Isolated Form***	***Primary Symbolism of Isolated Letters in Ibn 'Arabī's works***
Alif	ا	*Divine Essence*
Lām-alif	لا	*Relationship between the Creator and the Created*
Alif with Hamza	أ	*Cloud*
Hamza	ء	*First Intellect/ Pen*
Hā'	ه	*Universal Soul/ Preserved Tablet*
'Ayn	ع	*Universal Nature*
Ḥā'	ح	*Prime Matter/ Dust Substance*
Ghayn	غ	*Universal Body*
Khā'	خ	*Shape*
Qāf	ق	*Heavenly Throne*
Kāf	ك	*Pedestal*
Jīm	ج	*Starless Sphere*
Shīn	ش	*Sphere of the Fixed Stars*
Yā'	ي	*Sphere of Saturn, First Heaven*
Ḍād	ض	*Sphere of Jupiter, Second Heaven*
Lām	ل	*Sphere of Mars, Third Heaven*
Nūn	ن	*Sphere of the Sun, Fourth Heaven*
Rā'	ر	*Sphere of Venus, Fifth Heaven*
Ṭā'	ط	*Sphere of Mercury, Sixth Heaven*
Dāl	د	*Sphere of the Moon, Closest/Seventh Heaven*
Tā'	ت	*Orbit of Fire*

Letter	Isolated Form	Primary Symbolism of Isolated Letters in Ibn 'Arabī's works
Zāy	ز	*Orbit of Air*
Sīn	س	*Orbit of Water*
Ṣād	ص	*Earth*
Ẓā'	ظ	*Minerals*
Thā'	ث	*Plants*
Dhāl	ذ	*Animals*
Fā'	ف	*Angels*
Bā'	ب	*Jinn*
Mīm	م	*Human Beings*
Wāw	و	*Step-levels of Spiritual Development*

The first person to establish the classification of Arabic letters as 'vocal' and 'voiceless' was an eighth-century grammarian by the name of Sībawayh (d. ca. 180/796). His division was based on the intensity of the flow of air in the human articulatory system and Ibn 'Arabī added nothing to it. Like Sībawayh before him, Ibn 'Arabī believed that the letters are formed as the breath faces obstacles in the articulatory system – and the nature and location of these obstacles were said to determine the properties of letters. On his side, Sībawayh identified sixteen points of obstruction in the human articulatory system which can result in the sixteen different points of articulation.[28] By taking these points as a foundation, Sībawayh went on to establish one of the earliest known sequences of the letters of the Arabic alphabet.

Sībawayh's sequence (Table 10) begins with *hamza*, a glottal stop that is pronounced in the larynx, the deepest point of the throat, and the furthest end of the vocal tract. From there on, the sequence proceeds by listing the points of articulation in ascending order until it ends with *wāw*, the labial sound produced at the lips, at the front end of the resonating system. In spite of the minor differences in their classification systems, Sībawayh's sequence was once thought

28 Sībawayh, *Al-Kitāb* vol.4, p. 433. Like Ibn 'Arabī, he noted that 'when the air is clipped along its exit path toward the bodily mouth, the sites of its clipping are called letters and the entities of the letters appear' (*Fut.*I:256; al-Manṣūb, 1/509; *FM.*I:168).

to have been inspired by the works of his teacher, Khalīl b. Aḥmad. Similar sequences have been used in Syriac, Ethiopian and several other Semitic alphabets as well.[29] However, in the first century of the Islamic era, Sībawayh's sequence was significantly altered. Medieval historiographers tend to attribute the innovative sequence which grouped letters of similar shapes together and introduced *alif* as the first letter of the Arabic alphabet to Naṣr Ibn ʿĀṣim al-Laythī (d. 89/707). His modifications are thought to have been inspired by the desire to simplify the memorization of twenty-eight letters of the alphabet.[30]

Table 10 Sībawayh's sequence of the letters of the Arabic alphabet

ء ا ه ع ح غ خ ق ك ض ح ش ي ل ر ن ط د ت ص ز س ظ ذ ث ف ب م و

Table 11 al-Laythī's sequence of the letters of the Arabic alphabet

ا ب ت ث ج ح خ د ذ ر ز س ش ص ض ط ظ ع غ ف ق ك ل م ن ه و ي

Ibn ʿArabī used both sequences in his works. While he relied on al-Laythi's sequence as he was working on the cryptographic scripts from *The Book of Emanations* and *The Book of the Fabulous Gryphon*, Sībawayh's sequence served as a basis for the analyses he conducted on the act of genesis. However, rather than attributing Sībawayh's order of letters to the physiognomy of the vocal tract, Ibn ʿArabī maintained that the sequence, human vocal tract and the universe alike owe their structure to God. Ibn ʿArabī primarily identified the letters as the building blocks of the universe which was created in a distinct order. This order, or so Ibn ʿArabī believed, corresponds to the order of the Arabic alphabet. 'The manifestation of letters from heart to mouth is similar to the manifestation of the cosmos from the Cloud,' Ibn ʿArabī maintained, and 'the emergence of letters and words along this path is akin to the emergence of the universe from the mist which

29 Among the notable supporters of this theory were Nassir (1985:25), Talmon (1997:1–90) and Bräunlich (1926:61). However, Danecki successfully argues that Sībawayh was unfamiliar with *Kitāb al-ʿAyn*. Danecki's hypothesis is primarily based on the fact that 1) while Sībawayh quotes Khalīl hundreds of times, not a single reference has been made to his purported phonetic system and 2) that the refined nature of theories from *K. al-ʿAyn* indicates that this work was created *after* Sībawayh's *al-Kitāb*. Danecki. 'Early Arabic Phonetical Theory', pp. $51–6.

30 al-Nassir, *Sībawayh the Phonologist*, p. 26.

is the breath of the True, the All-Merciful.'[31] In Ibn ʿArabī's works, the breath represents the life-force in general: it stands for the act of genesis and the human life alike. To create Adam, God was said to have blown some of His breath into him – and when He wished for people to die 'He removes breath from them'.[32] The Breath of the All-Merciful has been commonly compared to the human breath – we were thought to have been created in His form. As a result, Ibn ʿArabī drew an analogy between the act of genesis and the extension of the divine breath across the void to create the twenty-eight levels of existence to the emergence of the twenty-eight letters of the alphabet from the human heart. A later commentator on Ibn ʿArabī's works offered an allegorical interpretation of this proposition: breath, words and letters reveal what lies in the heart.[33] In this case, however, the meaning was also quite literal. As he was unfamiliar with the anatomy of larynx and vocal cords, Ibn ʿArabī believed that the heart plays a crucial role in the physiological process of breathing. Upon entering the lungs, it was thought that the air passes into the heart in order to be heated and purified by its fire. From the heart, Ibn ʿArabī believed, the air enters pulsatile arteries and reaches all parts of the body. On its way back, the air passes through the heart once again, enters the lungs and exits through the throat and mouth, passing through the eight points of articulation on its way out (Fig. 13). The air flowing through the vocal tract is the ultimate prerequisite of life and speech alike. Although the air we breathe in is always one and the same, the place where it gets blocked by the articulatory organs determines the properties of the pronounced letter: will it be *hāʾ*, *ḥāʾ* or *khāʾ*?

While the Breath that creates the letters is one of the same, the ranking in excellence occurs because of the place of articulation and form (i.e. the sound) of the letters.[34] In Ibn ʿArabī's works, the same principle applies for the inanimate objects and living beings. Although both have been associated with death, Azrael, the archangel of the sphere of Saturn, is quite different in nature from angels of the sphere of Mercury.[35] If a spirit of the upper realms were to descend into the lower realms of existence, his form would be transformed in accordance with his place of manifestation. For example, upon

31 *Fut.*IV:36; al-Manṣūb, 6/154; *FM.*II:394.
32 *Fut.*III:497; al-Manṣūb, 5/619; *FM.*II:331.
33 See Bosnevi, *Sharḥ Fuṣūṣ* vol.1, pp. 89.
34 *Fut.*IV:35–6, 115, al-Manṣūb, 4/153; *FM.*II:394.
35 *Fut.*I:164; al-Manṣūb, 1/333; *FM.*I:105.

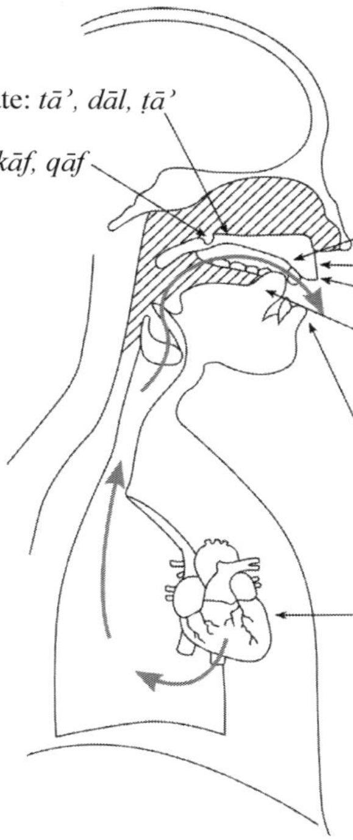

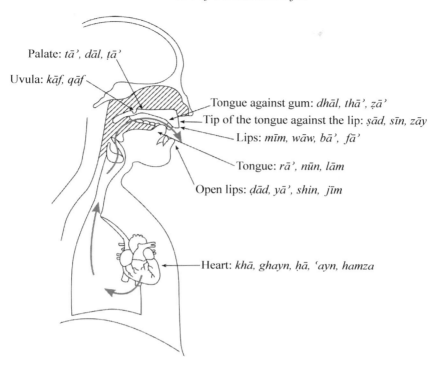

Fig. 13 The letters of the alphabet and their points of articulation according to Ibn 'Arabī

encountering archangel Gabriel in the Sphere of Saturn, below the Lote-tree, the Prophet Muhammad noted that it had 600 wings. Had he encountered the archangel in the realms of hell, his form would have changed accordingly.[36] In the Arabic language, letters have been traditionally divided into throat, medial and labial letters. These three categories served as a basis of Ibn 'Arabī's division of letters on the letters of the world of *Mulk*, *Malakūt* and *Jabarūt*:

1. The Supreme *Jabarūt* as the Great World: *hamza, hā'*
    a. Possible medial letters between Higher *Jabarūt* and *Malakūt*: *ḥā'*
2. The world of *Malakūt* as the Higher World: *ḥā'*, *khā'*, *'ayn* and *ghayn*
    b. Possible medial letters between *Malakūt* and *Jabarūt*: *kāf, qāf, ṭā', ẓā', ṣād, ḍād*

36 al-Qayṣarī, *Foundations of Islamic Mysticism*, p. 132.

3. The world of *Jabarūt* as the Middle World: *tā'*, *thā'*, *jīm*, *dāl*, *dhāl*, *rā'*, *zāy*, *ẓā'*, *kāf*, *lām*, *nūn*, *ṣād*, *ḍād*, *qāf*, *sīn*, *shīn*, *yā'*
    c. Possible medial letters between *Mulk* and *Jabarūt*: *fā'*
4. The world of *Mulk* as the Lower World and the Seen: *bā'*, *mīm*, *wāw*.[37]

Ibn ʿArabī's reasoning for the division was as follows: assuming that human beings were created in God's form, the human heart would correspond to the divine Essence, which is the source of all things in existence. 'The letters, all of them, emerge from the heart, just like the universe as a whole emerges through the creative process based on the imperative *kun*.'[38] The first to be created, and thus closest in proximity and nature to the divine being is the world of *Malakūt*. The First Intellect and the Universal Soul belong to this world – and the same goes for *hā'* and *hamza*, the letters that brought them in existence. In the human articulatory system, these two letters are pronounced deep in the throat, which is the point of articulation closest to the heart. According to this scheme, medial letters of the Arabic alphabet correspond to *Jabarūt*, the medial world between the angelic realm and the visible world. On the cosmological level, the visible world was thought to have the least in common with the purity of the divine Essence. Labial letters, which are pronounced the furthest away from the heart, thus came to be associated with it.[39] The fact that human beings have a potential to master the science of letters was partially based on the fact that the anatomy of their vocal tract, with its sixteen points of obstruction, supports the pronunciation of all twenty-eight letters of the Arabic alphabet in ascending order – beginning with the glottal stop *hamza* and ending with the labial *wāw*. In addition, Ibn ʿArabī claimed to have received a revelation that led him to draw a parallel between the points of articulation (*makhārij*) in the throat, mouth and lips with the step-levels of spiritual ascension (*maʿārij*).[40] Through the analysis of Sībawayh's phonetic scheme, an understanding of the act of genesis and the mystical ascension suddenly appeared possible.

---

37 *Fut.*I:95; al-Manṣūb, 1/190; *FM.*I: 58.

38 *Fut.*III:526–527;. al-Manṣūb, 5/355; *FM.*II:352. The properties of the divine essence will be analysed in detail in the chapter dedicated to the letter *alif.*

39 This correspondence is established on the points of articulation. In addition, *Mulk*, *Malakūt* and *Jabarūt* were sometimes symbolized by the letters *fā'*, *ʿayn* and *lām* respectively (*Fut.*IV:31–2; al-Manṣūb, 6/144–5; *FM.*II:391–2).

40 Chittick, *The Sufi Path of Knowledge*, p. 42.

Islamic cosmology speaks of four arrangements of the universe, with the first three referring to the spatial, temporal and qualitative relations of different levels of existence. The fourth arrangement follows the order of letters. Correspondences between the human vocal tract, the stages of the genesis and the order of the Arabic alphabet could easily lead to the conclusion that the letters were created over a certain period of time – alongside the segments of the universe they were said to represent. However, this idea was generally foreign to Sufi literature and the Islamic normative tradition. Abū ʿAbd Allāh b. Idrīs al-Shāfiʿī (d. 204/820), the founder of the Shāfiʿī school of law, was thus said to have declared: 'Do not say that the letters were created in time, for the first cause of the ruin of the Jews was in believing this.' According to Goldziher, this sentence was intended as a refutation of scholars who believed that the creation of letters accompanied the creation of the universe. In the eyes of al-Shāfiʿī, letters were uncreated and eternal: just like the Divine being and the Qur'an.[41] They always existed. As a result, the existence of letters was thought to have preceded the act of genesis.

Echoes of similar beliefs can be found in Ibn ʿArabī's *Book of Mīm, Wāw and Nūn*. Like al-Shāfiʿī, he held that the existence of letters precedes spatiotemporal relations. 'When' is a question pertaining to time and time belongs to the world of relations,' Ibn ʿArabī noted. 'Don't let these grammatical particles veil you from realizing the truth.'[42] His reasoning was mostly based on belief that it is theoretically impossible to speak of time before the creation of the heavenly spheres took place. In the eyes of Ibn ʿArabī, time was but an illusion created by the progression of heavenly bodies. As such, it was thought to belong to the material domain of existence. In the works of the later Akbarians, letters came to be associated with the domain of the Universal Soul, which knows neither space nor time. For example, al-Qashānī's glossary of Sufi terminology identifies the All-soul as eternity without a beginning and an end. 'All present moments are

41 Goldziher, 'Mélanges judéo-arabes XXIV: La création des lettres', p. 89. This is similar to the tenth-century debates of the (un)createdness of the Qur'an. On his side, al-Shāfiʿī believed that letters have always existed. As a result, there was no need for God to create them.

42 Quoted according to Chittick, *The Self-Disclosure of God*, p. 13. In Ibn ʿArabī's works, the term *ḥarf* can also stand for human beings in general. While nouns, verbs and particles have been traditionally perceived as the three basic elements of speech in the Arabic language, particles cannot be used on their own to form a meaningful sentence. In the same way, Ibn ʿArabī argued that no creation, including human beings, could outlive its Creator.

united within it. That is why it is called mystical time and the source of time for moments of time are simply patterns and alternations within it, by which its laws and forms are made manifest; while it endures exactly as it is, forever, endlessly – though it can combine with the subjective presence.'[43] In the works of al-Qashānī, 'the beginning of all things in Eternity without the beginning' is symbolized by the letter *alif*.[44] Nevertheless, in the material domain of existence all things have a beginning and an end. Ibn 'Arabī held that the circle of letters which brought forth the universe begins with *hamza* and ends with *wāw*.[45] However, our story begins and ends with *alif*: the letter that is not a letter.

43 al-Qashānī, A *Glossary of Sufi Technical Terms*, p. 7.

44 Ibid. pp.3–4.

45 *Fut.*IV:36; al-Manṣūb, 4/154–5; *FM.*II: 395.

'I raised my head and saw, indeed, that alif was in everything.'

Ibn 'Arabī[46]

46 Ibn 'Arabī, *K. Mashāhid al-asrār*, p. 215.

2.2. The Isolated Alif (ا) as the Divine Essence

A popular saying attributed to al-Hallāj states that the alphabet is a kingdom whose king is *alif*.[47] According to al-Sulamī, *alif* is God and the gifts of God'.[48] Both authors associated the first letter of the Arabic alphabet with the Creator. However, the Islamic normative tradition held that even if we were to focus only on the meaning of *alif* at the beginning of *al-Fātiḥa*, the weight of the interpretation would overburden seventy camels.[49] 'If *alif* was to be described by a noun, the noun would be "Allah" – and if it was to be described by an adjective, the adjective would be "self-standing",' noted Ibn ʿArabī on the matter.[50] To know *alif* meant seeing God as He truly is, before He created the world. To do so, al-Qashānī advised, 'obliterating from the mind all worldly impressions whilst maintaining awareness of the eternal presence of Oneness' was required.[51] On his side, Ibn ʿArabī was stricter. This is evident from the notes he made on Allah, which is the name the Creator was thought to have chosen for Himself. The name comes from the root *alif-lām-hā'*, one of whose meanings is 'to be perplexed'.[52] Ibn ʿArabī believed that His choice was far from whimsical. Throughout the centuries, countless voices have worshipped the Creator under many different names and attributes. Contradictory, divergent and man-made, these names were eventually discarded by Ibn ʿArabī as arbitrary descriptions. Ibn ʿArabī interpreted the Creator's choice to name Himself 'Allah' as twofold. By choosing for Himself the name which is ill-suited to serve as a root word of morphological derivations, the Creator 1) wanted to caution mankind against associating Him with other deities. Due to the fact that the name Allah betrays no characteristic of the One being named, 2) it also serves to imply that God in His Essence (*alif*) cannot be known[53]. In the Qur'an, the term *alif* is never used in association with God. However, Ibn ʿArabī relied on the Islamic normative tradition to establish the definition of *alif* as the divine Self and the ultimate reality with neither relation nor association with any other thing. The term *alif* is generally used without a definite article – a fact that Ibn ʿArabī approved of since

47 Böwering, 'Sulamī's Treatise on the Science of the Letters (*'ilm al-ḥurūf*)', p. 354.
48 al-Sulamī, *Sharḥ ma'ānī al-ḥurūf*, p. 371.
49 Bosnevi, *Sharḥ Fuṣūṣ* vol.1, p. 59.
50 *Fut.*I:106; al-Manṣūb, 1/207; *FM.*I:65.
51 al-Qashānī, *Glossary of Sufi Technical Terms*, pp. 3–4.
52 Ibn Manẓūr, *Lisān al-'Arab* vol.1, p. 96.
53 *Fut.*III:262; al-Manṣūb, 182-3; *FM.*II:174.

the article would implicitly serve to define something that is indefinable and unknowable.[54] Being fully independent of God's creations, His Essence is beyond limitations and cannot be known. Adjectives such as 'unlimited' and 'eternal' cannot be used to describe it. *Dhāt* is above such distinctions – there is always a little more, something else. The only thing that can be ascertained about *alif* is that it exists. Any attempt to analyse its nature could thus be labelled as the luxury of thinking.[55] In the surviving works of Ibn ʿArabī, the divine Essence is represented by *alif*, the first letter of the Arabic alphabet.

> According to those who smell the truth, *alif* is not a real letter. However, people usually label it as letter. When one who has verified this for himself (*muḥaqqiq*) refers to it as letter, he is doing i for the sake of convenience. The station of *alif* is the station of totality (*jamʿ*).[56]

Written as a single vertical stroke (ا), the letter *alif* owes its name to the root *alif-lām-fā'*, which conveys the notion of intimacy, familiarity and harmony between the units brought together. Ibn ʿArabī associated the meaning of this letter with the number one. This was found to be appropriate in the light of the fact that just as *alif* 'is not a real letter', number one 'is not one of the numbers'.[57] Ibn ʿArabī's reasoning was as follows. If the number one, *alif*, is followed by two (which symbolizes the First Intellect), two is followed by three (the Protected Tablet) – 'and like that up to infinity, until the genesis of the world is completed'.[58] However, when 1 is subtracted from 1000, the result we would get is not 999 ($1000 - 1 \neq 999$) but non-existence (0). 'When one is voided from something, the thing in question turns to void. When one is firmly there, the thing is found (i.e. it exists).'[59] Ibn ʿArabī believed that the creation could not outlast its Creator. Without the Creator to support it, the world would cease to exist. However,

54 For a detailed overview of the impact of the Islamic normative tradition on Ibn ʿArabī's notion of *dhāt*, see Alsamaani, *An Analytic Philosophical Approach to Ibn Arabi's Conception of Ultimate Reality*, pp. 152–63.

55 The Creator and the created, *dhāt* and the world, were compared by Ibn ʿArabī to the Craftsman and a chair. The chair does not recognize its maker. As a passive subject of His craftmanship, it only serves to prove that He exists (*Fut.*I:146; al-Manṣūb, 1/305–6; *FM.*I:93–4).

56 *Fut.*I:106; al-Manṣūb, 1/207; *FM.*I:65.

57 *Fut.*I:102; al-Manṣūb, 1/201; *FM.*I:63.

58 Ibid.

59 Ibid.

God and the universe share no essence. *Dhāt*, the divine Essence, does not manifest in the created world. Strictly speaking, it is not even proper to say that *alif* is the cause of all things since the cause (*ʿilla*) always seeks its effect (*maʿlūl*), just as the effect seeks its cause[60]. Ibn ʿArabī appears to have felt that every type of correlation between two things could be perceived as the one's dependence upon the other. And according to the Qurʾan (Q.3:97), Allah is fully independent of His creatures. In the works of Ibn ʿArabī, the term *alif* is therefore never used to indicate that Allah is the master and creator of all things – for this would mean that His Essence is dependent on His creations. Ibn ʿArabī maintained that the cause depends on the thing caused and that *alif* is too transcendent to be dependent on anything. While God was thought to exist through His Essence, cosmos is existent through Him. For this reason, Ibn ʿArabī held that it would be pointless to discuss the issue of cause and effect when it comes to *alif* and the universe, since the universe has no independent existence *per se*. He perceived *alif* as an embodiment of the eleventh verse of the Sura *al-Shūra*: *There is nothing like Him* (Q.42:11). In order to describe the properties of the unique relationship between the Creator and the created, Ibn ʿArabī turned to the letter *alif* and its relation to other letters of the Arabic alphabet:

> *Alif* is the line (ا) all letters are formed from and to *alif* they return once they are decomposed. *Alif* is therefore the root of all letters.[61]

All letters may be dissolved and reduced to *alif* and all of them are composed of it. However, *alif* itself is not reduced to any of them as, reiterating, it gets dissolved into its own spirit-being.[62]

> *Alif* is pronounced in the letters but the letters are not pronounced in *alif*. The letters are constituted of *alif* and *alif* always accompanies them, without them being aware of it.[63]

60 Chittick. *The Self-Disclosure of God*, p. 17.

61 *Fut.*III:182–3; al-Manṣūb, 5/33; *FM.*II:122.

62 Ibn ʿArabī wrote in a similar way of the number one. See *Fut.* I:282; al-Manṣūb, 1/547; *FM.*I:185.

63 Ibn ʿArabī, *K. Mashāhid al-asrār*, p. 217.

The quoted excerpts from Ibn ʿArabī's works evoke the Qurʾanic image of an exalted, transcendent God who is closer to a man than his jugular vein (Q.2:165, 50:16, 57:3). It is a well-known paradox which influenced Ibn ʿArabī's analyses of the orthographic form of *alif* and its relation to other letters of the Arabic alphabet. In the eyes of Ibn ʿArabī, *alif* was the underlying principle and subsistence of all letters (*qayyūm al-ḥurūf*). When pronounced, it sounds like the long vowel /ā/. Ibn ʿArabī compared this sound to the sigh of a man experiencing the greatness of God.[64] The Arabic grammar tradition held that the letters are formed when air meets an obstacle in the articulatory organs. In the case of *alif*, Ibn ʿArabī held that these standards were to be imposed strictly. Due to the fact that air meets no obstacle as *alif* is being pronounced, he deemed that *alif* is not a real letter. While other letters were perceived as an outcome of the interrupted flow of air, *alif* was the flow itself. Having identified it with the (divine) breath, Ibn ʿArabī went on to ascertain that all letters are morphological and orthographical changes of *alif*. Like the life-giving breath, the first letter of the Arabic alphabet was thought to have infused all letters with its presence.[65] Sometimes *alif* could appear explicitly, in the names of letters: this is the case with *wāw, lām, dāl* and nineteen other letters of the Arabic alphabet. Its presence could also be implicit – for Ibn ʿArabī reasoned that all letters owe their written forms to the transformations of *alif*. This theory was based on the fact that the isolated form of *alif* is a line (ا): the basic geometrical shape that could be adjusted to assume the form of any other letter. It could thus be said that while the letter *ḥāʾ* (ح) is the hunchback *alif*, *mīm* (م) is the circular *alif*. ʿAṭṭar of Nishapur (d. ca. 618/1221) famously expressed a similar conviction in the verses of *Ushturnāma*:

Alif was the first one in origin,
Then it produced the number of connections.
When it becomes crooked it is counted as *dāl*
When it puts another bend upon itself,

64 *Fut.*II:55–56; al-Manṣūb, 2/487; *FM.*I:414.
65 Ibn ʿArabī, *Kitāb al-Alif*, pp. 270–1.

Then it becomes *rā'*, o Ignorant one!
    When *alif* is bent like a reed,
Then both its ends become crooked and it is *bā'*,
    When *alif* becomes a horseshoe, then it is a *nūn*.[66]

Ibn ʿArabī taught that the letters come in three basic shapes: rounded (*mustadīr*), straight (*mustaqīm*) and bent (*muʿwajj*). In his works, the rounded shape of letters stands for the meditations on *alif*. Ibn ʿArabī associated this shape with a spiral curved in the direction of negating. This was due to the fact that, from the human point of view, *alif* can be discussed in negative attributes only. For example, it could be safely assumed that it is neither corporeal, manifested nor ethereal. These (negative) attributes were referred to by Ibn ʿArabī as the silence (*ṣamt*), the Great Unknown. In contrast, horizontal letters represent an adept's attempts to establish a bond with the Creator – while bent letters were seen as an attempt to reconcile the two approaches. Bent letters stand for 1) the acknowledgement of the transcendent, hidden nature of *alif* and 2) the state of unity between the Creator and the created. The three shapes of the letters in Ibn ʿArabī's works are represented with *alif*, *lām* and *hā'*: i.e. with the archigraphemes that form the name Allah (Fig. 14). *Alif*, when serving as the first letter of God's name, has an identical meaning to the isolated form of *alif*:

Fig. 14 The Divine Name Allah

Allah, it is the name of the essence (*ism al-dhat*) and the personal name (*ism al-alif*) of God in His Essence and totality. Remove *alif* and the rest symbolizes the three worlds: *dunya* (this world), the invisible heaven and starry firmament, *barzakh* and heaven and the hereafter (*al-akhira*). *Alif*, the first letter, is the source of all there is while *hā'* is *hu* [HE], the attribute of God free from all associations.[67]

66 ʿAṭṭār, *Ushturnāma*, p. 95.

67 See Ibn ʿArabī, *Journey to the Lord of Power*, p. 50.

The Meccan Revelations clarify that the two *lām*s, i.e. the second and the third letters of God's name, represent *Mulk* and *Malakūt*, the visible and the invisible worlds. The line that joins them is yet another symbol of *Jabarūt*, which is 'the place of the soul'.[68] The line between the second *lām* and *hā'* was seen as a mystery by means of which revealed knowledge is transferred from God to man 'and this is the centre of knowledge, *alif*, which is the place of fading away'.[69] According to Ibn 'Arabī, this *alif* represents 'the True, the One that does not join up'.[70] The three archigraphemes that form the name Allah were concurrently seen as symbols of the movements of a body during the prayer. The purpose of these postures was to articulate the name of God name simultaneously, by tongue and body alike (Fig. 15).

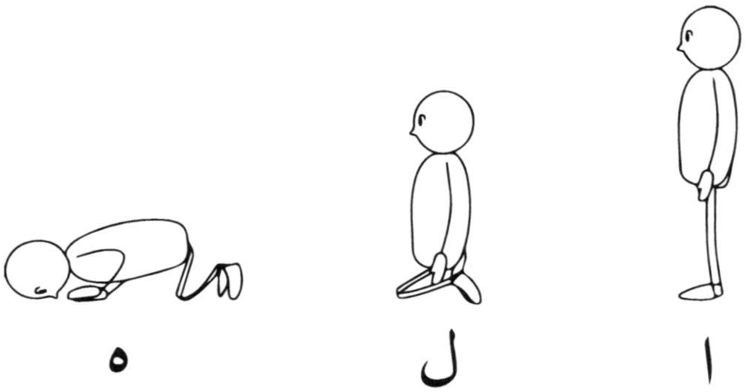

Fig. 15 Letters and the act of prayer

By means of prayer, a man reaches the state of unity with God. Ibn 'Arabī and the later interpreters of his works compared the orthographic form of *alif* with a standing human being. In traditional Islam, *alif*, the standing position in prayer, was thought to encompass all other positions like sitting, bowing and placing forehead to the ground.[71] As a result, *alif* came to be perceived as a symbol of unity and piety. However, the orthographic form of *alif* could also stand for the proud and arrogant individual. Any sort of arrogance in human beings was, however, deemed to be inappropriate. According to Ibn 'Arabī, the human nature is more evident in the shape of the letter *bā'*: that is,

68 *Fut.*I:162; al-Manṣūb, 1/330; *FM.*I:104.
69 Ibid.
70 Ibid.
71 See *Fut.* II:55–6; al-Manṣūb, 2/487; *FM.*I:414; al-Jīlī, *The Elucidation of Difficulties*, p. 90, and Ibn 'Arabī, *The Seven Days of the Heart*, p. 164.

when an individual is lying down ill, asleep and/or in pain (Fig. 16). *Alif*, the upright position, and all that it implies, was thought to be a symbol that is more befitting for the Creator.[72]

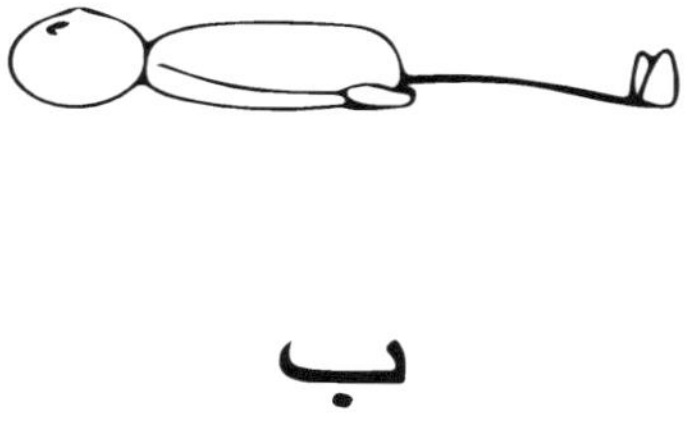

Fig. 16 Human nature

The rules of Arabic orthography specify that the vertical line which forms the letter *alif* is never to be joined to the letters that follow it: thus evoking the image of the sacred, isolated *alif*. As a result, the symbol of unity also came to be perceived as a symbol of self-standingness and transcendence. Precisely because *alif* (i.e. the divine Essence) is self-standing, our world is able to exist as it is.[73] Due to the fact that God and the world share no essence, little can be said on the nature and properties of *alif*. Ibn ʿArabī identified familiarity with *alif* as a secret that transcends revealed knowledge and the rational mind alike. The meaning of this letter is one of the insights that should not be sought. The consequences for the (un)fortunate receiver of a revelation concerning *alif* were thought to be dire: 'His soul, lost, baffled and unjust as it was, would return to God – while his body would sink to the lowest grade, to clay.'[74] When it comes to the divine Essence, 'no one knows God but God'.[75] However, Alsamaani pointed out that Ibn ʿArabī seemingly contradicts himself upon asserting that religious experiences, in fact, offer an insight into the nature of *alif*. Provided that one has come to terms with the notion of divinity (*ulūhiyya*), certain familiarity with *alif* could be achieved[76]. In Ibn ʿArabī's works, this issue was addressed in his reflections on the cherubim letters and the star of *lām-alif*.

72 In his commentary on *The Meccan Revelations*, al-Jīlī noted that as he sleeps, a man's body assumes the shape of *bā'*, but in spite of the fact that the body can assume the form of every letter of the alphabet, *alif*, the standing position, is its primary shape (*Elucidation*, p. 90). In addition, Aḥmad b. Ḥanbal condemned the Baghdad Sufi Sari al-Saqati, who identified *alif* as the letter of Iblis and the only letter that did not prostrate itself in front of Adam. See Massignon, *La Philosophie Orientale*, p. 14.

73 *Fut.*I:404; al-Manṣūb, 2/75; *FM.*I:368.

74 Elmore, *Islamic Sainthood*, pp. 331–32.

75 Quoted according to Chittick, *Sufi Path of Knowledge*, p. 62.

76 Alsamaani, *An Analytic Philosophical Approach*, p. 161.

'Had I remained silent, you would not exist,
if you had not spoken I would not have been
known. Speak then, so that I may be known!'

Ibn 'Arabi[77]

77 Ibn 'Arabī, *K. Mashāhid al-asrār*, p. 217.

2.3. The Creator and the Created, as Symbolized by the Cherubim Letters and the Star of Lām-Alif (لا)

According to Schimmel, *lām-alif* appears as one of the principal symbols in Islamic mysticism from the ninth century CE. Ibn Sawdakīn believed that it stands for the creative impulse of the Divine Self (*ulūhiyya*). Essentially One, through the act of genesis God brought forth the many – and this was the beginning of a relationship between the worshipper and the One being worshipped. In earlier times, however, this symbol was primarily used in profane poetry to signify the tightness of an embrace and the quick succession of events.[78] The surviving works of Ibn ʿArabī indicate that he was aware of this development. *The Meccan Revelations* refer to the star of *lām-alif* as the intertwined bodies of lovers 'floating through the year like a dream' and the two sapphires which are to be sought in the ocean of the Qur'an.[79] Ibn ʿArabī's works compare *lām-alif* to the plates of a shell that hide a pearl within and the bond between the Creator and the created. In *The Contemplations of the Holy Mysteries*, Ibn ʿArabī also demonstrates a tendency to identify the star of *lām-alif* with its orthographical equivalent: the negative determiner 'no' (*lā*).

> Look at what is hidden in the negation (*lā*) and then say whatever you like – that they are two or that they are One. In the link between *lām* and *alif* there is the undisclosed secret which I have deposited in My saying: God is He who raised the heavens without any support.[80]

In the quoted paragraph, Ibn ʿArabī alludes to the second verse of the Sura *al-Ra'd* and the image of God who created heaven with no pillars to support it (Q.13:2). Within the star of *lām-alif*, the shape of one letter is concealed in another. Written as a single orthographic unit (لا) which is composed of two letters (*lām* (ل) + *alif* (ا) = *lām-alif* (لا)), *lām-alif* thus came to be known as the 'the double letter'.[81] As the orthographic symbol of unity between the Creator and the created, *lām-alif* was deemed to be of equal importance to any other letter. Today, it is generally assumed that the Arabic alphabet has twenty-eight letters.

78 Schimmel, *Calligraphy*, p. 101.
79 *Fut.*I:119; al-Manṣūb, 1/227; *FM.*I:75.
80 Ibn ʿArabī, *K. Mashāhid al-asrār*, p. 225.
81 Ibn ʿArabī, *Tarjumān al-ashwāq*, p. 139.

The same number can be found in Ibn 'Arabī's works. However, Ibn 'Arabī reaches this number by omitting *alif*, the letter that is not a letter, and adding *lām-alif* to the sequence. This was in accordance with the saying attributed to the Prophet Muhammad, which states that whoever refuses to accept *lām-alif* as a real letter will never be accepted among his followers. Such a person is bound to suffer in hellfire for eternity.[82] While Ibn 'Arabī's sequences typically include *lām-alif*[83], they also demonstrate a tendency to put *alif* at the first place of the sequence of twenty-nine letters. In *The Meccan Revelations*, *lām-alif* is thus positioned before *yā'* and analysed as the twenty-eighth letter of the sequence. A similar arrangement can be observed in *The Book of Theophanies* (Fig. 17).

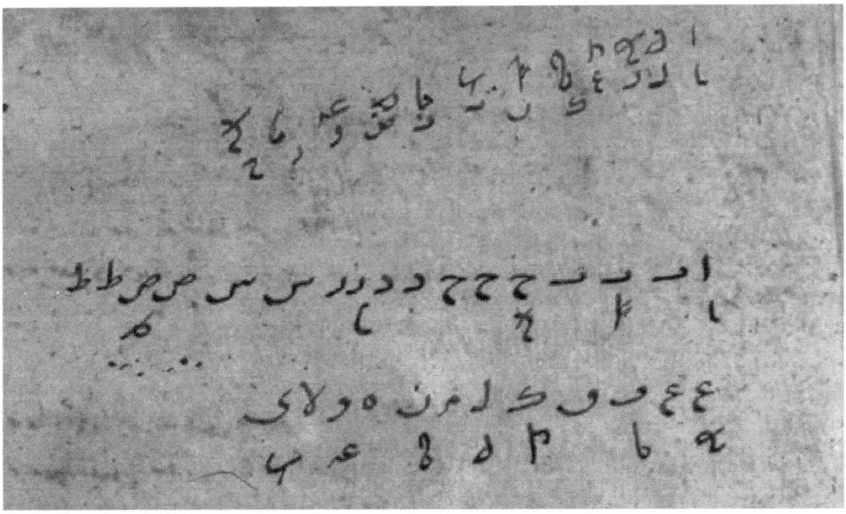

Fig. 17 Ibn 'Arabī's sequence of letters with lām-alif

However, *The Orientations of the Letters* (*Tawajjuhāt al-ḥurūf*), Ibn 'Arabī's compilation of twenty-nine prayers – one prayer for each letter of the Arabic alphabet – puts *lām-alif* at the end of the sequence. This sequence was intended as an allusion to the description of the Creator in the third verse of the Sura *al-Ḥadīd*: 'He is the First

82 Goldziher, *Aus Literatur der muhamedanischen Mystik*, p. 782.

83 A notable exception is the chapter 198 of *The Meccan Revelations*, which analyses the sequence of the letters of the Arabic alphabet based on their points of articulation and the correspondences between the Breath of the All-Merciful and the human breath. In this sequence, *lām-alif* is omitted (*Fut.*IV:36; al-Manṣūb, 6/154; *FM.*II:335).

and the Last, the Manifest and the Hidden, and He is the Knower of all things' (Qur'an 57:3). *Alif*, 'to whom the firstness belongs', hides itself in the shape of one of the last letters of the alphabet, *lām*, 'so as to combine the first and the last, the visible and the invisible'.[84] Manṣūr al-Ḥallāj popularized a similar view three centuries earlier. He believed that the two 'spikes' of *lam-alif* (لا) stand for the origins and purpose of all living beings – as presented in the Sura *al-Baqara*: *innā lillāhi wa inna ilay-Hi rāji'ūn* ('we belong to God and to Him we return') (Q.2:156). Al-Ḥallāj referred to the meeting point of the two spikes as *nuqṭa*. This term, which is usually translated as 'dot', was originally used in the Arabic grammar tradition to denote diacritical marks which distinguish one letter from another. According to al-Ḥallāj, an insight into the nature of all things could be obtained by means of familiarity with the disjoined letters of the Qur'an. While knowledge of the disjoined letters was thought to be hidden in *lām-alif*, 'the allusion of *lām-alif* is hidden in *alif* and the allusion of *alif* is hidden in the dot.'[85] Sufis generally identified familiarity with the dot as the primordial intuitive knowledge (*al-ma'rifa al-aṣliyya*).

On his side, Ibn 'Arabī compared this issue to the ocean without a shore and the great waves which cause ships to sink. The interpretation of the dot was thought to be close to impossible to convey in words. In his attempt to express the ineffable, Ibn 'Arabī found it convenient to rely on diagrams. 'If it [the act of genesis] must be put into form,' wrote Ibn 'Arabī in explanation of the second diagram of *The Meccan Revelations*, 'then let it be a dot within a circumference. While the dot is the Real (a), the emptiness outside the circumference stands for non-existence (c). Between them are all possible things.'[86] In this diagram, *alif* is represented by the centre of a circle. The universe, all that exists, lies between the circumference of the circle and its centre. As such, the circle contains all living beings, objects and planes of existence.[87]

When One gives birth to many, its essence neither multiplies nor increases in size. Ultimately, the creation has no impact on the Creator – and for this reason, in Fig. 18, the divine Essence appears to be isolated from other things in existence. Ibn 'Arabī believed that nothing steps into existence except by the power of the Divine will. The will of God, imbued with knowledge and power, is voiced and

84 Böwering, 'Sulamī's Treatise', p. 352.
85 Böwering, p. 392. See also al-Sarrāj, *Kitāb al-Luma'*, pp. 88–9.
86 *Sifr* 24: fol.87. See *Fut.*V:406; al-Manṣūb, 8/520; *FM.*III:275.
87 *Fut.*I:393; al-Manṣūb, 2/58; *FM.*I:260.

directed through the command '*kun!*'. The creative word of God is depicted in Fig. 18 as a circumference of the circle.

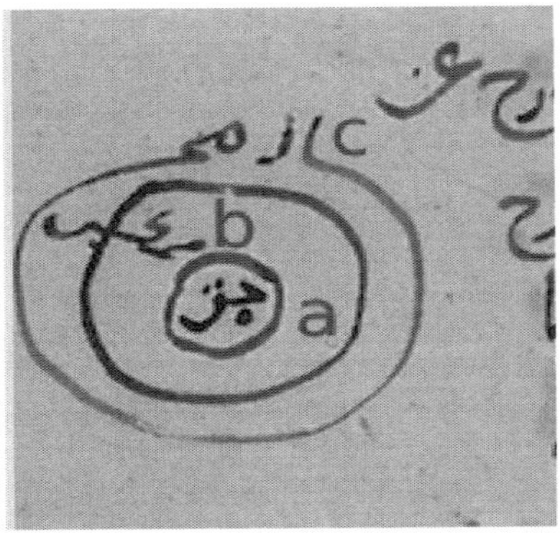

a) Dot, the Real
b) All things in existence
c) Non-existence

Fig. 18 The Act of Genesis

Alternatively, this circumference could be interpreted as a visual representation of the name Allah.[88] Ibn 'Arabī noted that the letter *alif* 'possesses a vertical movement and due to its condition of subsistent Self-standingness (*qayyūmiyya*) everything stands in existence'.[89] Possibly inspired by this passage, Winkel offered an innovative description of the centre and the circumference. His interpretation was depicted in Fig. 20 by the author of the present study. According to Winkel, *alif* can be perceived as a symbol of three-dimensional space coming into existence. Viewed from the top, a three-dimensional model of the letter *alif* looks like a two-dimensional dot (Fig. 19). The dot is the centre from which the universe expands as a circumference. When angled to the side, the model becomes a stick: a three-dimensional image. The rotation of the stick would then create a circumference – i.e. the universe.[90]

The Meccan Revelations also preserved the following description of the Divine omnipresence and the universe as a circumference of the circle:

> If you were to imagine the lines projecting from the dot to the circumference (*muḥīṭ*), these will terminate but unto a dot. The whole circumference bears the same relationship to the dot,

88 Bosnevi, *Sharḥ Fuṣūṣ* vol.1, p. 216.
89 *Fut.*III:182–3; al-Manṣūb, 5/32; *FM.*II:122, cited in Ibn 'Arabī, *Seven Days of the Heart*, p. 164.
90 See Winkel's introduction to Ibn 'Arabī, *The Openings Revealed in Makkah*, Changes, p. 19.

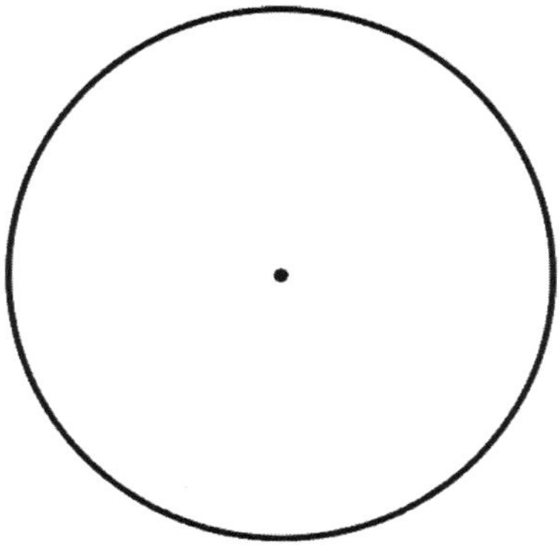

Fig. 19 Alif, the Divine Essence

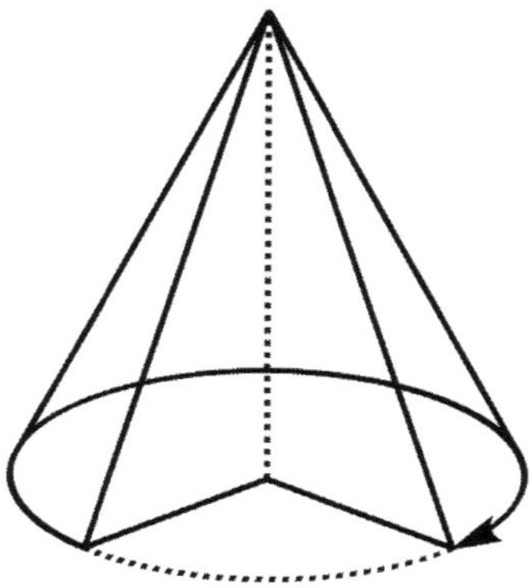

Fig. 20 The Act of Genesis according to E. Winkel

> which is [represented in] His saying: 'And God, all unseen, surrounds them,' and His saying: 'Is He not surrounding (*muḥīṭ*) all things?[91]

Ibn ʿArabī held that *alif* infuses other letters of the alphabet with its presence. In a similar way, the world was thought to be engulfed by the Divine presence. It could not be otherwise, as the universe was believed to be existing through God and not by itself. Standing for the intertwined bodies of two lovers, the star of *lām-alif* was also perceived as a symbol of the divine omnipresence.

> As we clasp and embrace to be the double letter,
> Although our bodies are dual, the eye sees only a single one.
> This is because of my leanness and his light.
> If it weren't for my sadness, I would be invisible to the eye.[92]

In Ibn ʿArabī's works, the star of *lām-alif* represents two aspects of the Divine being: *alif* and its attributes. 'As such, the *alif* of the *lām* belongs to the deep recognition of essences and revival of the bones decayed.'[93] What *alif* is, one cannot know – we will never know

91 *Fut.*V:406; al-Manṣūb, 8/520; *FM*.III.275, cited according to Akkach, *Cosmology and Architecture in Pre-modern Islam*, p. 72, referring to Q.85:20 and 41:54.
92 Ibn ʿArabī, *Tarjumān al-ashwāq*, p. 139.
93 Ibn ʿArabī, *Contemplation of the Holy Mysteries*, pp. 90–3.

God in His Essence. But of God as Creator (*ilāh*), certain things can be ascertained. For example, Ibn ʿArabī assures his reader that the world was created due to the fact that God is Living, Knowing, Wanting and Powerful – 'nothing else'.[94] These attributes were identified as the roots of all existence. God exists – and therefore He is Living. Knowing, God laid out a plan for the universe He Wanted to create. Speaking, He uttered the command: 'Be!' – and the fact that His command brought forth the desired result implies that His determination and wisdom were united through power. It can thus be assumed that the Creator is Powerful as well. But while *alif* is one, its properties are many. In accordance with the Islamic normative tradition, Ibn ʿArabī speaks of the 99 (or 100) divine attributes which are generally referred to as the Most Beautiful Names. These Names stand for the many properties of the single *alif*: 'for what is understood by Living is not by Wanting, Powerful, Measuring. It is the same with the letter *ṣād* and other letters (…). His *alif* does not multiply and is not completed by any addition – God is too great for that.'[95] In Ibn ʿArabī's works, the Most Beautiful Names of God also represent His relationship with each thing He created (Fig. 21). For this reason, it comes as no surprise that some of these Names appear to be mutually opposed to one another. For example, God describes Himself in the Qurʾan as the One who is benevolent and terrible, beaming with pleasure and burning with rage. The world He created also seems to be endowed with disparate forms of existence, with people being torn by opposing desires and with letters of the alphabet such as *ṭāʾ* being simultaneously classified as 'curved' and 'mixed', 'elevated and 'lax'[96].

The later commentaries of Ibn ʿArabī's works divide the Most Beautiful Names of God into manifested and non-manifested Names. The same division could be applied to letters. As such, manifested Names and letters were compared to active, male forces that imprint themselves onto passive matter. Apart from the ninety-nine manifested Names of God and the twenty-eight letters of the Arabic alphabet, countless more were thought to exist. These non-manifested, sublime Names and letters were perceived as 'individual qualities that lie dormant in the most hidden part of the hidden world – like the tree

94 *Fut.*II:324; al-Manṣūb, 3/415; *FM.*I:258–9.

95 *Fut.*IV:48; al-Manṣūb, 6/175; *FM.*II:403.

96 See *Fut.*I:112; al-Manṣūb, 1/217; *FM.*I:70, and *Fut.*IV:36; al-Manṣūb, 6/153; *FM.*II:394.

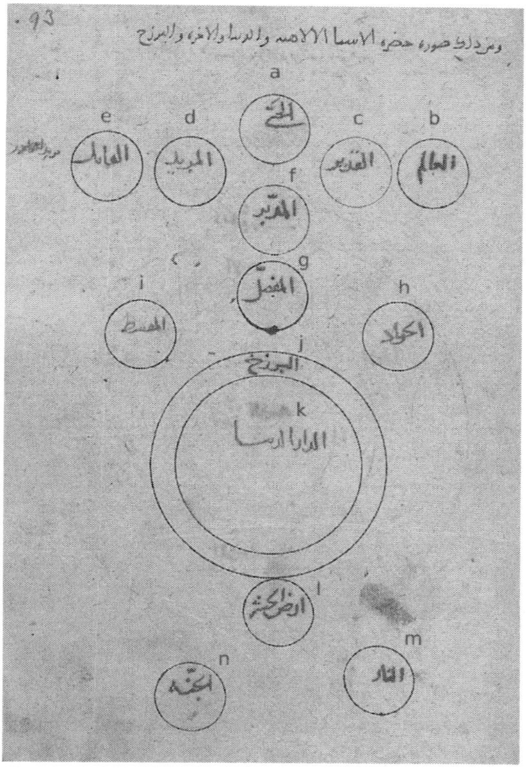

a. *al-Ḥayy, the Living*
b. *al-ʿĀlim, the Knowing*
c. *al-Qadīr, the Powerful*
d. *al-Murīd, the Wanting*
e. *al-Qāʾil, the Speaking*
f. *al-Mudabbir, the Ordainer*
g. *al-Mufaṣṣil, the Distinguisher*
h. *al-Jawād, the Most Generous*
i. *al-Muqsiṭ, the Impartial*
j. *Barzakh*
k. *Corporeal world*
l. *Land of Resurrection*
m. *Hellfire*
n. *Heavenly gardens*

Fig. 21 The Most Beautiful Names of God and the world

latent in the date-stone'.[97] As such, they have no impact on the material world and cannot be known.[98] Ibn ʿArabī taught that it is in the nature of the mind to analyse visual properties of an object separately from the meaning of an object in question: human nature induces it to make a distinction between a pen and the function of a pen. As a result, the mind fancies that each letter carries an allegoric, divine meaning which differs from its 'human' meaning – that there is another world, hidden and unseen, whose existence is separated from what can be seen. However, from the ultimate point of view, there is neither inner nor outer, microcosmic nor macrocosmic. There is only God. In reality, all is He, all is One. While God in His Essence is invariably represented by *alif*, God as the Living, Knowing, Wanting and Powerful Creator is usually represented by the star of *lām-alif* and associated with the first part of the Shahada: there is no God but God (*lā ilāha illā Llāh*). In the

97 al-Qashānī, *Glossary of Sufi Technical Terms*, p. 26.
98 al-Sulamī, *Sharḥ maʿānī al-ḥurūf*, p. 372–5.

eyes of Ibn ʿArabī, these attributes were something that is neither He nor other than He. To resolve this paradox, he relied on the properties of ice: a naturally occurring crystalline solid that is formed when water is frozen into solid state. As such, ice can be perceived as a potential state of water. If the potential manifests itself, we give it a new name: 'ice'. However, when ice melts, it turns to water once again: gone are its unique form and properties. According to Ibn ʿArabī, ice is neither water nor anything other than water. In a similar way, divine attributes were perceived as something that is neither He, nor anything other than He. Another example he provides is the relationship between ink and the twenty-eight letters of the alphabet. While the letters stand for divine attributes, ink was used to represent *alif.* The colour of ink was though to originate from the properties of all letters brought together.[99] Ḥaydar ʿĀmulī (d. 787/1385) subsequently developed Ibn ʿArabī's argument, which was summarised by Toshihiko Izutsu as follows:

> Letters written with ink do not really exist as letters. This is because the letters are nothing but various forms to which the meanings have been assigned through convention. What really and concretely exists is nothing but the ink. The existence of the letters is in truth no other than the existence of the ink, which is the sole, unique reality that unfolds itself in many forms of self-modification. One has to cultivate, first of all, the eye to see the selfsame reality of ink in all letters, and then to see the letters as many intrinsic modifications of the ink.[100]

> When they [the letters] are hidden in ink they are ink; when they are on the point of the pen they are on the point of the pen; but when they are written upon the tablet they differ both from the ink and the pen.[101]

Ibn ʿArabī referred to familiarity with ink as the gnosis of the ruby (*maʿrifat al-yāqūt al-aḥmar*). As such, this knowledge cannot be discerned, delimited and described.[102] In theory, through the analysis of letters, a certain familiarity with ink could be achieved. Al-Qashānī's *Glossary* thus identifies them as 'keys to the secrets of the invisible

99 *Fut.*III:450; al-Manṣūb, 5/547–8; *FM.*II:300.
100 Izutsu, 'The Basic Structure of Metaphysical Thinking in Islam', p. 66.
101 Cited in Johns, 'Daḳā'iḳ al-Ḥurūf by ' Abd al-Ra'ūf of Singkel', p. 72.
102 Elmore, *Islamic Sainthood*, p. 335.

world and the illumination of the Essence'.[103] However, in light of the fact that comprehensive knowledge of the properties of each letter would equal familiarity with all things in existence, Ibn ʿArabī dismissed this task as impossible. He relied on the Divine Name *al-Raḥmān*, 'the All-Merciful', to represent the unity of divine attributes and the properties of the twenty-eight letters brought together. Jovan Kuzminac, an eminent translator of Ibn ʿArabī's works into Serbian, observed that this Name comes from the same root as *raḥm*, which is the Arabic word for womb. For this reason, Kuzminac argued that it would be more accurate to associate *al-Raḥmān* with the act of genesis and the Breath of the All-Merciful (*nafas al-Raḥmān*) than to have it identified it with compassion.[104] This is not entirely correct. While Ibn ʿArabī was aware of the root *rāʾ- ḥāʾ- mīm* and the implications it contains, he also noted that 'mercy is a universal quality – for He is the All-Merciful (*al-Raḥmān*) of this world and the next.'[105] Aside from *alif*, the Name *al-Raḥmān* consists of five different archigraphemes: *lām, rāʾ, ḥāʾ, mīm* and *nūn*. These are the so-called cherubic letters. The five cherubic letters were the subject of several different interpretations in Ibn ʿArabī's works. In all cases, however, their meaning remains close to the star of *lām-alif*. Ibn ʿArabī primarily used these letters as a symbol of Knowing (*alif*), Wanting (*lām*), Powerful (*rāʾ*), Speaking (*ḥāʾ*), Hearing (*mīm*) and Seeing (*nūn*) God. In addition, these letters represent an organic body (*rāʾ*), nourishment (*ḥāʾ*), sensing (*mīm*) and articulation (*nūn*).[106] The cherubic letter *alif* also came to be associated with the *alif* 'that is beyond articulation'. Hence it has the same meaning as the disjoined letter *alif* and the isolated form of *alif*. However, Ibn ʿArabī also used the cherubic letter *alif* as a symbol of Living, the existing God:

> *Alif* is a dagger that floats above the other six letters of the Name (*al-Raḥmān*). It is the Life that floats to enliven the six letters (i.e. the six attributes): Knowing (*rāʾ*), Wanting (the first *fatḥa*),

103 al-Qashānī, *Glossary of Sufi Technical Terms*, p. 46.

104 Kuzminac, *Dragulji mudrosti*, p. 24.

105 *Fut.*I:158; al-Manṣūb, 1/324; *FM.*I:102. Ibn ʿArabī believed that every name has a form (*ṣūra*) and a meaning (*maʿnā*). If Allah is the name whose meaning is God, 'All-Merciful' would be its form.

106 *Fut.*I:162; al-Manṣūb, 1/331; *FM.*I:104.

Powering (*ḥā'*), Speaking (*mīm*), Hearing (the second *fatḥa*) and Seeing (*nūn*).[107]

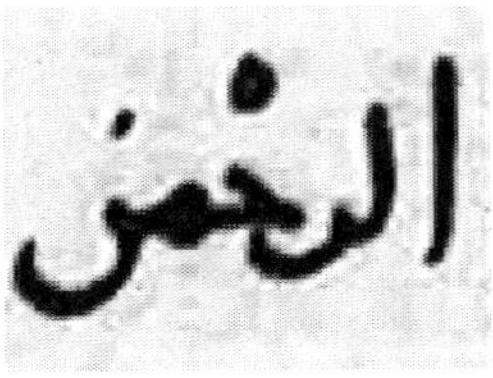

Fig.22 The Divine Name al-Raḥman

The five consonants of the word *al-Raḥmān* were among the major symbols of the relationship between the Creator and the created in Ibn 'Arabī's works. While he interpreted *rā'* as power (the Creator), *ḥā'* was the object of power (the created). These letters served to convey that the path to God begins with recognition of our ignorance towards Him.[108] Among the cherubic letters, the most prominent symbol of the relationship between the Creator and the created was *nūn*. The shape of this letter was thought to conceal 'strange mysteries within – such that it cannot be heard except by the one who is strongly wrapped in submission and the one who is receiving the truth of a spirit like a corpse would receive it. A corpse cannot imagine resisting what's happening to it, let alone actively stirring to look around.'[109] The shape of *nūn* is the shape of the universe. Ibn 'Arabī associated the orthographic form of *nūn* with the embrace of *lām* and *alif*. The need for Him is the reason for the spiritual passion between them (i.e. between *lām* and *alif*), particularly when they appear in a written, inscribed word. This is a mystery yet undisclosed – except to those who have straightened *alif* up from its reclining position and loosened the letter *lām* from its knot (Fig. 23).

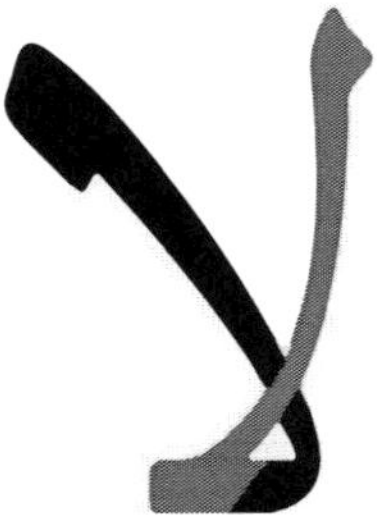

Fig. 23 The universe and the knot of lām-alif

107 Ibn 'Arabī, *Interactions II*, p. 256.
108 *Fut.*I:167; al-Manṣūb, 1/338; *FM.*I:108.
109 *Fut.*I:88; al-Manṣūb, 1/180; *FM.*I:53.

Ibn ʿArabī compared the shape of the *nūn* to an inkpot – or, alternatively, to the *omphalos*, the centre of the world. Ibn ʿArabī's *nūn* is a symbol of the visible and the invisible world. 'Whereas He made *alif* the first of all letters,' Ibn ʿArabī wrote, '(…) *nūn* is the last.'[110] *Alif*, which needs no vowel to be pronounced, was said to represent the nature of the divine Essence. It was deemed to be perfect like the Sun. *Nūn*, akin to the Moon, is imperfect. The Moon waxes and wanes and its glow is borrowed from the Sun. While Ibn ʿArabī used the Full Moon as a symbol of purity and the ascension of the heart in the presence of God, the waxing of the Moon symbolizes the fleeting human existence in general. However, the Moon in general could also stand for the bond between the Creator and the created.[111] Assuming that the orthographic shape of *nūn* consists of a full circle, only one half of it is visible to us (Figs. 24a, 24b). The other half is invisible. The visible half of the letter *nūn* stands for the material world. 'If it were transferred from the spiritual world, we would see the full circle,' noted Ibn ʿArabī. Only the diacritical mark, a sign from God, indicates that the other half exists: 'the physical [form of] *nūn*, like the physical world, indicates what lies beneath'.[112]

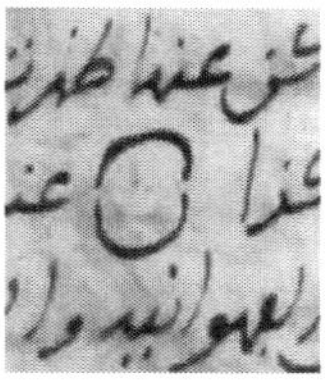

Fig. 24a The letter nūn and the visible and the invisible world

Fig. 24b The circle of nūn

The letters of the Arabic alphabet have been traditionally divided into fourteen sun letters and fourteen moon letters (Table 12). These were thought to represent the division of the universe into light and shadow: the manifested *nūn* and the transcendent, mysterious *alif*.

110 *Fut.*I:98; al-Manṣūb, 1/194; *FM.*I:60.

111 Ibn ʿArabī, *K. al-Mīm*, fol.40;

112 Alternative interpretation: while the letter *mīm* of the Divine Name *al-Raḥmān* stands for the world of *Malakūt*, *nūn* and its diacritical are the symbols for *Mulk* and *Jabarūt*. *Fut.*I:166; al-Manṣūb, 1/336; *FM.*I:107.

Table 12 Sun letters and moon letters

Sun Letters	ن	ل	ظ	ط	ض	ص	ش	س	ز	ر	ذ	د	ث	ت
Moon Letters	ي	و	ه	م	ك	ق	ف	غ	ع	خ	ح	ج	ب	ا

While familiarity with *alif* was thought to be unachievable, an attempt to come to terms with the limited number of divine attributes could also leave the seeker perplexed and confused.[113] Although difficult, this task was deemed to be feasible. This was due to the fact that God was thought to have created the world out of love. In his works, Ibn ʿArabī differentiates between three types of love: divine, spiritual and nature-based love. While nature-based love is fixated on certain objects, spiritual love leads men to God. However, love that led to the creation of the world was thought to be divine. Divine love usually manifests in God's efforts to lead mankind towards happiness, away from danger.

> He teaches His servants that, provided that they follow His messenger, God will love them. This is the second type of love, quite unlike the first. The first type of love is a divine Grace (*ʿināya*) (a), and the second type of love is reward and generosity (i.e. the Honouring Love (c)), by virtue of being a beloved visitor (*wāfid*) through the first love. The Love of the Servant (b) for his Lord is something that is safeguarded between these two types of divine love. The servant is constrained in his servanthood, compelled by what God prescribes for him, so that he becomes aware that he is enclosed within the tight embrace (*qabḍa*) of the Real, without being able to be freed or pass through it in any way. The matter is as we depicted it here.[114]

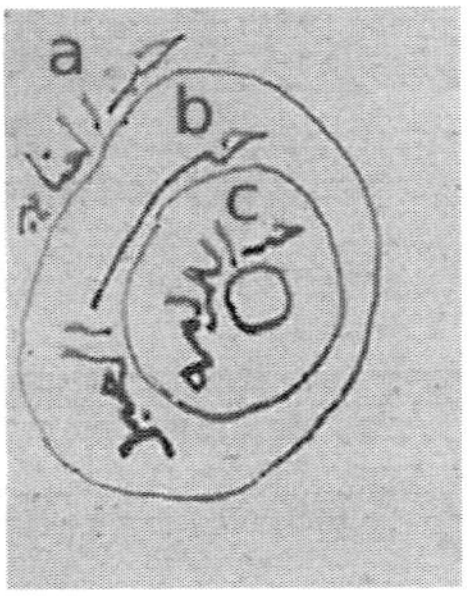

Fig. 25 The Divine Love and the Love of the Servant

113 Elmore, *Islamic Sainthood*, p. 329.
114 *Sifr* 30, fol.60; *Fut.*VII:151; al-Manṣūb, 10/434; *FM.*IV:102–3.

Divine love also manifests through God's desire to introduce Himself to His creations. Perfect and all-powerful, He was the hidden treasure that loved to be known. As a result, knowledge of divine attributes remains a possibility. 'If I were not the Lord, the servant would not exist. If it were not for the servant, the Lord would not have been described by attributes. Existence is from the Lord, attributes are from the servant,'[115] reads a line from *Bezels of Wisdom*. Al-Nābulusī subsequently interpreted this passage as an implication that while each man needs God to sustain his existence, God needs a man in order to be known by something other than Himself.[116] If the bond between the One and the many was to be expressed in grammatical terms, one could say that a noun is *alif* whose creations are verbs. In this case, *ḥarf* would be the bond between the two.[117] Ibn ʿArabī taught that there are three possible relations between the Creator and the created: 1) transcendence, 2) divine mercy and 3) the act of revealing Himself to the seeker. In the early Sufi interpretations of the relationship between man and God, the concept of personal love was predominant. However, Ibn ʿArabī sided with the later interpreters who held that knowledge is more eminent than love. He interpreted the Qurʾanic advice to 'flee to God' (Q.51:51) as a flight from ignorance to knowledge. In this case, however, rational knowledge was thought of as a side-product of one's flight towards happiness and unity with the Creator. Throughout the centuries, men have sought unity with God by means of religious studies, rational observations and self-reflection – for 'he who knows himself (*lām*) knows his Lord (*alif*)'.[118]

In his works, Ibn ʿArabī differentiated between four types of seekers: 1) recipients of divine revelations, who are experts in making a distinction between contradictory reports, 2) people who seek unity with God by means of imagination, intimacy and ecstasy, 3) seekers of any kind of sign from the Divine and 4) intellectuals, who are incapable of comprehending that God is always close at hand – closer to a man than his jugular vein. While some seekers expect to see the fruit of their efforts, others do not. Ultimately however, it is up to the Creator to reach out and establish the bond between His creations and Himself. 'Even if you expand everything on Earth, entirely, you will

115 al-Nābulusī, *Sharḥ Jawāhir al-nuṣūṣ* vol.1, p. 36.

116 al-Nābulusī, *Sharḥ* vol.1, p. 21.

117 Word play: in the Arabic language, this term can be used to signify letter and particle alike – and the letters were thought to be pointing a way towards God.

118 *Fut.*I:173; al-Manṣūb, 1/346–7; *FM.*I:112. See also *Fut.*I:19; al-Manṣūb, 1/74–75; *FM.*I:5.

not succeed in making this link on your own,' reads a line from *The Meccan Revelations*.[119] In spite of the fact that human beings were said to have been created for the sole purpose of knowing and worshipping the Creator, without His help, they would be incapable of either. For this reason, reads the fifty-third verse of the Sura *Fuṣṣilat*, they were provided with the signs to follow: *We shall show them our signs upon the horizons and in themselves until it is clear to them that He is the Real* (Q.41:53). 'If the True did not want them to obtain knowledge,' Ibn 'Arabī observed, 'there would no directions [from Him]'.[120] While the visible, delimited world has the least in common with the Absolute, Nondelimited Creator, Ibn 'Arabī taught that it is among the greatest sins to think that God is removed and isolated from the world. 'He is with us, but we do not know Him.'[121] Having concealed Himself behind His creations, God demanded to be sought. As a result, signs that conceal Him were also seen as stairs upon which they ascend when they seek Him. 'He hid his Essence out of sight, behind the veils of attributes, thus He concealed Himself behind the phenomena that reveal him in the Universe.'[122] Once a virtuous man turns his eyes towards the corporeal world (a), the world will provide him with signs that will lead him towards the invisible world (b) and its Creator (c) (Fig. 26).

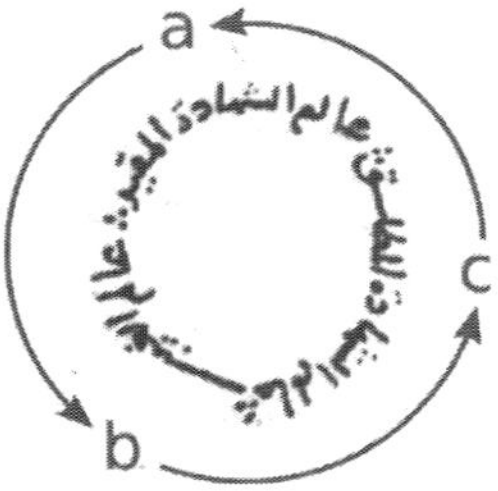

Fig. 26 The material world as a sign

Sometimes, God introduces Himself by means of revelations. Other signs include ground-shattering earthquakes, eclipses and miracles such as the occurrence of a sound from the mouth of an animal. Ibn 'Arabī believed that the whole world is composed of signs, down to the worms in the ground. The two words 'world' (*'ālam*) and 'mark' (*'alāma*) share the same root in Arabic. From this root, the Arabic words for 'knower, adept' (*'alīm*) and 'knowledge' (*'ilm*) are

119 *Fut.*III:183; al-Manṣūb, 5/35; *FM.*II:123.
120 *Fut.*I:291; al-Manṣūb, 1/261; *FM.*I:192.
121 *Fut.*III:85; al-Manṣūb, 4/423; *FM.*II:56.
122 al-Shādhilī, *Qawānīn ḥikam al-ishrāq*, p. 33.

also formed. With several appropriate synonyms at his disposal, Ibn ʿArabī claimed to have intentionally used these terms to underline that the created world consists of signs that can lead an adept towards God. He believed that the world is a word with meaning – and the meaning is God.[123] While the goal of each adept is to know God, the goal of the world is to direct him towards Him.

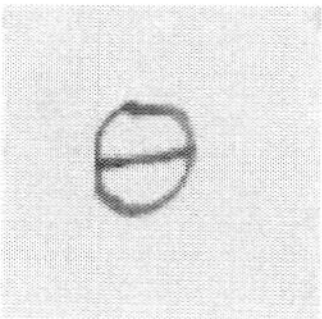

Fig. 27 The two arcs

If you cut through the circle with a line, two arching bows will appear.
That is the closeness of the Real;
So cross over to the Reality of 'closer' from the two of them![124]

This poem alludes to the ninth verse of the Sura *al-Najm*, which states that the Prophet Muhammad (or some say, the archangel Gabriel) stood at the 'distance of two bow lengths or closer' (Q.53:9). In Sufism, this is usually interpreted as a metaphorical expression for the Prophet's unparalleled closeness to the presence of God. In the Akbarian tradition, profound metaphysical meditations have been dedicated to the symbolism of the two arcs that Ibn ʿArabī depicted (Fig. 27).[125]

In the Qur'an, God is described as omnipresent and closer to a man than his jugular vein. *Wherever you turn there is the face of Allah*, reads the second verse of the Sura *al-Baqara* (Q.2:115). The divine presence was thus thought to be evident in the murmur of water, whistling of wind and the song of birds – one had only to practise to see:

123 Quoted according to Chittick, *The Self-Disclosure of God,* p. 5.
124 *Sifr* 28, fol.126. *Fut.*IV:281; al-Mansub 6/624; *FM.*II:558.
125 For a detailed overview of the symbolism of the two arcs in the works of Ibn ʿArabī and later Akbarians, see Paolo Urizzi's presentation, 'The Symbolism of the Two Arcs: some reflections' (https://ibnarabisociety.org/p-p-2020-ibn-arabi-and-the-geometry-of-reality-2/).

My heart can take any form.
  For gazelles a meadow – for monks a cloister,
For the idols sacred ground – Ka'ba for the circling pilgrims;
  The tablets of the Torah and the scrolls of the Qur'an.[126]

Ibn 'Arabī also compared the relationship between the Creator and the created to the relationship between a man and his shadow.

> Know that the relationship between the Real and that which is other than Real (*siwā al-ḥaqq*), i.e. that which is called the universe, is the relationship between a shadow and that which casts a shadow. The universe is the shadow of God.[127]

Al-Qashānī maintained that while divine attributes can be perceived as shadows of the qualities of *alif,* existing things are shadows of His attributes.[128] This commentary echoes Ibn 'Arabī's meditations on the relationship between the Sun and Moon, *alif* and *nūn*, when he stated that 'the appearance of the Sun in the mirror of the Moon is the appearance of the True in the creation.'[129] While it is impossible to come to terms with the nature of *alif*, familiarity with its shadow can be obtained through analyses of the ethereal, impermanent world around us. Two obstacles were, however, thought to obstruct the process. The first obstacle emerges from the immeasurable distance between the Absolute (God) and the relative (man). The five senses can be deceiving. For this reason, hills that appear dark and distant to the naked eye are not necessarily dark in colour.[130] In a similar way, Ibn 'Arabī observed, his contemporaries were aware of the astronomical calculations stipulating that the Sun is 160 times bigger than the Earth. Nevertheless, they still went on to compare its size to the size of a shield. Attempts to come to terms with divine attributes can also be thwarted by the fact that many of them remain hidden in potentiality, never to be manifested in the created world. Like *alif*, these attributes were thought to be among the things one can have no knowledge of.[131] While God is perfect, the world is not.

---

126 Ibn 'Arabī, *Tarjumān al-ashwāq,* p. 13. See also Ibn 'Arabī, 'Gentle now, Doves', p. 73.

127 Ibn 'Arabī, *Fuṣūs*, p. 101.

128 al-Qashānī, *Glossary of Sufi Technical Terms*, p. 46.

129 *Fut.*II:386; al-Manṣūb, 3/509; *FM.*I:642.

130 Bosnevi, *Sharḥ Fuṣūṣ* vol.3, p. 98.

131 Ibid. p. 99.

> Contemplate Me in the attributes, but not in the essences, because I am not contained by them. Although he may listen, understand, know, allude, communicate, particularize or summarize, he will not comprehend Me.[132]

Nonetheless, each person was expected to come to terms with as many divine attributes as possible. It was only important to avoid the pitfall of worshipping inanimate objects. Whereas the Creator is omnipresent, no form of existence can be rightfully worshipped as Him. However, to deny God's likeness to anything would mean that we are limiting the Creator – and Ibn ʿArabī held that only a man who is foolish or corrupted by evil would dare to do so. On the authority of Abū Saʿīd al-Kharrāz, he deemed that God cannot be known except as a synthesis of opposites. As he put it in a poem in the *Fuṣūṣ al-ḥikam*:

> If you insist only on His transcendence (*tanzīh*),
> you restrict Him
> and if you insist only on His immanence (*tashbīh*)
> you limit Him
> and if you maintain both aspects,
> you are in the right.[133]

According to al-Qashānī, the key was in 'witnessing the creation being sustained by Truth and seeing unity in multiplicity and multiplicity in unity without the subject being veiled by either of them'.[134] Ibn ʿArabī held that each adept has several research objects at his disposal. These choices correspond to the three great books of the science of letters. For those who choose to seek the truth in the Qurʾan, Ibn ʿArabī gave the practical advice to pay attention whether God speaks of Himself in the singular or the plural. When He speaks in the singular, the Creator refers to His Essence and the search should be abandoned. But if He speaks in the plural, using words like 'We' (*naḥnu* or *innā*), He is thought to refer to His attributes.[135] Like the Qurʾan, the human body was also perceived as the Book of God. Not only was he deemed to be a Book – a man was also provided with the knowledge to read it. Knowledge of anatomy and self-reflection could

132 Ibn ʿArabī, *K. Mashāhid al-asrār*, p. 216.
133 Ibn ʿArabī, *Fuṣūṣ*, p. 47.
134 al-Qashānī, *Glossary of Sufi Technical Terms*, p. 90.
135 Quoted according to Chodkiewicz, *An Ocean Without Shore*, p. 36.

thus lead to familiarity with the nature of the world and the twenty-eight letters of the alphabet.[136] To seek the truth in the natural world was also deemed to be appropriate. In the eyes of Ibn ʿArabī, the universe was 'a book whose meaning is God[137]. Ibn ʿArabī believed that it is possible to rely on letters to come to terms with the divine attributes. As a matter of fact, his *Book of Mīm, Wāw and Nūn* identifies familiarity with letters as a prerequisite for the successful analyses of the Most Beautiful Names. This was due to the fact that the existence of letters was thought to precede the existence of The Most Beautiful Names of God. In Akbarian thought, what is simple always precedes what is complex in nature. As a result, Ibn ʿArabī reasoned that the science of letters 'precedes that of the Names'.[138]

When it comes to signs from God, the letters of the Arabic alphabet were thought to be second to none. In their own way, each testifies that there is no god but God. The shared function of the letters as signs was compared by Bosnevi to the physiognomy of the human body. While Zayd is one man, Bosnevi observed, his body is composed of many organs which ensure that it functions properly. At the same time, however, the unity of these organs testifies to the individual existence of the man in question.[139] On his side, Faḍl Allāh Astarābādī held that the letters of the Arabic alphabet are the only symbols which contain an organic connection between the signifier and the signified. For example, it would be necessary to use the orthographic form of *alif* to write down the name of the first letter of the Arabic alphabet.[140] In Islamic culture, a personal name and handwriting have been commonly taken as a hint of one's nature, his future deeds and the events to come. According to legend, Dajjāl, the Antichrist of the Islamic normative tradition, was thus set to wear the letters *kāf, fā'* and *rā'* on his forelocks – though none but the true believer will be able to read them.[141] The prophet David was also said to have been named 'David' as a sign that God distinguished him among the people. While each letter of the Roman alphabet can be connected to the previous and the following letter, seven letters of the Arabic alphabet do not connect to any of the

136 Correspondences between the microcosm, macrocosm and the twenty-eight letters of the alphabet will be discussed in detail in the chapter concerning the letter *mīm*, which stands for human beings.

137 *Fut.*II:176; al-Manṣūb, 3/96; *FM.*I:497.

138 Ibn ʿArabī, *K. al-Mīm*, fol.15.

139 Bosnevi, *Sharḥ Fuṣūṣ* vol.4, p. 256.

140 See also Bashir, *Fazlallah Astarabadi and the Hurufis*, p. 65.

141 al-Qayṣarī, *Foundations of Islamic Mysticism*, p. 132.

following letters. Among them are *dāl, alif* and *wāw*, the archigraphemes that form the name 'David' (داود). According to Ibn ʿArabī, David had the power to induce mountains to sing praises to God. In addition, he was blessed with an exceptional son, the future prophet Solomon. The ruling power (*taḥakkum*) and influence (*taṣarruf*) he possessed over the material world transcend average human capabilities – and this fact came to be reflected in the archigraphemes that form his name.[142] In the Arabic language, nothing was thought to be accidental. While Ibn ʿArabī's works endorse connected letters as symbols of the flow of time and interconnectedness of all things, the letters that do not bind were thought to stand for the timeless ocean of being and man vanishing into timelessness. Apart from orthography and lexicography, morphology and syntax, especially when it comes to the gender of words in Arabic, were also held to be an important part of successful inquiries into ontology, cosmology and Islamic religious law.[143] *The Meccan Revelations* thus tell a story of Mālik b. Anas (d. 93/795), who was lauded as the leading jurisprudent of his time. Upon being asked if Muslims are allowed to consume the flesh of a dolphin, Mālik b. Anas ruled that this was to be considered illegal. His argument was based on the fact that the Arabic word for dolphin can be directly translated as 'water pig' (*khinzīr al-māʾ*). And according to the Islamic religious law, pork was prohibited to believers. According to Ibn ʿArabī, Mālik's argument was not unanimously accepted:

- Doesn't this animal belong to the family of marine animals?
- He said: Certainly, but you just named it 'pig'.[144]

Ibn ʿArabī believed that the twenty-eight letters of the Arabic alphabet are capable of expressing realities (*ḥaqāʾiq*) of the created world and he had no doubts that Mālik's reasoning was sound. In his works, the first of the spoken letters and the first sign pointing towards God was *hamza*.

142 Bosnevi, *Sharḥ Fuṣūṣ* vol.4, p. 112.

143 For an analysis on the gender of nouns in Ibn ʿArabī's works, see Shaikh, *Sufi Narratives of Intimacy*, pp. 173–7.

144 *Fut.*IV:164; al-Manṣūb, 6/396; *FM.*II:481.

I am – and there is nothing with Me in the Cloud.

Ibn ʿArabī[145]

145 Ibn ʿArabī, *The Meccan Revelations* vol.1, p. 35.

2.4. Image of the Primordial Cloud and All It Contains: Hamza and Its Elongations

Ibn ʿArabī's works endorse *hamza* as a symbol of the Creator determining Himself with the Most Beautiful Names. *The Meccan Revelations* identify *hamza* as a symbol of the original teaching and knowledge upon which God created the world. This was the teaching of the Self-realization and Self-disclosure of the Creator. Ibn ʿArabī's *hamza* stands for the Creator's knowledge of Himself and His absolute, divine imagination (*al-khayāl al-muṭlaq*). Without imagination, there would be no creation. Ibn ʿArabī referred to the act of genesis as the Self-disclosure of God. Two phases of this process were distinguished: 1) the essential self-disclosure (*al-tajallī al-dhātī*) and 2) the self-disclosure through the Names (*al-tajallī al-asmā'ī*).[146] The first phase refers to God's knowledge of His Essence. During this phase, *alif* is observed by Itself, in Itself. The essential self-disclosure is an inward act with no visible manifestations.[147] At this point, the world and its entities exist only within the divine knowledge, awaiting His command to emerge as distinct beings, seemingly independent from divine Essence. Imbued with knowledge and power, the command is eventually voiced as: '*kun!*'. This was the self-disclosure through the Names and the beginning of a visible manifestation of God's knowledge. During the self-disclosure through the Names, the Creator observes Himself through the prism of divine attributes. Bosnevi compared this process to a man in front of a mirror. A mirror always assumes the form of a looker. Although a man might not be aware of it, there is little or no difference between him gazing in a mirror and an act of introspection. It is only the surface of a mirror that creates the illusion of otherness between him and his reflection. On the divine level, an act of introspection corresponds to the essential self-disclosure of God – while gazing in a mirror can be compared to the self-disclosure through the Names.[148] However, Ibn ʿArabī also held that the act of genesis corresponds to the Self-realization of the divine being:

146 See Izutsu, *Sufism and Taoism*, pp. 131–2.

147 'The universe does not reach God nor does it know Him the way He knows Himself,' reads a line from Bosnevi's commentary on Ibn ʿArabī's *Bezels of Wisdom*. See Bosnevi, *Sharḥ Fuṣūṣ* vol.1, p. 337.

148 Ibid, p. 224.

> The material domain of existence becomes manifest in the form of kun! Kun is His command, His command is His speech, His speech is His knowledge and His knowledge is His Essence. Hence the world became manifest in His form.[149]

> He knew the cosmos as a part of His knowledge of Himself so He made nothing manifest in engendered existence save what He is in Himself. It was as if He was internal and invisible (*bāṭin*) and then, by means of the universe, He became outward and visible (*ẓāhir*).[150]

Not only did Ibn ʿArabī believe that God created the world through His knowledge of Himself – he also implied that only by knowing Himself does the Creator know His creations! Upon being asked where God was before He created the world, the Prophet is reported to have said that He was in the Cloud with no air above or below.[151] This is also what Ibn ʿArabī believed. It was a cloud unlike any other. By emphasizing the fact that there is no air above it, the Prophet meant to say that nothing can stand above God. The absence of the air below meant that the material world was yet to be created. Ibn ʿArabī identified the Cloud as the first thing to step out from divine knowledge into the realm of existence:

> Then came out the Breath, which is the Mist. The reason why the Lawgiver referred to it as the Mist is because the Mist, which is the Cloud, is also generated from warm vapour (…). It filled the nothingness, all of it, which is the space of the universe, or its vessel.[152]

> The essences of divine words, which are twenty-eight in number and are endowed with multiple aspects, emanate from the Breath of the All-Merciful, which is the Cloud, where our Lord stood when He created the world. The Cloud corresponds to the human breath, and the manifestation of the world out of the void and into the various levels of being is like the human breath emanating from the heart, spreading out through the

149 Chittick, *The Self-Disclosure of God*, p. 56.
150 Ibid, p. 70.
151 *Saḥīḥ al-Tirmidhī*, #468.
152 *Fut.*III:366; al-Manṣūb, 5/570–7; *FM.*II:310.

> mouth and forming letters on its way. These letters are like the manifestation of the world from the Cloud, which is the breath of God, the Real, the All-Merciful, spreading into distinct levels [of existence] within the void.[153]

In Ibn ʿArabī's works, the Cloud is represented by *alif* with *hamza* (أ). While the sound of *alif* has been traditionally associated with the uninterrupted flow of air, *hamza* (ء) is a glottal stop. It is produced by blocking and releasing the flow of air in the vocal system. Sībawayh described the articulation of *hamza* as 'a spasm in the chest which requires certain effort to be produced – a sound akin to belching'.[154] In the Phoenician script, which the Arabic alphabet came from, a glottal stop and the long vowel /*ā*/ were both marked by the letter *ālep* (𐤀). The same method can be observed in early copies of the Qurʾan. Prior to the late eighth century, *alif* was used in the same way as its Phoenician counterpart for a glottal stop and the long vowel /*ā*/. Khalīl b. Aḥmad is traditionally identified as the first to introduce the orthographic symbol for *hamza* to make a distinction between the two phonemes. In order to indicate that a glottal stop was to be used, Khalīl suggested that *hamza* should be added diacritically to the body of *alif*.[155] In the works of medieval grammarians, *hamza* was generally believed to be devoid of phonetical value. It was also thought to have shared its point of articulation with *alif*. For this reason, *hamza* came to be recognized as a distinct consonant phoneme – but not as a 'full' letter which could be listed on a par with other letters of the alphabet.[156] *Alif*, the first [letter] of the alphabet, is the graphical symbol of *hamza*, noted Ibn Jinnī (d. 392/1002) in the late tenth century.[157] However, Ibn ʿArabī had a somewhat different view on the matter. While he acknowledged the soundness of arguments which challenged the status of *hamza* as one of the written letters of the alphabet, he held that there can be no doubt

153 *Fut.*IV:36; al-Manṣūb, 6/154; *FM.*II:395, cited according to Lory, 'The Symbolism of Letters', p. 143.

154 Sībawayh, vol. 1, p. 548.

155 Ibn Durustawayh, *Taṣḥīḥ al-faṣīḥ*, p. 56.

156 In the Arabic grammar tradition, *hamza* has been perceived as the articulatory gesture by means of which sound is produced. However, it was not deemed to be a letter endowed with phonetic value. As such, *hamza* was thought to share its point of articulation with *alif*. In his *Kitāb al-ʿAyn*, Khalīl b. Aḥmad described *hamza* as follows: 'The *hamza* is air, it has no place of articulation.' See Ibn Jinnī, *Sirr ṣināʿat al-iʿrāb* vol.1, p. 46; al-Sirāfī, *Sharḥ Kitāb Sībawayh* vol.1, p. 13, and Nassir, *Sībawayh the Phonologist*, p. 27.

157 Ibn Jinnī, Abū al-Fatḥ, *Sirr ṣināʿat al-iʿrāb* vol.1, p. 46.

of its status as one of the real, spoken letters.[158] Ibn ʿArabī's reasoning was based on the fact that letters have been traditionally identified as interruptions of the flow of air. *Hamza*, the glottal stop, fulfils this condition. For this reason, Ibn ʿArabī's works endorse *hamza* as the first of the spoken letters. *Alif*, which he acknowledged as the first of the written letters, was thought to have no place of articulation. This was due to the fact that the pronunciation of *alif* has been compared to the uninterrupted flow of air. When someone speaks, we do not hear the flow of air – what we hear is the pronunciation of letters as the air is being blocked. As there can be no talk of blockages in the case of *alif*, Ibn ʿArabī argued that *alif* needs *hamza* in order to be voiced in the human speech. In a similar way, *alif* needs the Cloud. Just as the naked eye perceives the difference between the orthographic forms of *alif* (ا) and *alif* with *hamza* (أ), the human mind tends to perceive the Cloud as something external to the transcendent, hidden *alif*. However, similarity between the two glyphs has been generally interpreted as an implication that the Cloud, *hamza*, mirrors certain features of *alif*. This is hardly surprising as *hamza* stands for the first Self-determination of God (*al-taʿayyun al-awwal*). In his commentary on Ibn ʿArabī's *Bezels of Wisdom,* Bosnevi went one step further. He maintained that *alif* has two faces: the one that can be named (*hamza*) and the one that cannot (*alif*)[159]. Bosnevi allegorically described the relationship between the two as a divine inhalation and exhalation. In this case, *alif* stands for the inhaled air before the exhalation, *hamza*, is to occur. 'However, prior to the [divine] Self-determination, there is neither inhaling nor exhaling.'[160] With imagination comes self-determination and with it – specification: 'like when *alif* gets *hamza* in order to be pronounced as a glottal stop. The human breath that comes from the heart is interrupted. Of all the diacritical signs, *hamza* is the one closest to the heart'.[161] Sufis and grammarians traditionally held that no other phoneme has a point of articulation that is located as deep in the throat as *hamza*. On the cosmological level, the Cloud, as its counterpart, stands in the nearest proximity to the divine Essence.

If *alif* is the absolute singularity and oneness (*al-aḥadiyya*), the Cloud is the absolute collectivity (*jamʿ al-jamʿ*) of the One.[162] The

158 *Fut.*I:106; al-Manṣūb, 1/207–208; *FM.*I:55–6.

159 Bosnevi, *Sharḥ Fuṣūṣ* vol.3, p. 75; see also vol.1, p. 84.

160 Ibid, p. 88.

161 Ibid, pp. 88–90.

162 However, there was no absolute consensus among the Akbarians on this matter. On his side, al-Qayṣarī identified the Cloud as the degree of singularity (*al-aḥadiyya*)

meaning of *hamza* thus came to be associated with the Divine Name *al-Raḥmān* and God's knowledge of the divine attributes. According to Bosnevi, 'God described Himself with the first exhalation which emerged from non-existence. The first exhalation is the Name *al-Raḥmān*. Through creation, other Names will appear as well.'[163] The Most Beautiful Names in Ibn ʿArabī's teachings were perceived as creative elements with a potential to bring forth a certain thing into existence. Omniscient, God is familiar with all of them – and through His knowledge of Himself, different properties of His Essence are manifested in the world He created. This knowledge led to the creation of living beings and other forms of existence.[164] As the absolute collectivity of divine attributes, the Cloud contains all Names, forms and beings. This is how it came to be referred as the shadow of the original unity of *alif*. In the created world, *alif* is veiled by its manifestations and the servant sees it in particulars but not in its reality. 'The world,' al-Qashānī maintained, 'is the second shadow – which is none other than the existence of the Truth made visible in all its contingent forms.'[165] The nature of *alif* is concealed by the *hamza* it carries. In other words, the Cloud stands as the first veil between the corporeal world and *alif*. For this reason, or so Bosnevi believed, Ibn ʿArabī referred to the Cloud as the cosmic blindness.[166] However, Ibn ʿArabī also perceived the Cloud as a transitional zone between form and the formless. The individual forms of all that was, is and will be emerge from the vastness of the Cloud. Ibn ʿArabī depicted this process twice, in the fourth and sixth diagrams of The *Meccan Revelations* (Figs. 28 and 34).

Simply labelled 'Image of the Primordial Cloud and All It Contains', Ibn ʿArabī's diagram is not artistically elaborate. Taken by a surge of inspiration, he often felt unwilling to pause his writing for long enough to draw an image he had in mind. As a result, his manuscripts are marred with empty spaces where diagrams were supposed to be added later on. While some of these diagrams never

---

and the reality of realities (*ḥaqīqat al-ḥaqā'iq*). See al-Qayṣarī, *Foundations of Islamic Mysticism*, p. 44.

163 Bosnevi, *Sharḥ Fuṣūṣ* vol.3, p. 241.

164 As such, it was identified as the One (*al-wāḥid*) by Bosnevi, i.e. as the comprehensive Divine Name (*al-ism al-jāmiʿ al-ilāhī*) that provides other Names with effusion and assistance. This Name is occasionally identified as the Muhammadan Light. See al-Qayṣarī, *Foundations of Islamic Mysticism*, pp. 44, 168.

165 al-Qashānī, *Glossary of Sufi Technical Terms*, p. 64.

166 Bosnevi, *Sharḥ Fuṣūṣ* vol.1, p. 264.

came to be drawn, others suffered from serious lack of space due to Ibn ʿArabī's inability to plan in advance. This seems to be the case with 'Image of the Primordial Cloud' – a fact that was lamented by Ibn ʿArabī due to the importance of the process it depicts:

> Unfortunately, the image I've drawn is too narrow to contain all that we wished to include in a single diagram. If I was only able to draw a bigger diagram, it would all be clearer to the reader...[167]

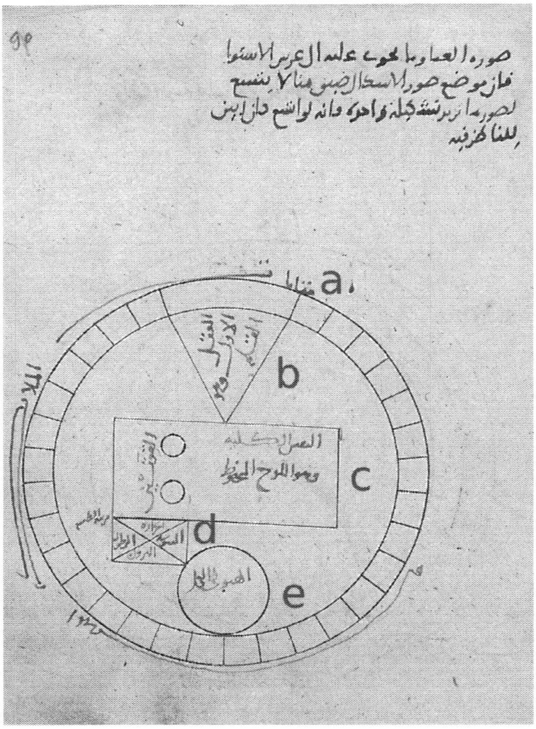

a) Thirty Stations of Angels Filled with Love
b) First Intellect
c) Protected Tablet
d) Universal Nature
e) Universal Body

Fig. 28 Image of the Primordial Cloud and All It Contains

Ibn ʿArabī's diagram depicts the Cloud in a circular shape and divides its perimeter into thirty stations of the angels filled with love (*maqamāt al-malā'ika al-muhayyama*). Sachiko Murata identified the perimeter of the Cloud as God's White Earth from the Islamic normative tradition, 'in which the Sun takes thirty days to cross the sky and each of these days is thirty times longer than the days of the lower world. That earth is filled with creatures who do not know that God has been disobeyed on Earth or that he has Created Adam and Iblis.'[168]

167 *Sifr* 26: 90 ff.
168 Murata, *The Angels*, p. 589.

Enraptured with the Divine presence, the angels filled with love are detached from the turmoil of the material world (Fig. 29). Ibn ʿArabī believed that they belong to the cherubim class of angels. Normally devoid of self-conscience, these cherubs live to sing praises to God. However, one of these angels was singled out to receive the knowledge of all things to pass before Judgement Day. In the Islamic normative tradition, this angel eventually came to be known as the White Pearl. Among his other names were the First Intellect and the Highest Pen. All three names were endorsed by Ibn ʿArabī as well. He associated the First intellect with the Divine Name *al-Badīʿ*, the Initiating. In his works, the First Intellect is represented by the isolated form of *hamza* (ء) – an orthographic shape he compared to the two horns of Aries (*sharaṭān*). According to Ibn ʿArabī, '*hamza* is the first letter that was brought forth by the Breath as the First Intellect.'[169]

The later interpreters of Ibn ʿArabī's works quickly traced this reference to the Prophet Muhammad and the Islamic normative tradition. 'As the Prophet said: 'The first thing God created was the White Pearl. And the first thing created by God was the Intellect.'[170] Ibn ʿArabī's 'Image of the Primordial Cloud' depicts the First Intellect as the first individual form of existence (Fig. 30). Having created it, 'God said to the Pen: Write down My knowledge concerning My creation until the Judgement Day.'[171] Ibn ʿArabī believed that it is only natural for each pen to yearn for a writing surface – and the First Intellect was no exception. 'When God created the First Intellect as a pen, its truth sought a place for its writings – because it is the Pen!'[172] The choice eventually fell on the Protected Tablet. Ibn ʿArabī's 'Image of the Primordial Cloud' depicts the Protected Tablet as the second individual form of existence (Fig. 31). While the First Intellect was the first transmitter of divine knowledge, the Tablet was deemed to be the second.

In his *Glossary*, al-Qashānī identified this Tablet as a record sheet containing all things in existence.[173] In the 'Image of the Primordial Cloud', the Tablet is depicted in a rectangular shape which contains two circles. These stand for the practical and intellectual capacities of

169 *Fut.*IV:76, 77; al-Manṣūb, 6/237; *FM.*II:421.

170 al-Qashānī, *Glossary of Sufi Technical Terms*, p. 16. See also Bosnevi, *Sharḥ Fuṣūṣ* vol.4, p. 341.

171 *Fut.*IV:79; al-Manṣūb, 6/241; *FM.*II:423.

172 *Fut.*IV:86; al-Manṣūb, 6/254; *FM.*II.428.

173 al-Qashānī, *Glossary of Sufi Technical Terms*, p. 21. See also *Fut.*I:171; al-Manṣūb, 1/343–4; *FM.*I:110.

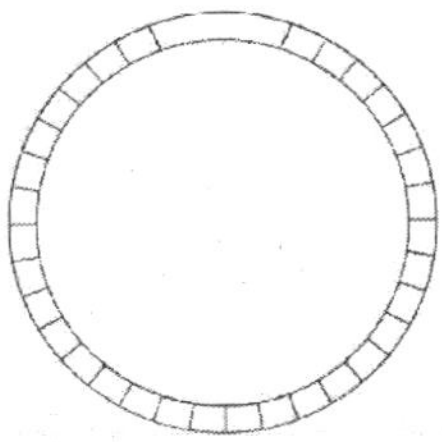

Fig. 29 The thirty stations of the angels filled with love

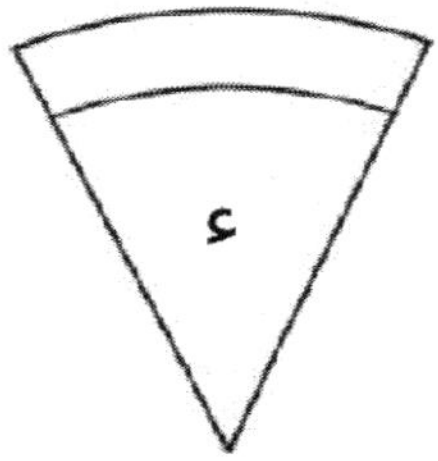

Fig. 30 Hamza, the Highest Pen

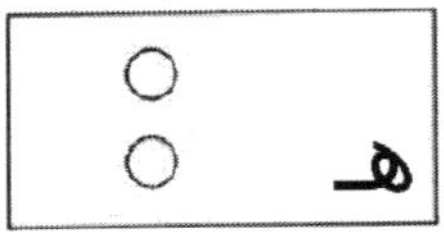

Fig. 31 Hāʼ, the Protected Tablet

the Universal Soul. Sufis like Ibn Sabʻīn (d. 669/1271) held that God created the Pen from a green emerald and the Tablet from white light. However, Ibn ʻArabī believed that the First Intellect and the Tablet are similar in nature. In accordance with the Islamic normative tradition, it was the Pen, and not the Tablet, that was explicitly associated with light in Ibn ʻArabī's works. Just like any other ray of light, the First Intellect also casts a shadow. *The Meccan Revelations* refer to the ontic shadow of the First Intellect as the Protected Tablet. In another place, Ibn ʻArabī identified the Tablet as yet another of the cherubs filled with love. Ibn ʻArabī associated this cherub with the letter *hāʼ* (ـه), which stands for the Divine Name *al-Ākhir,* the Last, and the emergence of organic bodies from the Dust. He also associated it with the divine exhalation, maintaining that the exhaled Breath of the All-Merciful serves to manifest the hidden realities of the Cloud. Our world and all in it were thought to be formed from the Dust. For this reason, Ibn ʻArabī believed, 'intellectuals named it *hayūlā*, prime matter.'[174] According to al-Qashānī, the term *hayūlā* was used by Sufis for 'any hidden thing in which a form can appear'.[175] Possibly due to the lack of space, the 'Image of the Primordial Cloud' does not contain a separate image of

174 *Fut.*I:184; al-Manṣūb, 1/364; *FM.*I: 119. See also *Fut.*IV:40; al-Manṣūb, 6/161; *FM.*II:398.

175 al-Qashānī, p. 18.

the Dust. Another reason for this 'omission' might be related to the fact that Ibn ʿArabī held that the Dust has no physical form of existence. As such, it was represented by the letter *ḥā'* (ح). This letter was perceived as an ideal symbol for the Dust because, when pronounced, it sounds like *alif*, the uninterrupted flow of air. Although there is almost no obstacle to be met in the articulation organs as the letter *ḥā'* is being produced, the human ear is capable of registering this sound. In a similar way, the nature of the Dust can be comprehended by the mind in spite of the fact that it has no visible form. Ibn ʿArabī maintained that prime matter possesses no determination other than existence. The Dust was perceived as a simple, ideal substance which cannot be detected by the five senses. As a result, it could not be depicted either. He therefore compared the Dust to the gryphon – a bird no one has seen but everyone has heard of – or alternatively, to ʿAlī b. Abī Ṭālib, the fourth caliph of Islam, who was long dead by the thirteenth century ce. Yet, due to ʿAlī b. Abī Ṭālib's impact on Islamic cultural history, no one doubted his existence.[176] Ibn ʿArabī perceived the Dust as a universal reality and one of the four things worth knowing in the world. Among the known forms of the Dust were light, air, water and minerals. However, the Dust was more than a passive substance:

> [This degree is] the Divine Name *al-Ākhir* ('the Last'), and His turning towards the creation of the Dust-substance, within which are manifest the forms of bodies and whatever resembles this substance in the world of compound entities, and His turning towards bringing into being the *ḥā'* among the letters and the two lunar mansions of the Taurus constellation.[177]

All living beings were thought to have emerged from the Dust. Since Ibn ʿArabī believed that the Dust is omnipresent, he compared it to the gypsum which a builder spreads over the entire wall he is working on. As such, the Dust was thought to be akin to whiteness in every white thing.[178] In light of the fact that the existence of the Dust precedes all other forms of existence, human beings tend to perceive it as something ancient, archetypal in nature. In reality, Ibn ʿArabī believed it neither old nor new. 'You see,' Ibn ʿArabī wrote, 'its properties did not arise until after the creation of (other) individual

176 *Fut.*IV:91–92; al-Manṣūb, 6/264; *FM.*II:430.
177 *Fut.*IV:91; al-Manṣūb, 6/264; *FM.*II:431.
178 *Fut.*I:188; al-Manṣūb, 1/369; *FM.*I:120.

forms of existence. So in a way, the Dust is also something new.'[179] While the Dust was thought to be receptive to all shapes, it has no shape of its own. Its nature mirrors the nature of its creations and it has no individual traits of its own. If it were not for the later creations, the Dust could not be known. Effectively, this would be as if it never existed. For this reason, Ibn ʿArabī chose not to depict it in his 'Image of the Primordial Cloud'. Nevertheless, he acknowledged its role in the formation of distinct entities. Devoid of form, the Dust gives birth to all forms in existence. For this reason, Ibn Masarra associated it with the letters of the alphabet in general. On the authority of Sahl al-Tustarī, Ibn Masarra held that 'letters are the Dust and the foundation of things at the beginning, when all things were created'.[180] On the cosmological scale, the Dust, *ḥāʾ*, was thought to be ruled by Universal Nature, *ʿayn* (ع).

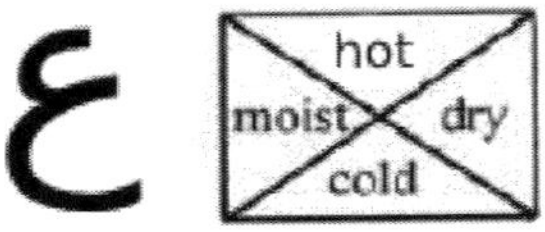

Fig. 32 ʿAyn, Universal Nature

Like Dust, Nature (*al-ṭabīʿa*) lacks a visible form of existence. In this aspect, Nature and Dust resemble the First Intellect, the Protected Tablet and other angels filled with love – for neither of these are corporeal entities. They are within the cosmos, cautioned Ibn ʿArabī, albeit they are neither inside nor outside physical bodies because they are not spatially confined. If Nature had a physical form of existence, Ibn ʿArabī wrote, 'it would be located below the [Universal] Soul'.[181] Ultimately, this where he drew it in 'Image of the Primordial Cloud' (Fig. 32). Ibn ʿArabī referred to Universal Nature as the shadow of the Tablet. In light of the fact that the Tablet was perceived as the shadow of the Pen, it can thus be said that Nature is a shadow of a shadow. Nevertheless, like all things created, it also testifies to the existence of God. For this reason, Ibn ʿArabī observed, 'God singled it out and granted it a step-level of existence' and a letter, *ʿayn*, to represent it.[182] While *ʿayn* has been traditionally identified as one of the twenty-eight letters of the Arabic alphabet, this term could also be translated as 'eye', 'essence' and/or 'entity'. 'Nature,' Ibn ʿArabī wrote, 'has its

179 *Fut.*IV:92; al-Manṣūb, 6/265-6; *FM.*II:430.
180 Ebstein and Sviri, *The So-Called Risālat al-ḥurūf*, p. 221.
181 *Fut.*IV:92; al-Manṣūb, 6/260; *FM.*II:430.
182 Ibid.

existence in entities (*a'yān*, sg. *'ayn*) of the material forms and this is why her letter is *'ayn.*'[183] Unlike the Dust, however, Universal Nature was thought to be distinguished by four qualities, hot, cold, moist and dry, whose existence is independent from other forms of existence. For this reason, it ultimately came to be depicted in Ibn 'Arabī's 'Image of the Primordial Cloud'.

> Between the Soul and Universal Matter there is the state of Nature. It, too, is based on four realities, two of which are active, and two are passive. Yet all are in the state of passivity with regard to the source whence they proceeded. These are heat, cold, moistness, and dryness. Dryness is passive in relation to heat, and moistness is passive in relation to cold. Heat is from the Intellect, and the Intellect is from Life; hence the nature of life in the sensible bodies is heat. Cold is from the Soul, and the Soul from Knowledge; hence knowledge, when settled, is usually described by the "cold of certainty" and by "snow" . As dryness and moistness are passive with regard to heat and cold, Will demands dryness because it belongs to its state, and Power demands moistness because it belongs to its state. And since Power is restricted to bringing-into-existence in particular, it is duly charged with imprinting the nature of life, that is, heat and moistness, in the bodies.[184]

In Ibn 'Arabī's works, the four qualities are occasionally referred to as the Four Mothers and the Four Natures. Rather than having them identified as independent forms of existence, Ibn 'Arabī cautioned that these stand for the interplay between Universal Nature and (in)organic bodies. In this aspect, the existence of Nature is akin to divine attributes. As it lacks a corporeal form, it is only possible to analyse it through the impact it has on the material world. Ibn 'Arabī held that the Universal Nature is an intelligible essence comprising of four qualities. The effects of these qualities on the nature-based, organic bodies are heating, drying, cooling and moisturizing.[185] Akkach perceived the four qualities of Universal Nature as the roots of spatio-

183 Ibid.

184 *Fut.*I:442; al-Manṣūb, 2/133; *FM.*I.293, cited according to Akkach, *Cosmology and Architecture*, p. 76.

185 *Fut.*IV:92; Manṣūb, 6/259–60; *FM.*II:430.

temporal existence.[186] However, the first visible form of existence was identified by Ibn ʿArabī as the Universal Body (Fig. 33). In his works, the Universal Body is linked with the letter *ghayn* (غ). Ibn ʿArabī perceived the Universal Body as an extension of divine imagination. It was perceived as an outcome of the spiritual marriage (*nikāḥ*) between Universal Nature and Dust:

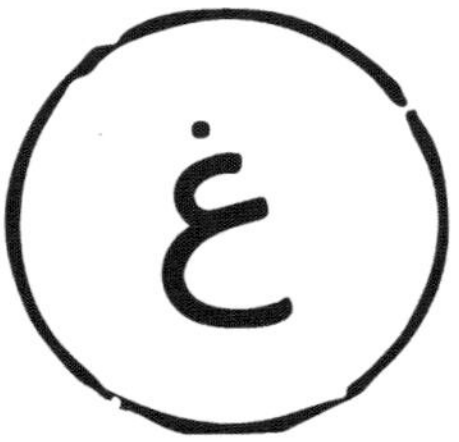

Fig. 33 Ghayn, Universal Body

> Dust and Nature are brother and sister, born to the same mother and father. He (i.e. the Creator) married Nature to Dust. The Universal Body, as the first outward, visible body, was born to these two. Nature is referred to as 'father' because it has an active role in the process, while Dust is 'mother' since her role is passive. The outcome [of this marriage] is the creation of organic bodies. (...) There is however disagreement on this matter between the six schools of thought. A certain group [of scholars] assumes that one of the four natures is the foundation [of existence]. Another group says: 'The element of fire is the foundation. What is denser than fire is air, what is denser than air is water and what is denser than water is earth.' Some other group says: 'The element of air is the foundation and what is less substantial than air is fire and what is denser than air is water.' Another group says: 'The element of water is the foundation.' Some other says: 'The foundation is the fifth element, not any of the four!' This corresponds to the possessions of the right hand. Our Law takes into consideration all arguments concerning the four elements in natural sciences and encompass all schools of thought. We deem that the school of thought which claims that the fifth element is the foundation is correct. The fifth element is called Nature, since Nature is single, intelligible. The element of fire and all other elements appear from Nature. One could say that the element of fire comes from Nature. However, this

186 Akkach, *Cosmology and Architecture*, p. 123.

> element is not Nature itself. It would also be incorrect to assume that Nature is a combination of the four elements since some of them are incompatible with one another. For example, fire and water are mutually incompatible from every perspective – and the same goes for air and earth. This is why God created the (hierarchical) levels of existence, precisely and wisely, on the account of the transferences from one level to another.[187]

Ibn ʿArabī believed that the Universal Body is in a state of constant movement, like a millstone rotating around its centre, 'never leaving nor transferring from its space'.[188] It fills the empty space of the universe, all of it, spinning endlessly – which is why Ibn ʿArabī remarked that it moves in stillness. From the moment it was created, the emptiness and stillness of the universe were no more.

> There is no space in the universe except for what is populated by this Body. As it necessarily moves, it moves in one place. It has a medial movement since there is nothing external to it and there is no empty space it could be moved to (…). God makes all forms of the universe to emerge from this Body, in this body mass, based on their different preparedness for each form – even though their totality is a single body and a single determiner. These forms accept the spirit from the Divine Breath, just like the letters become meaningful upon exiting the mouth.[189]

The corporeal and imaginal bodies of all living beings owe their form to *ghayn*. Thus it came to be associated with the Divine Name *al-Ẓāḥir*, the Manifest – as something that can be perceived through sensory faculties. The visible form of the Universal Body, whose symbol is *ghayn*, is the main point of difference between it and the letter *ʿayn*, which is the Dust. The orthographic forms of the two letters, *ʿayn* (ع) and *ghayn* (غ), differ in a single dot. While the isolated form of *ʿayn* was occasionally used by Ibn ʿArabī as a symbol of the soul and the Self, the difference between *ʿayn* and *ghayn* is more evident in his meditations on the Arabic term for knowledge, *ʿilm*. Ibn ʿArabī interpreted the first letter of this term, *ʿayn*, as a symbol of the intelligible world (*ʿalām bil-ʿilm*) and the absolute, pre-

187 *Fut.*I:216; al-Manṣūb, 1/403–4; *FM.*I:140.
188 *Fut.*IV:95; al-Manṣūb, 6/269; *FM.*II:434.
189 Ibid.

existing knowledge awaiting to be embodied in material substance (as symbolized by the letters *lām* and *mīm* respectively). While *ʿayn* represents the absolute knowledge of the Creator, *ghayn* is the knowledge manifested and the world made corporeal. As such, *ghayn* can be interpreted as a cloud that obscures reality. In his *Prayers for the Week,* Ibn ʿArabī thus asks of the Creator to banish the dot of *ghayn* so that he may witness the hierarchy of laws which govern the universe:

> O, my Master, You are the author of the causes and their order, and the director of the hearts and their turner. I ask of You, by the Wisdom which determines the arrangement of the prime causes and the effect of the highest upon the lowest that You cause me to witness the arrangement of the causes, ascending and descending so that I may thus witness the interior of them by witnessing the exterior and the first of them in the last. Let me view the wisdom of the ordered arrangement by witnessing the Arranger and how the Author of the causes precedes causation, so that I am not veiled from the *ʿayn* [Eye-Essence] by [the dot of the] *ghayn* [of otherness].[190]

The Meccan Revelations identify prayer as the state of encompassing unity between the Creator and the created. When one prays, one is required to be present and focused. During prayer, the tongue becomes 'the existential state of outwardness, where the Divine becomes visible'.[191] Good intentions and pure language were thought to be crucial in prayer. Those who do not disobey God linguistically were thus set to be endowed with 'the angelic language' and the knowledge of the higher causes. In particular, Ibn ʿArabī sought to escape from the dot of *ghayn* so that he could come to terms with the emergence of organic matter. *The Meccan Revelations* offer certain insight into the nature of this process, whose symbol is *alif madda* (آ). In the Arabic grammar tradition, *alif madda* usually marks a glottal stop that is followed by the long vowel /*ā*/. Alternatively, it can be interpreted as the orthographic symbol for any long vowel. Ibn ʿArabī appears to have been aware of both interpretations since he compared *alif madda* to the twisted pronunciation of the verb *jā'* as *jāāāā'* (جاااء) and the forceful elongation of long vowels in everyday speech. In his works, *alif madda* is mostly used as a symbol of the creative potential of the

190 Ibn ʿArabī, *The Seven Days of the Heart*, p. 95.
191 *Fut.*II:338–9; al-Manṣūb, 3/438; *FM.*I:608–9.

First Intellect. However, it could also be used to represent all elements of 'the Image of the Primordial Cloud', in order of appearance (Fig. 34).

آ

The Higher Pen

↓

Universal Soul

↓

Universal Nature

↓

The Dust

↓

Universal Body

Fig. 34 The Primordial Cloud as alif madda and
the world as the dripping of ink from the Higher Pen

> … The basis (*aṣl*) is the existence of the entity of the Intellect and what is additional (*zā'id*) is the existence of the [Universal] Soul, which is in accordance with the measure of the Intellect; then [there is] the [Universal] Nature, which is in accordance with the measure of the Intellect; then the Dust, which is in accordance with the measure of the Intellect; then the Universal Body, which is the fourth. Beyond it there is nothing except images. Likewise, the natural stretching-out (*madd*) corresponds to the Intellect, like the lengthening of *alif* in [saying] *qāla* and suchlike.[192]

192 *Fut.*IV:77; al-Manṣūb, 6/238–9; *FM.*II.422.

A popular Sufi narrative reads that the first movement of the Pen towards the Tablet produced a single drop of ink. When it fell on the surface of the Tablet, the ink spread to form a straight line. This line was *alif*, the first letter of the Arabic alphabet. When God saw the line, He decided to use it as the first letter of His name, Allah. According to legend, this is how *alif* became the first of the written letters and the source of all things in existence.[193] While similar narratives are widespread in the Sufi literary circles, it is highly unlikely that Ibn ʿArabī took them for granted. On his side, he maintained that the writings of the Pen are secure from omissions and alterations. Like any other angel, the First Intellect was thought to be free of wilfulness and neglect – and thus perfectly suited for the task it was entrusted with. 'God chose the Pen (…) and made it a simple element so that it wouldn't become neglectful, sleepy or forgetful. As a result, it is the most preserving and the most guarding of all created beings.'[194] The two cherubs, the Pen and the Tablet, were thus seen as the active and receptive principles that dictate the process of creation.

> God dictates to the Higher Pen what it should write on the Protected Tablet. The speech of the whole cosmos, both the absent of it and the witnessed, derives from this presence – and all is the speech of God – for this is the First Presence.[195]

Al-Qayṣarī referred to the First Intellect and the Universal Soul as 'the Mother of the Book' and 'the Manifested Book'. While the vast knowledge of the Mother of the Book encompasses all things in existence, the Manifested Book sees that this knowledge is firmly established in the form of writing of the three great books.[196] Schimmel sought the origins of these teachings, which led to the increasing popularity of calligraphy among the Sufis, to the activities of the Brethren of Purity:

---

193 As in al-ʿAlawi's verses: 'Indeed the *alif* is none other than the Point itself which is an eye that wept or a drop that gushed forth and which in its downpour was named alif.' Quoted according to Lings, *A Sufi Saint of the Twentieth Century: Shaikh Ahmad Al-ʿAlawi*, p. 156.

194 *Fut.*IV:78; al-Manṣūb, 6/240; *FM.*II:422.

195 Quoted according to Chittick, *The Self-Disclosure of God*, p. 116.

196 al-Qayṣarī, *Foundations of Islamic Mysticism*, p. 122.

The world found name and fame from the Pen
If the Pen were not there, there would not be the world
Anyone who did not get the share from the Pen
Don't think that he is noble in the eyes of the intelligent.[197]

Ibn ʿArabī perceived the Tablet and the Pen as the mother and father of the world. He maintained that 'everything below the Tablet is a product of sexual reproduction'.[198] In his 'Image of the Primordial Cloud', the Pen is depicted above the Tablet. In spite of this fact, Ibn ʿArabī compared the relationship between the Pen and the Tablet to 'the gushing water that reaches a female's womb. The meanings produced in this act of writing, which are entrusted to the divine letters, are akin to spirits of children that are then entrusted to physical bodies.'[199] In another diagram (Fig. 35), Ibn ʿArabī established the connection between 'the Image of the Primordial Cloud', the star of *lām-alif* and the opening words of the Shahada.

This diagram depicts the quadruple force which gives birth to the universe. The force is quadruple since the Shahada opens with four words: *lā ilāha illā Llāh* (there is no God but God). These words correspond to the four divine attributes: Living, Knowing, Wanting and Powerful. Ibn ʿArabī perceived these attributes as the roots of all existence. They were thought to correspond to the four elements depicted in 'the Image of the Primordial Cloud': i.e. to 1) First Intellect, 2) Preserved Tablet, 3) Universal Nature and 4) Universal Body.

> God brought the First Intellect into existence from the attribute of Life, and the Universal Soul from the attribute of Knowledge. The Intellect became a condition for the existence of the Soul just as Life is a condition for the existence of Knowledge. The two passive forces in relation to the Intellect and the Soul are the Dust and the Universal Body. These four are the origins of the manifesting of forms in the world.[200]

The four attributes, Living, Knowing, Wanting and Powerful, were also associated with the four elements (fire, water, air, earth) and

---

197 Habib, *Khaṭṭ u khaṭṭāṭān*, p. 222. Quoted according to Schimmel, *Calligraphy*, p. 80.
198 *Fut.*IV:91; al-Manṣūb, 6/258; *FM.*II:492.
199 al-Ḥakīm, *al-Muʿjam al-Ṣūfī*, p. 996.
200 *Fut.*I:442; al-Manṣūb, 2/133; *FM.*I:293.

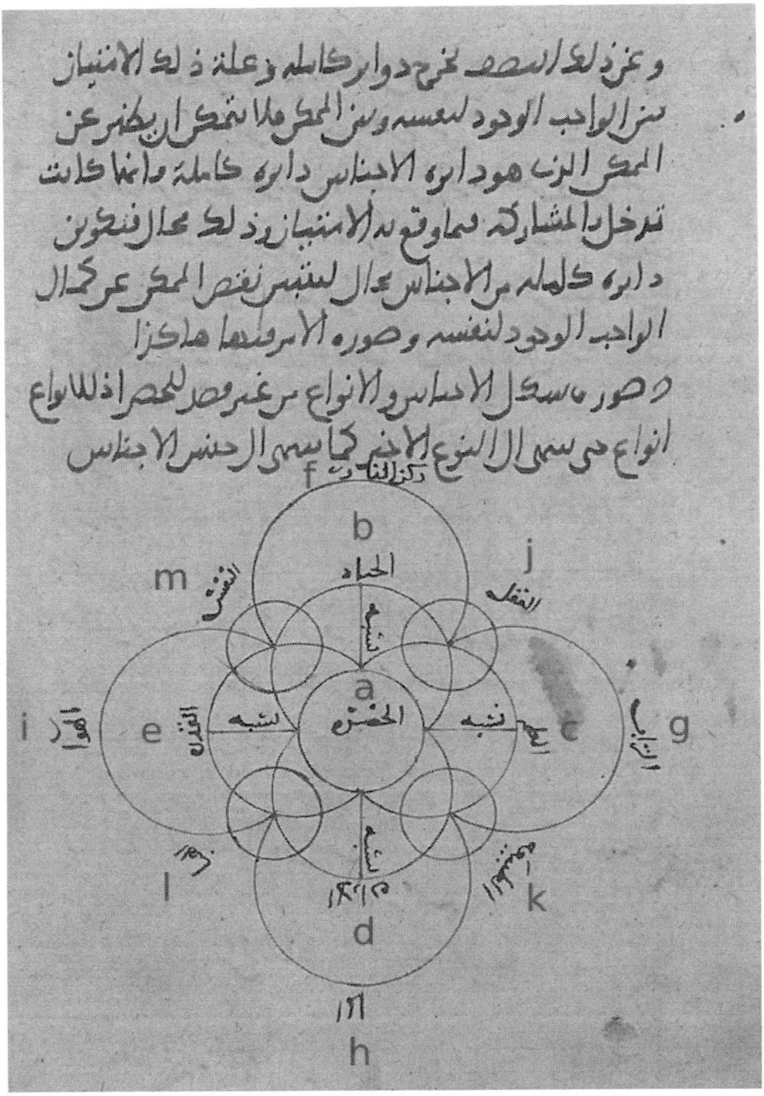

a) *Divine Presence*
b) *Life*
c) *Knowledge*
d) *Will*
e) *Power*
f) *Fire*
g) *Earth*
h) *Water*
i) *Air*
j) *First Intellect*
k) *Nature*
l) *Dust*
m) *Universal Soul*

Fig. 35 The Roots of Existence

four qualities of the natural world (hot, cold, dry, moist). Ibn ʿArabī's reasoning was mostly based on analogy: in both Arabic and English, life is associated with warmth and fire. In contrast, knowledge is usually described in everyday speech as cold and calculating. As a result, Ibn ʿArabī reasoned that knowledge is appropriately represented by water. The remaining attributes, Wanting and Speaking, were ascribed dry and moist characteristics. While the four qualities emerge from the divine attributes, the four qualities were thought to dictate the emergence of the four elements.

> Hot and dry combine to create fire. Hot and wet create air. Cold and wet create water. Cold and dry create earth. Examine the creation of air from hot and wet: this is the Breath and the life itself. Everything moves by the power of breath: water, earth and fire alike. All things move with the movement of the Breath since the Breath is life and the movement is the result of life. These four foundations are born from the First Mothers (i.e. from the Four Natures). [201]

Evaporations of the four elements were thought to dictate the creation of the visible, material world. These will later provide the foundation for the emergence of human beings, animal kingdom and, presumably, all forms of existence (Table 13).

Table 13 The roots of all existence

Roots of the Universe	Living	Knowing	Wanting	Saying
	↓	↓	↓	↓
Roots of Organic Bodies	Hot	Cold	Moist	Wet
	↓	↓	↓	↓
Roots of Animal kingdom	Yellow Bile	Black Bile	Blood	Phlegm
	↓	↓	↓	↓
Roots of Human Beings	Body	Nourishment	Senses	Articulation

According to Ibn ʿArabī, one of the first tasks of the Pen was to create the Shape, by means of which one thing could be distinguished from another. In his works, the notion of the shape is represented by the letter *khāʾ* – and the first thing to take shape in the universe was *qāf*, the Divine Throne.

201 *Fut.*I:91; al-Manṣūb, 1/184; *FM.*I:55.

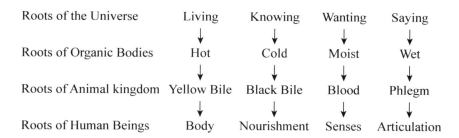

Haven't the infidels realized that heavens and earth were one solid mass before We tore them apart and made every living being out of water? Will they, then, still not believe?

Q.21:30

2.5. The Throne and the Heavenly Spheres

When God tore the mass of the Universal Body in half, the seven heavens, Earth and the heavenly Throne were created. Ibn ʿArabī believed that the Throne was created at the furthermost end of the universe. 'He made it a boundary where He settled and created the Pedestal (of the Throne). From this point downwards extend the Earth and the higher heavens.'[202] In accordance with the Islamic normative tradition, Ibn ʿArabī taught that the Throne stands on water. From water it was created and water was thought to sustain it. A vivid description of this process is preserved in the preface to *The Meccan Revelations*:

> [Allāh was] the first Name written by the sublime Pen, above [all] other Names. 'It was for your sake, Muhammad, that I wanted to create the world, which is your kingdom. So I created the water-jewel: I created it beneath the veil of guarded inaccessibility. I am, as I always was, and there was nothing with Me in the Cloud.' Thus He created water as a frozen solid, like a precious jewel in roundness and whiteness. He deposited within it in potential the realities of [all] bodies and contingent things. Then He created the Throne and settled upon it as *al-Raḥmān*, the All-Merciful. Then He erected the Footstool (Pedestal) and lowered His feet on it. He looked at that substance with the eye of Majesty, and it dissolved in shyness, its parts melted and water flowed. His Throne was on that water (Q.11:7), prior to the existence of earth and heaven, and there was nothing in existence apart from the realities of Him settling on it, it being settled upon and the act of settling. Then He sent the Breath, and the water swelled from the violent gale, foamed and resounded with the praise of Praise, most praised and true, as it struck against the shoreline of the Throne. The leg stirred and He/he/it said to it: 'I am Ahmad [the Greatest in Praise, Q.61:6]' – and the water became abashed and flowed back, yearning for its middle-height and leaving on the shoreline the foam that it generated, for it is the churning of that water which embraces most things. Then from that foam He brought out the Earth, in its spherical configuration, with height and breadth spread out. Then He brought out smoke from the fire of the Earth's frictions

202 *Fut.*I:62; al-Manṣūb, 1/136; *FM.*I:36.

when He split it apart. He cleaved asunder the high heavens and made it a place of lights and abodes for the highest angels. And He counterposed the shining stars that adorn [the heavens] with the flowering plants that adorn the earth.[203]

The main symbols of the Throne in Ibn ʿArabī's works are the letter *qāf* (ق) and the Divine Name *al-Muḥīṭ*, the Encompassing. This letter was thought to conceal the secret of life and the origins of organic matter. Ibn ʿArabī taught that the heavenly Throne was the first and the biggest corporeal object in existence. The enormous mass and proportions of the Throne were perceived as a symbol of its power over life and matter.[204] In his study on Islamic architecture and cosmology, Akkach refers to the Throne as 'the circumference of creation'.[205] However, this does not mean that its shape is circular.

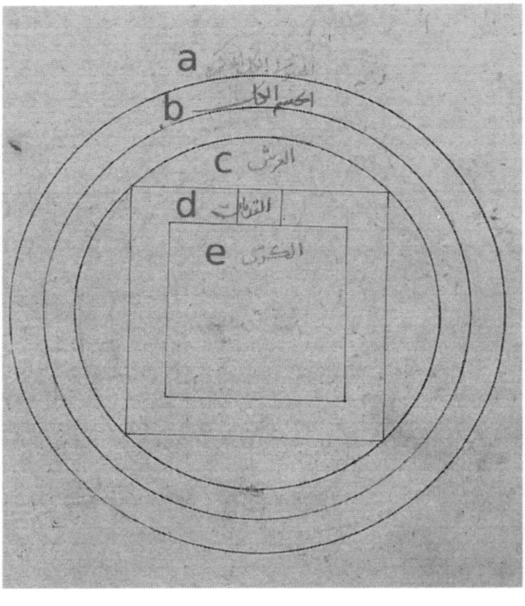

a) Prime Matter
b) Universal Body
c) Throne
d) Two feet of God
e) Pedestal

Fig. 36 The Throne and its surroundings

As a matter of fact, Ibn ʿArabī depicted the heavenly Throne (c) as an angular body that emerged from the Prime Matter (a) and the Universal Body (b). He maintained that it stands on four legs – a fact

203 *Fut.*I:17; al-Manṣūb, 1/72–73; *FM.*I:4.

204 Among Sufis, a popular narrative reads that Harquaeel, the angel with 38,000 wings, could not encircle one pillar of the Throne even after he was flying for 9,000 years. Kabbani, *Angels Unveiled: Sufi Perspective*, p. 43.

205 Akkach, *Cosmology and Architecture*, p. 129.

he claimed to have witnessed with his own eyes in 1201 CE, when the spark of revelation brought him before the Throne. The legs of the Throne appear in Sufi literature as a recurring symbol for the Living, Knowing, Wanting and Powerful Creator. Sufis traditionally held that its legs were created from green emerald stone, with the pillars made of ruby to support them – however, Ibn ʿArabī's vision contains no such details. What he offers is a vivid description of 1) the treasures beneath the Throne, which might or might not have been intended as an allusion to the wonders of creation, and 2) the four angels that hold it: Isrāfīl, Jibrāʾil, Mikhāʾil and Riḍwān. *The Meccan Revelations* contain the following description of these angels:

> Their light resembles the light of a lightning bolt. Nevertheless, I saw that the Throne has a shadow whose measures are limitless. This shadow was like a shade in the interior of the Throne, concealing with a curtain of light the One who is settled there, the All-Merciful.[206]

Apart from the letter *qāf*, the letters of the Basmala appear in Ibn ʿArabī's works as a recurring symbol of the Throne and its bearers. The Basmala consists of four words: *bismi Llāhi r-raḥmāni r-raḥīm*; in the name / of Allah / the Merciful / the Compassionate. When combined, these words symbolize the Throne in general.[207] Having conducted the analysis of the Divine Names Allah, the Merciful (*al-Raḥmān*), the Compassionate (*al-Raḥīm*) in several research units dealing with the isolated letters *alif* and *hamza*, Ibn ʿArabī does not return to this topic in his discussions on the heavenly Throne. Instead, he chose to focus on the word *bismi* (Fig. 37). In his works, the first word of the Basmala emerges as yet another symbol of the Creator and the created. Written as a single orthographic unit, the word *bismi* consists of two elements: *ism*, which is the Arabic word for noun, and the particle *bi*. In the Arabic language, this particle conveys the meaning of connection and association. For this reason, Ibn ʿArabī identified the first consonant and vowel of the Basmala (ب and ـِ) as the symbols of coming together and uniting of the opposites (*ittiṣāl wa wuṣla*). In accordance with the rules of orthography, *alif* between *bāʾ* and *sīn*, the first and the second consonant of the Basmala, is to be omitted in writing. Ibn ʿArabī interpreted the Basmala's invisible *alif* as the truth of Him standing

206 *Fut.*IV:98; al-Manṣūb, 6/274; *FM.*II:436.
207 *Fut.*I:169; al-Manṣūb, 1/340; *FM.*I:109.

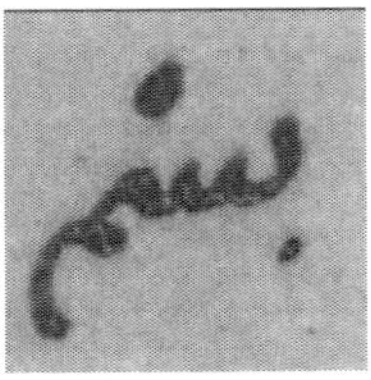

Fig. 37 Bismi

above everyone, exalted as He is. The truth of standing above everyone is veiled, as kindness on His part, by the dot underneath the *bāʾ*.[208] Ibn ʿArabī believed that this *alif* was veiled by the act of divine mercy. For had it been otherwise, the world would perish before its glory. *It was never meant for human beings that God should speak to them – except by means of revelation or from behind the veil or by sending them a messenger and revealing what He wishes through him. Allah, indeed, is the most High and Wise* (Q.42:51). In this model, the spark of revelation and the timeless power of the Creator are represented by *hamza* underneath the first, invisible *alif*. However, if this *alif* were to be interpreted as a divine messenger (which is also a possibility), the letters *bāʾ, sīn* and *mīm* would stand for the universe and all in it.[209] *Bāʾ*, the first consonant of the Basmala, thus emerges as a symbol of the corporeal world. Alternatively, this letter could be interpreted as a symbol for the creation in general. In this case, the archigrapheme of the letter *bāʾ* (ٮ) stands for the celestial realm of *Malakūt*. *Kasra*, the vowel it carries (ـِ) in the Basmala, symbolizes the world of *Mulk*. Ultimately, the intermediary world of *Jabarūt* is represented by the diacritical mark underneath this letter (ب). Ibn ʿArabī recorded how shaykh Abū Madyan (d. ca. 594/1198) claimed that everything he sees has the letter *bāʾ* written above it. This *bāʾ* is the first consonant of the Basmala. Since it carries the vowel *kasra*, it can be read as *bi* (Eng. *through me*) – thus indicating that everything any individual does is actually done by God. While we perceive ourselves as independent forms of existence – just as the dot underneath the letter *bāʾ* appears to be separated from its archigrapheme – Ibn ʿArabī taught that this is nothing but an illusion. There is the unity of the letter and the unity of existence. As evidence to his claim, Ibn ʿArabī cites the seventeenth verse of the Sura *al-Anfāl*: *It was not you who killed them – Allah killed them. And it was not you who threw when you threw, but it was Allah who threw so that He might test the believers with a good test. Indeed, Allah is Hearing and Knowing* (Q.8:17). Irrespective of his spiritual

208 *Fut.*I:158; al-Manṣūb, 1/325; *FM.*I:102.
209 *Fut.*I:159; al-Manṣūb, 1/324; *FM.*I:102.

rank, no friend of God is ever to be mistaken for God Himself. On the authority of al-Shiblī, Ibn ʿArabī taught that the dot underneath the letter *bāʾ* could also be interpreted as a rift between the worshipper and the object of his worship. 'I am the dot under the *bāʾ*,' al-Shiblī is reported to have said. The same words also came to be attributed to Imam ʿAlī. As a symbol of the worshipper, the letter *bāʾ* came to be perceived among the Sufis as an unassuming, modest letter next to the proud *alif*. In Sufi literature, this letter is often compared to the undemanding, broken heart.[210]

Out of 114 suras of the Qurʾan, 113 begin with the Basmala. As a result, *bāʾ*, the first letter of the Basmala, came to be perceived as a door to the secrets of the Qurʾan. 'I went out and saw everything that was written on the outside of this door,' asserted Ibn ʿArabī in *The Contemplations of the Holy Mysteries*.[211] Elsewhere he recounts a friend's vision in a spiritual gathering, in which he heard a voice informing him that 'all things manifest through *bāʾ*, and *bāʾ* has a certain matter within it'.[212] Ibn Sawdākin's commentary on *The Contemplations of the Holy Mysteries* later interpreted Ibn ʿArabī's answer as a reference to the first letter of the Basmala. He believed that, in this context, *bāʾ* stands for every Name of God and any attribute attributed to the Real (*al-ḥaqq*). In *The Meccan Revelations*, Ibn ʿArabī recorded the following anecdote:

> One of the people versed in Jewish lore said: 'You Muslims have no share in *tawḥīd* because the chapters of your Holy Book start with *bāʾ* instead of *alif*'. I answered him: 'nor do you, since the Torah begins with *bāʾ* (= *bereshit*)!' He understood the point I was trying to make - and nothing else would be possible since nothing begins with *alif*![213]

Apart from *hamza*, the first consonant of the Basmala appears as a recurrent symbol of the First Intellect in Ibn ʿArabī's works. In the universe, only the existence of the Creator precedes the emergence of the First Intellect. However, just as *alif* is not a real letter, one is not a number. 'It is only after the arrival of the *bāʾ*, which is at the second

210 Cole, *The World as Text: Cosmologies of Shaykh Ahmad al-Ahsa'i*, p. 154. See also Schimmel, *Calligraphy*, p. 98.

211 Ibn ʿArabī, *K. Mashāhid al-asrār*, p. 223.

212 Ibn ʿArabī, *K. al-Bāʾ*, p. 2.

213 *Fut.*I:131; al-Manṣūb, 1/243; *FM.*I:83.

level of existence, that the existence of numbers appear' – i.e. it is possible to speak of the existence of numbers.[214] As a symbol of the First intellect, the first *bā'* of the Basmala stands for 'the principial state of utterly impenetrable secrecy where there is neither separation nor union, neither after nor before, neither breadth nor length, and all the letters were obliterated in its hidden Essence.'[215] As for *sīn*, the second consonant of the Basmala, it was used as a symbol of the relationship between the Creator and the created. As such, it stands for dependence and humility of a human being in the presence of the Creator.[216] If the letter *mīm* had any special meaning when serving as a part of the Basmala, its symbolism remains unknown. However, in Ibn ʿArabī's works, all letters of the Basmala could be interpreted as symbols for the bearers of the heavenly Throne.[217]

Ibn ʿArabī believed that the bearers of the Throne are responsible for the management of the natural world. While one of these angels appeared to him in the form of a man, the other three were endowed with the head of a lion, eagle and bull.[218] Although there were only four bearers to be seen, Ibn ʿArabī observed that the Throne has eight pillars. When the horn of Riḍwān sounds the beginning of the Judgement Day, reads the sixty-ninth verse of the Sura *al-Haqqa*, *Eight will hold the Throne of their Lord.*[219] Ibn 'Arabī interpreted this verse as an implication that eight angels will lift the Throne by its pillars on Judgement Day, thus causing it to separate heaven from hell. He depicted this moment in *The Meccan Revelations* (Fig. 38), where the Throne (a) is surrounded by archangel Gabriel (b) and inhabitants of the heavenly gardens (c). Underneath the seat of God lies the scale that measures good and bad deeds committed by each person. On each day in every man's life, these are recorded by the angels Raqib and Atid. In accordance with the Islamic normative tradition, Ibn ʿArabī referred to these angels as 'the honourable scribes' (*kirāman kātibīn*). In order to be worthy of the gardens of heaven, the right pan (e), which measures

214 Ibn ʿArabī, *K. al-Bā'*, p. 12.

215 Quoted according to Lings, *Sufi Saint of the Twentieth Century*, p. 152.

216 *Fut.*I:160; al-Manṣūb, 1/326; *FM.*I:103.

217 The symbolism of the isolated letter *mīm* will be analysed in a separate sub-chapter of the present study.

218 These angels appear in the Islamic normative tradition as well. While the angel with the head of a lion was thought to intercede for the beasts of prey, the angel with the head of an ox prays for pastured animals, the eagle-headed angel prays for birds, and the angel with the human appearance intercedes for human beings. See Kabbani, *Angels Unveiled: Sufi Perspective*, p. 43.

219 *Fut.*IV:98; al-Manṣūb, 6/275; *FM.*II:436. For the original reference see Q.69:17.

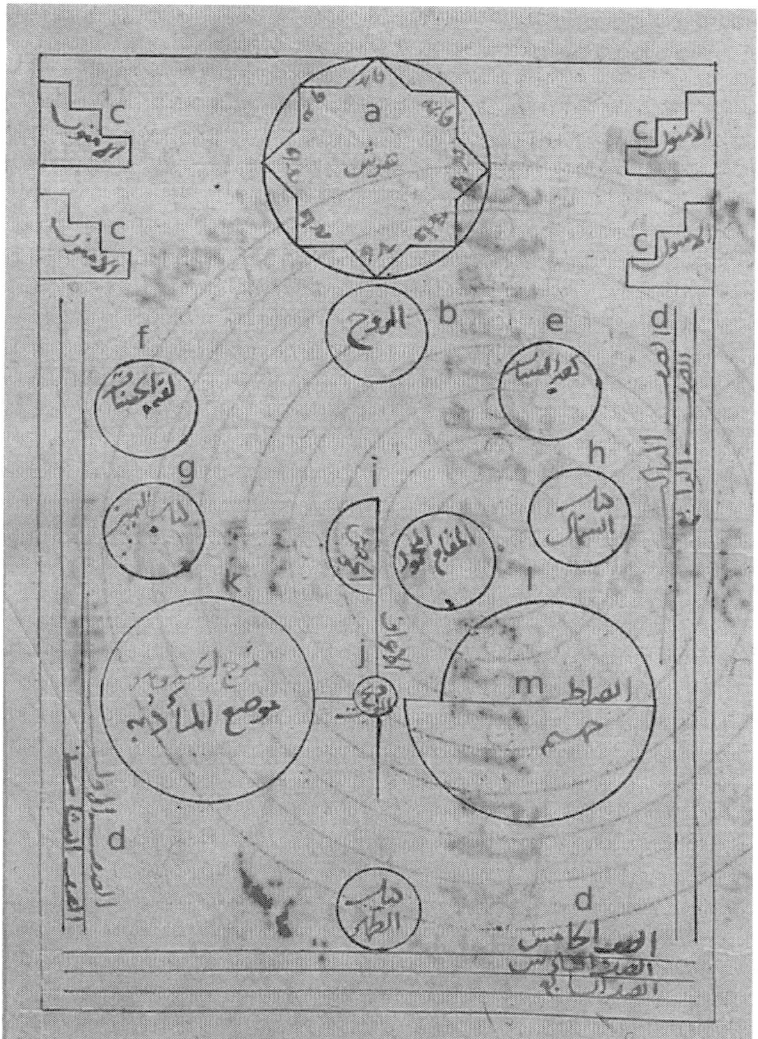

a) *The Throne and its pillars*
b) *The Spirit (i.e. archangel Gabriel)*
c) *The Just Ones*
d) *Rows of angels*
e) *Right pan*
f) *Left pan*
g) *The Book of Good Deeds*
h) *The Book of Bad Deeds*
i) *Border between heaven and hell*
j) *Prophet Muhammad*
k) *Heavenly gardens*
l) *Hell*
m) *The bridge Sirat over hell*

Fig. 38 The Throne on the Day of Resurrection

good deeds from the books of Raqib and Atid (g, h), has to outweigh bad deeds from the left pan of the scale (f).

Until Judgement Day, the seat of God was to remain in a different position, so that it can 'encompass the universe on the account of its circling'.[220] For this reason, the Throne was associated with the Divine Name *al-Muḥīṭ*, the Encompassing. In light of the fact that the Throne encompasses the creation, Ibn Masarra defined it as '*al-Mulk*, which is the divine kingdom in entirety'. In his works, Ibn ʿArabī went one step further: he identified the Throne as the synthesis of the created world. While Ibn Masarra associated the Throne with the world of *Mulk*, Ibn ʿArabī held that it would be more accurate to associate it with the second letter *lām* from the Divine Name Allah. While the first *lām* was perceived as a symbol of *Mulk*, the second *lām*, *Malakūt*, shines its light on *Mulk* as it stretches out to support it. In a similar way, the Throne supports the existence of the material world. For this reason, Ibn ʿArabī preferred to compare it to *Malakūt*.[221] He believed that the first divine revelation took place in front of the Throne, where all beings were summoned before the Creator to answer a simple question: 'Am I not your Lord?' Sura *al-Aʿrāf* testifies that the answer was unanimous: 'Yes, indeed' (Q.7:172). Having provided Him with the proper answer, the summoned beings were sent down through space, spiralling down the zodiac towers and heavenly spheres, in order to be born in the lower realms of existence.[222] A vivid description of this process was preserved in Ibn ʿArabī's poem on the letter *khāʾ* (خ):

> I experienced the being of the world in every state,
> and I saw it having reached the stage of transmutation:
> treacherous, reliable, truthful and lying—
> and such states can meet only through cooking.[223]

In this context, 'cooking' is to be interpreted as an allusion to the merging of the four elements and the chaotic nature of the corporeal world. However, before the act of genesis could begin in earnest, the power of the Throne had to be stabilized and directed through the letter *kāf* (ك). In Ibn ʿArabī's works, this letter was used as a symbol of stability. It stands for the Pedestal of the Throne, the

---

220 *Fut.*IV:97; al-Manṣūb, 6/272; *FM.*II:436.
221 *Fut.*I:162; al-Manṣūb, 1/330; *FM.*I:104–5.
222 Winkel, *The Youth*, pp. 18–9.
223 *Dīwān*, p. 221. Quoted according to McAuley, *Ibn Arabi's Mystical Poems*, p. 182.

Divine Name 'Thankful' (*al-Shakūr*) and the resting place for the feet of the Creator. Inside the Throne, God created the Pedestal, square in shape, and lowered His feet upon it.[224] From the moment it was created, the Pedestal stabilized the power of the creative word *kun*. For this reason, the just souls of the heavenly gardens were also thought to be able to use the creative word of God to shape the world in accordance with their wishes. The creation of the Pedestal also marked a division between the Creator and the created. While the Throne is Whole, the Pedestal is Separation.

> When He created the Pedestal, the world was split in two. His two feet were lowered on the Pedestal and on the account of this lowering the world was split – His are the creation and command.[225]

Ibn Abī Jumhūr (d. ca. 901/1495), a fifteenth-century interpreter of *The Meccan Revelations*, proposed that Ibn 'Arabī's notions of the First Intellect, the Protected Tablet and the heavenly Throne should be treated as synonyms.[226] While the surviving works of Ibn 'Arabī offer little support to this claim, in *The Meccan Revelations* the Throne and its Pedestal are represented by two dots underneath the letter *yā'* from the Divine Name *al-Raḥīm*, the Compassionate (Fig. 39). The diacritical marks underneath this letter were sometimes interpreted as a symbol of divine blessings and prohibitions. In this context, the other letters of the Name *al-Raḥīm* could be interpreted as symbols of divine knowledge (*alif*), desire (*lām*), power (*rā'*), the heavenly Throne (*ḥā'*) and the world it surrounds (*mīm*).[227] On the authority of the Prophet, Ibn 'Arabī depicted the Pedestal 'in the interior of the Throne, like a ring tossed in the empty desert of the Earth'.[228] Comparing it to a ring, or so Ibn 'Arabī believed, the Prophet wanted to allude to the circular shape of the heavenly spheres. Ibn 'Arabī taught that the spheres are located inside the Pedestal. In the eleventh diagram of *The Meccan Revelations* (Fig. 40), he depicted the world as a multitude of concentric spheres. This diagram was intended as a visual representation of the Primordial Cloud, the Throne, the heavenly spheres, heaven and hell and the

224 *Fut.*IV:100; al-Manṣūb, 6/277; *FM.*II:437.
225 *Fut.*IV:95; al-Manṣūb, 6/269; *FM.*II:434.
226 Nasr, *Cosmography in pre-Islamic and Islamic Persia*, p. 51.
227 *Fut.*I:171; al-Manṣūb, 1/343–4; *FM.*I:110.
228 *Fut.*IV:97; al-Manṣūb, 6/275; *FM.*II:436.

presence of the Divine Names. As such, 'it stands for the world in its entirety and the ranking of its levels, in spirit and body, highness and lowness.'[229]

Fig. 39 The Divine Name al-Raḥīm

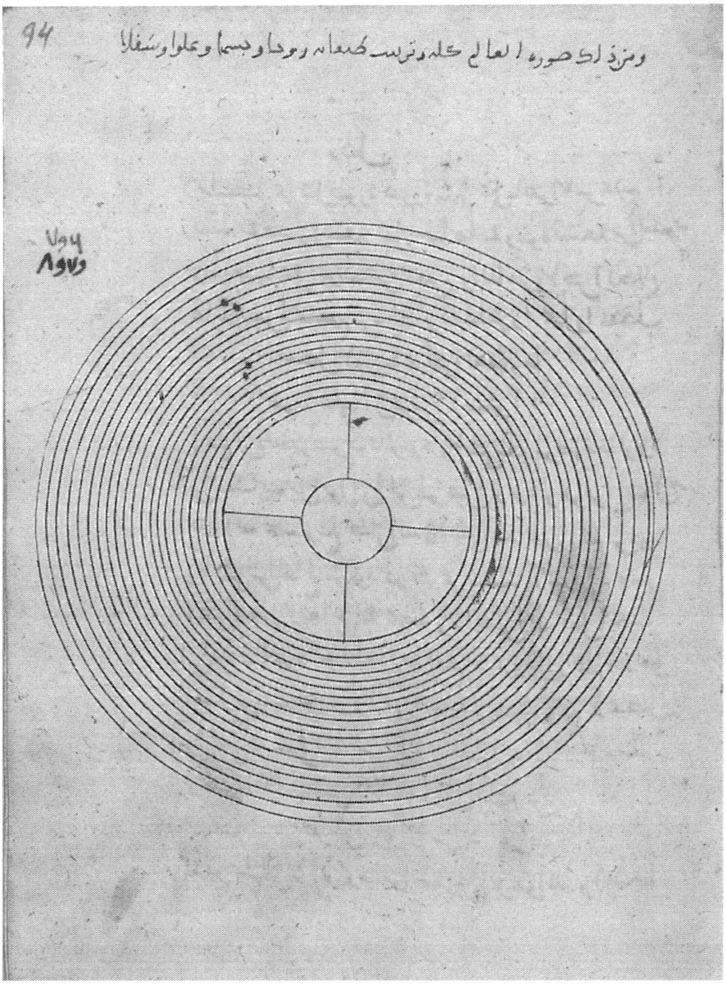

Fig. 40 The World

229 *Sifr* 26: 94 ff. *FM*.III:429.

Each work of God, including the world, was thought to be perfect. To emphasize this, Ibn ʿArabī depicted it in the form of a circle. He believed that the circle is the first and the most perfect shape to be created.[230] As such, it was represented by the letter *ṣād* (ص).

According to Ibn ʿArabī, *ṣād* is 'one of the letters of the truth, well-formed and guarded'. He identified familiarity with this letter as 'a strange mystery' and the knowledge of circle. Being round, *ṣād* was thought to be receptive of all shapes. Having extended it 'downwards and beyond', God went on to create the universe (Fig. 41).[231]

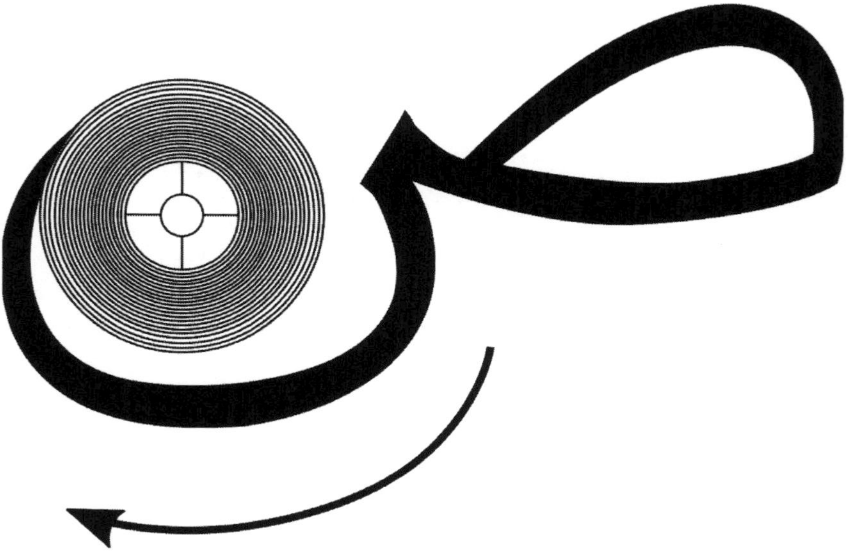

Fig. 41 The letter ṣād. Having extended it downwards and beyond, God went on to create the universe

In light of the fact that its shape is circular, the universe beneath the Throne was thought to have retained the nature of a circle. As a result, Ibn ʿArabī taught that meditations on this shape offer a certain insight into the genesis of the world and the laws that govern it. This was demonstrated in the first diagram of *The Meccan Revelations,* which explains the reason why the world is in the state of constant change and turmoil (Fig. 42). This diagram, which reflects on the circular nature of the universe, is conveniently constructed as a circle divided in eight segments.

230 *Fut.*I:114; al-Manṣūb, 1/220; *FM.*I:71.
231 Ibid.

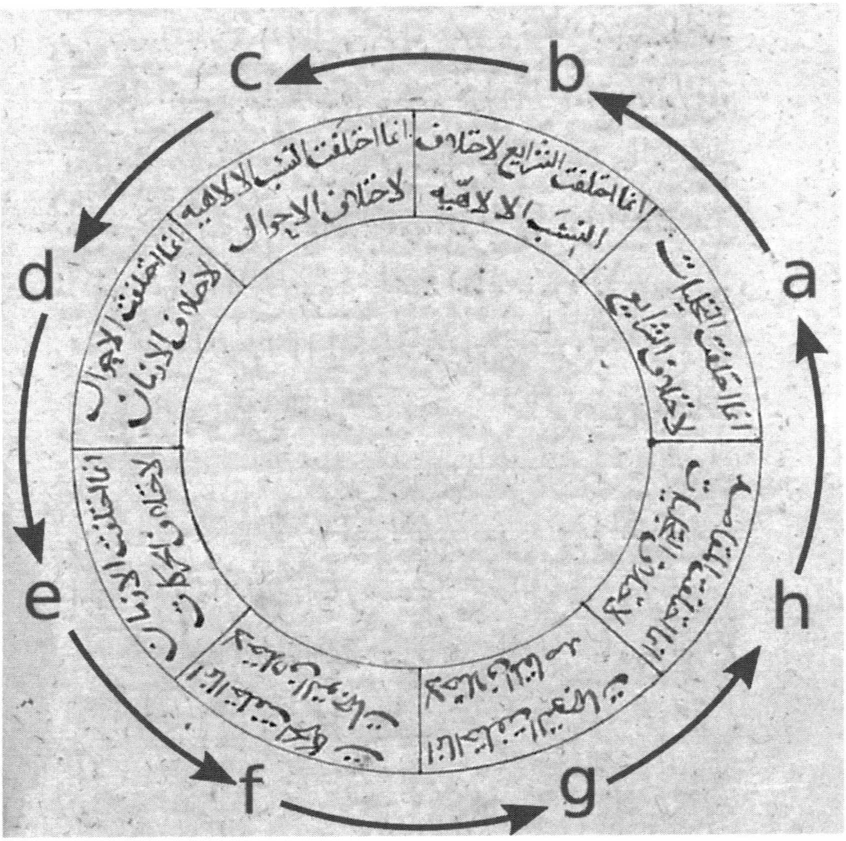

Fig. 42 – The ephemeral nature of the world and the laws that govern it

The first segment of the diagram (a) reads that 'divine laws are relative because of divine relations'. Ibn 'Arabī elaborates on this fact by stating that the Islamic normative tradition knows of a few cases when a certain thing was deemed to be absolutely forbidden by the prophets. Since divine revelations typically state that certain things are forbidden under certain circumstances, this leaves space for theological debates concerning the divine laws. The second segment of the diagram (b) explains the fluctuating nature of divine relations. It states that divine relations differ from one another because of different states: for while some people are just, others are corrupt – and while some are healthy, others are sick. The third segment of the diagram reads that states differ because of time (c) i.e. while we enjoy the warmth of summer, in winter we suffer from cold. In the fourth segment, time changes are attributed to the movement of celestial bodies (d), which are still used to measure time. However, movements tend to differ because of the divine attention: when His attention is directed towards something, it comes into existence (f). Divine attention is, however, governed by intention, which is also changeable (g), and while sinners are punished once their deeds catch divine attention, just people are rewarded. Ultimately, intentions were thought to differ from one another due to the fact that divine laws, which were brought by the prophets, vary from one community to another. So while divine laws are determined by divine relations, relations are determined by states, states are determined by time, time is determined by the movement of celestial bodies, whose movement is dictated by divine attention, which is determined by intentions. Intentions are, however, determined by divine laws – and this is how the circle closes.[232]

> Our saying that verily, the laws differ because the divine relations vary is primary, and so the circle turns. At every stage of these issues that you grasp, it is proper that there be a first, a last and an in-between. In this way, every order is circular, each part of which through the act of bisecting accepts a first, a last and what lies in between.[233]

Ibn ʿArabī taught that meditations on circles could also be used to come to terms with the act of genesis. His reasoning was based on the fact that each circle consists of a circumference and a centre. In order to form a circle, the first and final point of a circumference must meet. The final point of a circumference thus unites with its source as the circle is being formed (Fig. 43). On a wider scale, this image symbolizes the ephemeral nature of human life: on his deathbed, a man looks back with longing at his beginnings. To prove his point, Ibn ʿArabī refers to the Qur'anic revelation: *He created us from nothingness. We are from God and to Him we return…* Just like a circumference yearns to form a full circle.[234] Had it been otherwise, i.e. if human beings and the world were created from a straight line, the authority of the Qur'an would prove to be groundless – and in the eyes of Ibn ʿArabī, such a possibility was not even worth considering. Apart from the letter *ṣād*, the *mīm*, *wāw* and *nūn* were also among the letters that

232 *Sifr* 4: fol.56. al-Manṣūb, 2/68; *FM*.I.265.

233 *Fut*.I:402; al-Manṣūb, 2/69; *FM*.I:266.

234 *Fut*.I:385–386; al-Manṣūb, 2/47–48; *FM*.I:255. The original Qur'anic reference can be found at Q.2:156.

could provide us an insight into the nature of the world. As a matter of fact, Ibn ʿArabī advised those who wished to obtain familiarity with cosmology to 'contemplate on the *mīm, wāw* and *nūn*, whose end is the beginning so that there is neither beginning nor end.'[235] His reasoning was based on the fact that the circular shape of these letters resembles the heavenly spheres. Ibn ʿArabī's works speculate that the fate of each being is determined by its form – for he was aware that the term 'form', *shakl*, comes from the same root as *shikāl,* which is the Arabic word for shackles. In his works, the term *shakl* is commonly identified with *khuluq*. For example, the curved shape of a bow is used in *The Meccan Revelations* as an illustration of its nature and purpose: had it been shaped otherwise, it would not be able to fire an arrow. In this regard, the heavenly spheres are not an exception. 'The curvature of the bow is its trueness, so don't be fooled! Don't you see? The empty space rules over the properties of a body by its circularity and thus He created it in the form of an orbit.'[236] Like Aristotle before him, Ibn ʿArabī taught that the perfect nature of the creation requires that all celestial bodies, including the spheres, move in circles. The shape (i.e. the nature) of the heavenly spheres thus 'shackles' them to their course.[237]

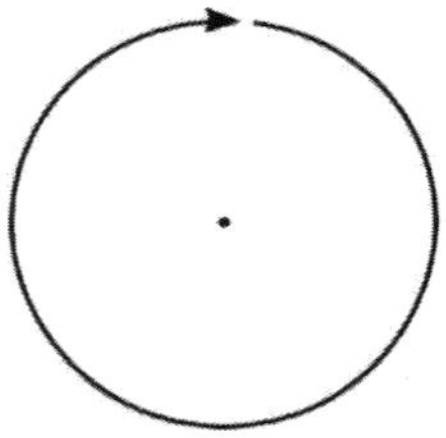

Fig. 43 Circumference of the Circle: We are from God and to Him we return

Aristotle argued, on purely philosophical grounds, that the Earth is located at the centre of the universe and surrounded by the heavenly spheres. Ptolemy's *Almagest,* an influential second-century treatise on astronomy, lists these spheres as the Spheres of Saturn, Jupiter, Mars, Sun, Venus, Mercury and the Moon. In the vast majority of Sufi diagrams, including those of Ibn ʿArabī, the names and arrangement of the heavenly spheres have remained the same (Fig. 44).

235 Ibn ʿArabī, *K. al-Mīm*, fol.14.
236 *Fut.*IV:97; al-Manṣūb, 6/271; *FM.*II:435.
237 *Fut.*IV:96–97; al-Manṣūb, 6/271; *FM.*II:435.

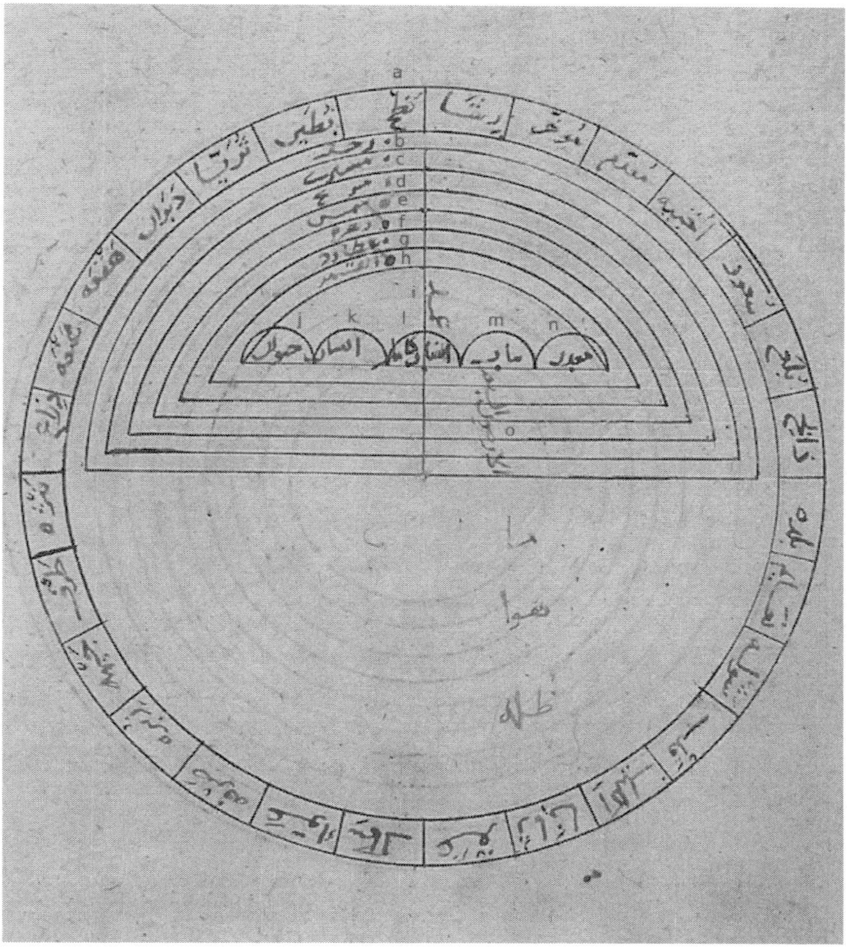

Fig. 44 The heavenly spheres

Figure 44, from top downwards: Underneath the Sphere of the Fixed stars lie the Spheres of a) Saturn b), Jupiter c), Mars d), Sun e), Venus f), Mercury g) and the Moon h). In the centre of the diagram is the Earth i) with its four kingdoms. The animal kingdom j) and the kingdoms of plants m) and minerals n) are ruled by man k) and the Perfect Human l) as the highest form of existence.

The earliest examples of Ptolemaic diagrams in Sufi literature can be traced from the late eleventh century CE.[238] In Ptolemy's system, the Earth is slightly displaced from the centre of the universe. This was

238 See Karamustafa, *Cosmographical diagrams*, p. 75; and Fitzpatrick, *A Modern Almagest*, pp. 5–6.

due to the fact that Ptolemy held that the Sun, Earth and the majority of planetary deferents have different geometric centres. As a result, he opposed the idealistic, philosophical model of the universe with the Earth at its centre. Another point of difference between Ptolemy's *Almagest* and Sufi diagrams is reflected in the fact that Ptolemy taught that the lower edge of each sphere touches the upper edge of the sphere below it. However, al-Bīrūnī (d.1050) argued that there is always a certain amount of space between the spheres to accommodate the celestial bodies they contain.[239] On his side, Ibn ʿArabī described the heavenly spheres as ceilings raised above the Earth (*saqf marfūʿ*).[240] These were traditionally compared to layers of an onion. The Earth lies at the centre of this 'onion', surrounded by the orbits of Air, Water and Fire. Above these orbits is the Sphere of the Moon, followed by the Spheres of Mercury, Venus, the Sun, Mars, Jupiter and Saturn. As they rotate, the spheres carry celestial bodies over the horizon. By the early thirteenth century, the works of Fakhr al-Dīn al-Rāzī (d.1210) put this model to the test – and Ibn ʿArabī advised his students to conduct independent astronomical observations instead of relying on outdated works and arbitrary measurements. Although his advice was sound, Ibn ʿArabī himself would be the first to ignore it. As a Sufi, he was chiefly interested in spiritual accomplishments and in his works, science mixes with religious beliefs. Ibn ʿArabī's diagrams thus supplemented Ptolemy's model of the universe with several recurring motives from the Islamic normative tradition. Among them are the Throne and its Pedestal, the Starless Sphere, the Sphere of the Fixed Stars with its zodiac watch-towers, orbits of Fire, Water and Air, the seven heavenly gardens and hell. As a result, Ibn ʿArabī's model of the universe has more in common with Sufi cosmology than with the scholarly works of al-Rāzī, Naṣīr al-Dīn Ṭūṣī (d. 672/1274) and other eminent astronomers of his time. Prior to the early twentieth century, cosmology was not recognized as a scientific discipline in its own right. Based on the classification system of Christian Wolff, it used to be perceived as a branch of metaphysics instead. Tamar Rudavsky identified cosmology as 'an enterprise which describes what the universe looks like'.[241] The name of this discipline comes from the Greek word κόσμος, which stands for the universe, meaning and order and λογία, which is the

239 For al-Bīrūnī's teachings, see Wright, *Elements of Astrology*, p. 43.

240 Elmore, *Islamic Sainthood*, p. 400.

241 Langerman, 'Arabic Cosmology', p. 185. See also Fatoorichi, 'The Problem of the Beginning: Modern Cosmology and Transcendent Ḥikmah Perspectives', p. 633.

Greek term for 'science' and/or 'discourse'. As its name suggests, cosmology is a scientific discipline concerned with structure, origins and hierarchy between the various parts of the universe. In this respect, Sufi cosmology is not an exception. Having conducted a comparative analysis of numerous schools of Islamic cosmological thought, Anton Heinen came to the conclusion that it would be impossible to speak of a universal model of the Islamic cosmos.[242] However, the majority of these schools shared a general notion of the nine heavenly spheres, surrounded by the Throne and its Pedestal (Fig. 45).

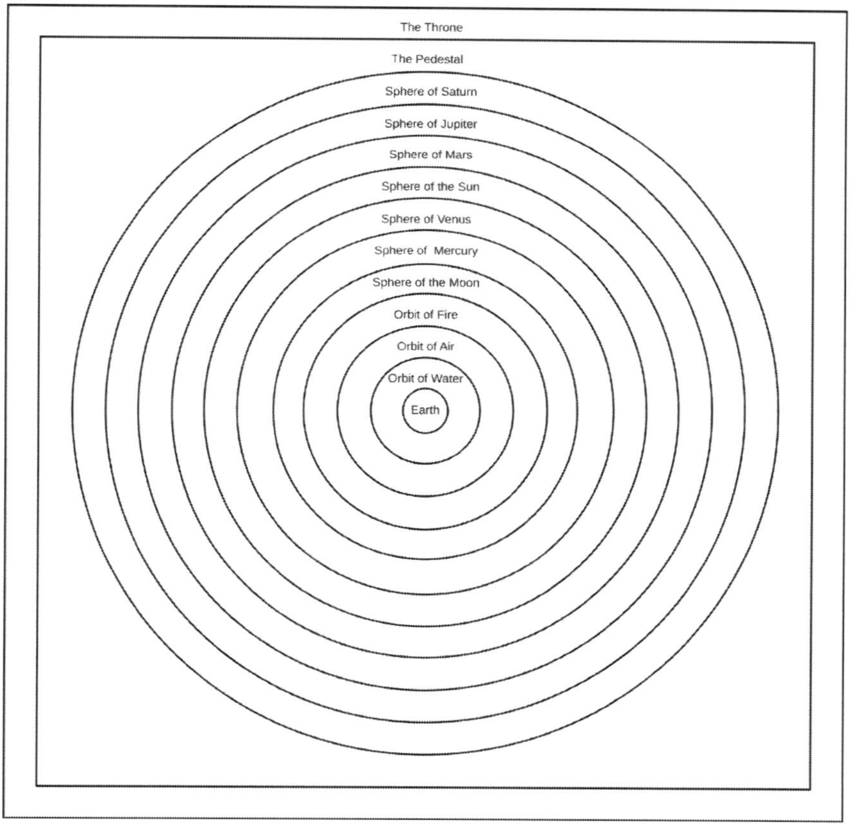

Fig. 45 Ibn 'Arabī's model of the universe

On his side, Ibn 'Arabī taught that this model was based on the science of letters. Apart from the human, angelic and jinn letters, he

242 Heinen, *Islamic Cosmology. A study of al-Suyūṭi's al-Hay'a as-sanīya fī l-hay'a as-sunnīya*, p. 7.

believed in the existence of the three Divine letters: *alif, zāy* and *lām*.[243] In addition, his works speak of three levels of existence: *Mulk, Malakūt* and *Jabarūt*. Each of these levels can be divided into three sub-levels (3 x 3 = 9). If the number of Divine letters is multiplied by the number of the worlds, the result is nine (3 x 3 = 9).

3 (*alif*, *zāy*, *lām*) × 3 (*Mulk*, *Malakūt*, *Jabarūt*) = 9

This number stands for the Starless Sphere, the Sphere of the Fixed Stars and the Spheres of Saturn, Jupiter, Mars, Sun, Venus, Mercury and the Moon. In accordance with the Islamic normative tradition, Ibn ʿArabī believed in the existence of seven heavens and earths one atop another.[244] Islamic jurisprudents held that the seven earths and their inhabitants are the exact copy of one another. The Prophet's companion ʿAbd Allāh b. ʿAbbās (d. 67/687) is thus reported to have said that there are fifteen Kaʿbas (Fig. 46) and seven other Ibn ʿAbbāses underneath the seven heavens. 'If I were to tell you the interpretation of these words, you would stone me.'[245]

Fig. 46 Bayt al-Maʿmūr, the Kaʿba of the highest heaven

But while Ibn ʿArabī's works contain relatively little information on the seven earths, the Earth as we know it, the one 'that radiates by the light of its Lord', is always depicted at the centre of his diagrams (Fig. 47). As such, it is symbolized by the connection between the two letters *lām* that form the name Allah.[246] This earth (a) was thought to be encircled with the Orbit of Water (b), followed by the orbits of Air (c) and Fire (d).

---

243 See the first chapter of the present study.

244 Elmore, *Islamic Sainthood*, p. 408.

245 *Fut.*I:56; al-Manṣūb, 1/125–6; *FM.*I:32.

246 *Fut.*I:162; al-Manṣūb, 1/330; *FM.*I:105.

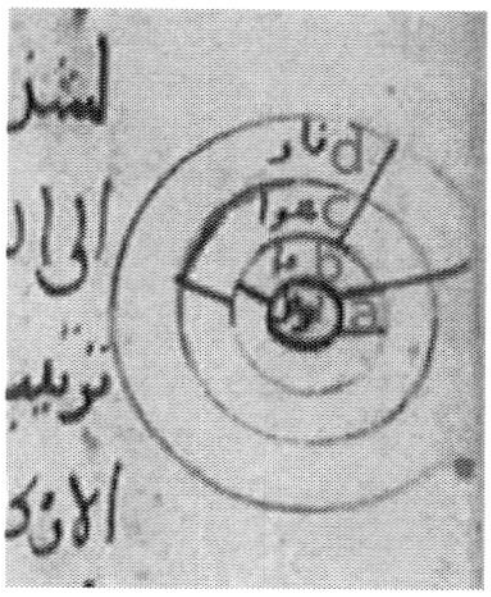

Fig. 47 The Earth (centre) surrounded by the Orbits of Water, Air and Fire in ascending order

Ibn ʿArabī taught that the four orbits were created before the heavenly spheres. According to legend, the letters of the Arabic alphabet emerged from the rotation of these orbits and/or the heavenly spheres.

> Letters are produced by the rotation and interaction of a specific number of heavenly spheres that move concentrically within the absolute, ultimate sphere [i.e. underneath the Starless Sphere]. Apart from bringing letters into existence, the rotation of the spheres combines physical qualities (hot, cold, dry and moist). As a result, the letters are located on the edge of the material world, since these qualities, which are the original elements, give birth to the four elements when combined.[247]

In another place, however, Ibn ʿArabī ascertained that the spheres, like all things in existence, owe their existence to the letters of the Arabic alphabet. These letters were also thought to determine the rotation of celestial bodies. 'By means of the letters, celestial bodies rotate in their whirling orbits in His higher kingdom, in the midst of the muted sleepers and those who are roused, alert.'[248] But regardless of whether letters gave birth to spheres or the spheres gave birth to letters, it is clear that, in Ibn ʿArabī's works, the science of letters cannot be examined independently of cosmology – for just like letters have a dominion over words, celestial bodies rule over seasons and Divine Names rule over created beings.

Ibn ʿArabī taught that the life on Earth and the properties of the four orbits are dictated by the rotations of the heavenly spheres. Out of nine heavenly spheres, seven were thought to contain planets. These are the Spheres of Saturn (*al-zuḥal*), Jupiter (*al-mushtarī*), Mars (*al-*

247 Ibn ʿArabī, *The Meccan Revelations* vol. 2, p. 108.
248 *Fut.*I:85; al-Manṣūb, 1/176; *FM.*I:51–2.

mirrīkh), Sun (*al-shams*), Venus (*al-zuhra*), Mercury (*al-'uṭārid*) and the Moon (*al-qamar*). Ibn Arabī identified the seven planetary spheres beneath the Starless Sphere and the Sphere of the Fixed Stars with the seven mothers of all Names of God, i.e. with the Creator who is Living, Knowing, Wanting, Powerful, Speaking, Generous and Just. In his *Book of the Fabulous Gryphon,* he also associated the planetary spheres with the following properties of Muslim sages:

> Sun is their life and their sight is Venus. Their speech is Mercury and the Moon is their knowledge. Their power is Saturn, their will is Jupiter and their hearing is Mars.[249]

Ibn 'Arabī's *Book of the Fabulous Gryphon* also compares the procession of the planets through the zodiacal watch-towers with the spiritual ascension through mystical stations (*sayruhum fī-l-maqāmāt*).[250] He believed that every moral debasement and spiritual elevation is reflected in the soul. As such, they were compared to the full Moon and eclipse on the horizon. In Ibn 'Arabī's works, the Sun and the Moon are also associated with the spirit (*rūh*) and soul (*nafs*) of sages. He therefore advises his reader to 'contemplate on this model and strive to set his Sun and Moon in motion' in order to achieve spiritual elevation.[251] Ibn 'Arabī taught that the heavenly spheres are the rest-stops for contemplation where one gets to know God. A similar opinion was advocated by Islamic jurisprudents and astronomers as well.[252] In Ibn 'Arabī's works, this theory is justified on the basis of the twelfth verse of the Sura *al-Ṭalāq*:

> God reveals His command to each heaven (…) A segment of what God revealed to His heavens and what he set up in His Preserved Tablet concerns the sending of the messengers. They gain [knowledge] from the Tablet by the means of revelation and, by being Divinely informed and they gain knowledge from each heaven through observation and reporting.[253]

249 Elmore, *Islamic Sainthood*, p. 443.

250 Ibid.

251 The remaining five spheres beneath the Fixed Stars have been compared to the five senses in this model. See Elmore, *Islamic Sainthood*, p. 443.

252 See Saleh, *Licit Magic: The Touch and Sight of Islamic Talismanic Scrolls*, p. 54.

253 *Fut.*I:492; al-Manṣūb, 2/251; *FM.*I:326.

Ibn ʿArabī taught that God created the seven heavens, zodiac watch-towers and the lunar mansions to serve as visible manifestations of the law that governs the universe. By the Breath of the All-Merciful, they were set to rotate for eternity, with letters swirling in their orbits. On the authority of Abū Ṭālib al-Makkī, Ibn ʿArabī maintained that the position of these orbits will remain unchanged 'till the Judgement Day, with fixed hierarchy between them.[254]

Ibn ʿArabī's model of the universe demonstrates a hierarchy that is both cosmological and ontological. The excellence of each sphere was thus thought to be proportional to its distance from the heavenly Throne. The spheres were also thought to be populated with inhabitants that match them in excellence, starting from the angels around the Throne to the inhabitants of Earth which is made of the four elements and distinguished by motion, change and contradiction.[255] Each of these spheres was thought to contain a unique piece of information concerning the Creator and the created. Having experienced his *miʿrāj*, a spiritual ascension through the heavenly spheres, Ibn ʿArabī claimed to have met the prophets associated with each of them. Like the spheres, divine messengers were also thought to be ranked in excellence – with their spiritual status being reflected in the position of the sphere they occupy. For example, the Sphere of the Moon, which Ibn ʿArabī associated with the prophet Adam, was thought to conceal the secret of the four elements and orbits that are associated with them. To learn how the four elements merge to form organic bodies, one has to reach the Sphere of the Moon. 'Depart from the rule of corporeal, elemental lust. For those who have succeeded in this endeavour, the heavenly gates of this world are to be opened, and a student who follows [his teacher] blindly will meet with Adam, peace be on him, delight in him and visit his realm.'[256] Each heavenly sphere was thought to contain the accumulated powers of all spheres underneath. Adam, whose place of residence is the lowest in the hierarchy of spheres, shares his knowledge with adepts who reach the Sphere of the Moon. This knowledge is proportional to the spiritual accomplishments of an adept. However, the highest state of spiritual development was associated with the Prophet Muhammad and the Starless Sphere he was affiliated with.

254 *Fut.*I:492; al-Manṣūb, 2/251; *FM.*I:326.
255 McAuley, *An A to Z of Sufi Metaphysics: Ibn ʿArabi's Muʿashsharāt*, p. 73.
256 *Fut.*III:411; al-Manṣūb, 5/481; *FM.*I:273.

> Just like the Starless Sphere includes all spheres, (...) so does the Master — once he attained unto the station of the Seal of the saints of his age — his fame and his influence spread throughout the world.[257]

The seventeenth-century astronomer Bahā' al-Dīn al-'Āmilī (d. 1030/1621) taught that the Starless Sphere and the Sphere of the Fixed Stars correspond to the heavenly Throne and its Pedestal.[258] However, Ibn 'Arabī's works provide no support for this theory – for he believed them to be located underneath the Pedestal. *The Meccan Revelations* thus inform us that the lower part of the Pedestal touches the Starless Sphere (*al-falak al-aṭlas*), where 'the celestial arks hide by the day'.[259] In another place, Ibn 'Arabī asserts that the Pedestal encircles the Starless Sphere and the Sphere of the Fixed Stars. In this model, the Starless Sphere is located alongside the upper edge of the Pedestal, 'like a ring that rotates eternally in a tight space'.[260] Ibn 'Arabī identified the Starless Sphere as the furthermost border of the material world, whose symbol is the letter *jīm* (ج). This is the dominion of the archangel Michael and the first sphere to be created. In Arabic, the term *aṭlas* usually stands for something that is effaced and obliterated; a perfect homogeneity with no distinguishable features. The Starless Sphere, *al-falak al-aṭlas,* thus came to be identified in Ibn 'Arabī's works as 'the sand swept clear of tracks, the featureless, background-free sphere'.[261] Seven centuries later, Titus Burckhardt described this sphere as nothingness from the formal point of view.[262] Ibn 'Arabī taught that the only way to determine the size of a heavenly sphere is to study the movement patterns of the celestial bodies it contains. However, the Starless Sphere contains none. For this reason, it would be impossible to estimate its size as there is nothing to compare it against. Ibn 'Arabī described the Starless Sphere as a great river whose volume no cup could measure. However, he speculated that the rotation period of this sphere takes 78,000 years.[263] In his works, the Starless Sphere is occasionally referred to as the All-encompassing Sphere

257 Cited from the commentary by al-Maqābirī, in Elmore, *Islamic Sainthood*, p. 314.
258 al-'Āmilī, *Tashrīḥ al-aflāk*, fol.2.
259 *Fut.*IV:78; al-Manṣūb, 6/240; *FM.*II:422.
260 Bosnevi, *Sharḥ Fuṣūṣ* vol.2, p. 265.
261 *Fut.*IV:78; al-Manṣūb, 6/240; *FM.*II:422.
262 Burckhardt, *Mystical Astrology According to Ibn 'Arabi*, pp. 14–5.
263 *Fut.*II:17; al-Manṣūb, 2/421; *FM.*I:388. See also Bosnevi, *Sharḥ Fuṣūṣ* vol.2, p. 268.

(*al-falak al-muḥīṭ*). This was due to the fact that Ibn ʿArabī believed that it encircles all other spheres, like the outer layer of an onion. All celestial bodies move underneath the Starless Sphere. In Ibn ʿArabī's model of the universe, this was the highest of all spheres, the biggest in volume. It was thought to be divided into twelve watch-towers, which Ibn ʿArabī compared to the observation posts that governors have in their kingdoms.[264] For this reason, it also came to be known as the Sphere of Towers (*falak al-burūj*). The twelve towers of the Starless Sphere were thought to be equal in size, with each of them occupying 30° of the ecliptic circle. Ibn ʿArabī believed that the reason why there are twelve watch-towers, neither more nor less, is to be sought in the fact that the creation of the Pedestal caused a division between the Creator and the created. This division is symbolized by the number 2. As it is located directly underneath the Pedestal, the Starless Sphere touches the two feet of the Creator. Ibn ʿArabī held that the two feet on the Pedestal stand for six things: 1) the Creator who is the cause of all things and His relation to His creations which includes instructions on what is 2) obligatory, 3) permitted, 4) forbidden, 5) recommended and 6) disliked by God. If six is multiplied by two, the number which, in this case, stands for the feet of the Creator, the result we would get is twelve. In Ibn ʿArabī's works, this number symbolizes the division caused by the Pedestal; where each of the twelve division units represent a single principle in the universe. The twelve watch-towers of the Starless Sphere were believed to be inhabited by twelve angels. In Sufi literature, these angels are collectively known as *al-Mudabbirāt*, 'Those Who See that God's Orders Are Being Done'.

> This heavenly sphere is divided into twelve general measures. He made this orbit a watchtower for the angelic spirits of different natures and each watchtower is called by the name of the angel for whom that zodiac measure was created for him to reside in. These are like the circular watchtowers around the walls of a land, like the observation posts the governors have in a kingdom.[265]

264 *Fut.*IV:95; al-Manṣūb, 6/270; *FM.*II:434. The towers in the sky (*al-samāʾ dhāt al-burūj*) from the first verse of the Sura *al-Burūj* (Q.85:1) were thought to be the reference to this sphere.

265 *Fut.*IV:95; al-Manṣūb, 6/270; *FM.*II:434. The watch-towers of the Starless Sphere are not to be confused with the mansions of the Moon, zodiacal constellations and/or the fixed stars.

According to Bosnevi, the angels of the Starless Sphere live to testify to the Oneness of God. In his commentary on Ibn ʿArabī's *Bezels of Wisdom*, he recorded that their individual names and duties are as follows: 1) Libra (*mizān*), the angel that regulates spiritual states and time since the creation of heaven and earth; 2) Scorpio (*ʿaqrab*), the angel of fire and immobility; 3) Sagittarius (*qaws*), the angel that presides over plants, light and dark bodies; 4) Capricorn (*al-jadī*) that holds the keys of day and night; 5) Aquarius (*dalw*), the angel of awe and dignity that guards the key of souls; 6) Pisces (*ḥūṭ*), the angel that holds the key of animals and, like Sagittarius, presides over light and dark bodies; 7) Aries (*kabsh*), the angel that rules over all accidents, properties and movements; 8) Taurus (*thawr*) who guards the keys of paradise and hell; 9) Gemini (*jawzāʾ*), the angel that was entrusted with the key of minerals; 10) Cancer (*saraṭān*), the angel with the key of the creation of the material world; 11) Leo (*asad*), the angel with the key of the creation of the other world (*al-akhira*); and 12) Virgo (*sunbula*), the angel that rules over human bodies. In addition to their individual duties, *al-Mudabbirāt* were also entrusted with the rotation of the heavenly spheres. Although Bosnevi maintained that these angels were named for their outward shape and appearances, he failed to elaborate on the fact that their names and positions of the towers they occupy correspond to the well-known zodiacal constellations.[266] The watch-tower of Aries thus extends between 0 and 30° of the ecliptic longitude, followed by the watch-tower of Taurus which is located between 30° and 60° – and so on until the watch-tower of Pisces, which is positioned between 330° and 360° of the ecliptic longitude. However, it would be mistaken to confuse the watch-towers of the Starless Sphere for the zodiacal constellations beneath them – for these actually belong to the domain of the Sphere of the Fixed Stars (Fig. 48).

266 Bosnevi, *Sharḥ Fuṣūṣ* vol.2, pp. 265–8. The names of the zodiacal constellations were also inspired by their shape.

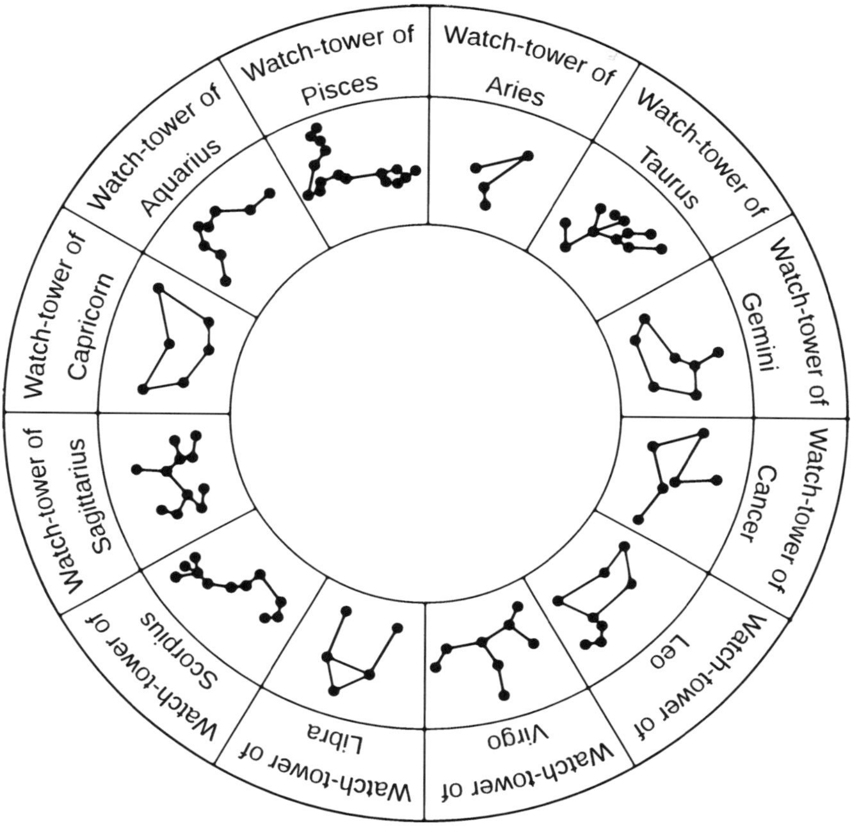

Fig. 48 Watch-towers of the Starless Sphere and the zodiac constellations of the Sphere of the Fixed Stars. The towers owe their names to the constellations beneath them.

On the authority of Ptolemy, Ibn ʿArabī taught that the Sphere of the Fixed Stars contains twelve constellations with 1025 stars. In his works, this sphere is commonly referred to as the Sphere of Constellations. Ibn ʿArabī believed that the heavenly gardens are located between the Starless Sphere and the Sphere of the Fixed Stars (Fig. 49). For this reason, he described the Sphere of the Fixed Stars as the floor of paradise and the ceiling of hell.[267]

267 *Fut.*IV:102; al-Manṣūb, 6/281; *FM.*II:493.

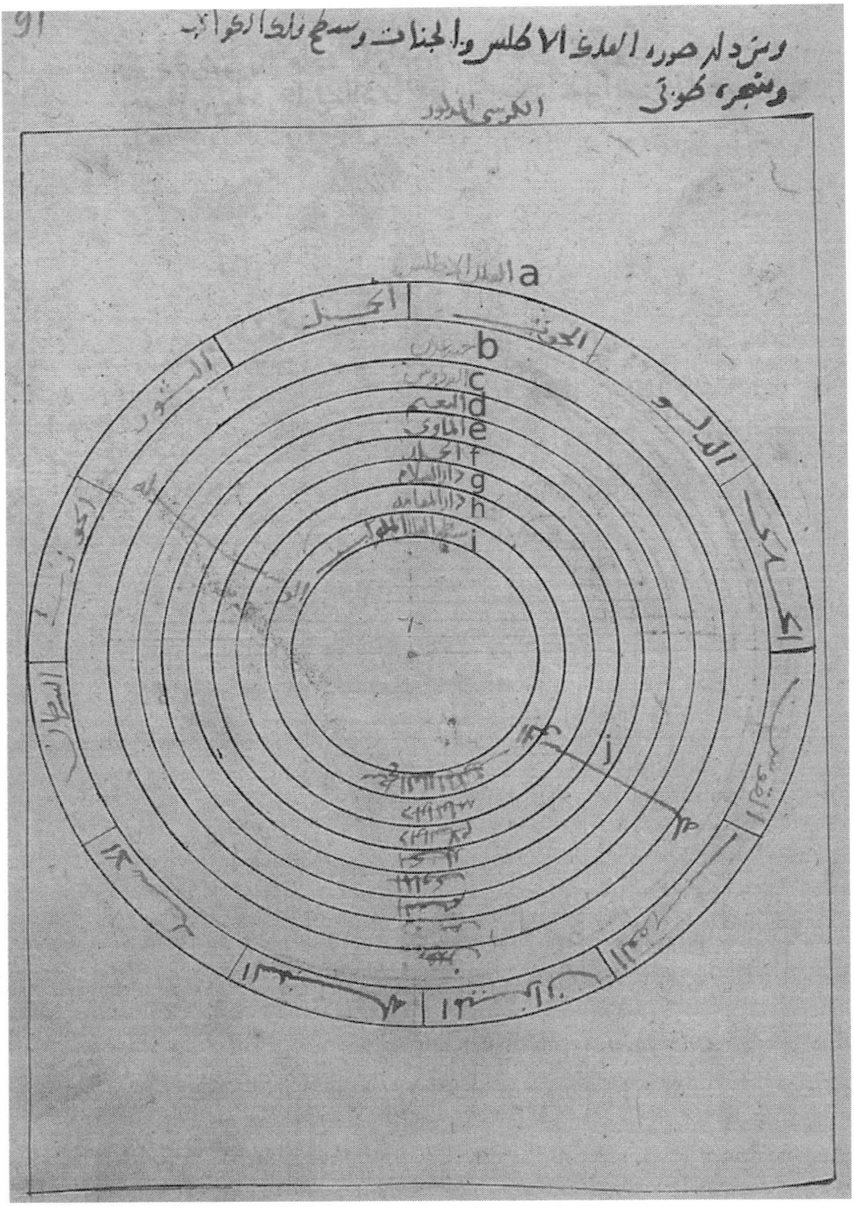

Fig. 49 The heavenly gardens. From top downwards: (a) the Sphere of the Fixed Stars, (b) Paradise of Eden, (c) Firdaws, the Highest Garden, (d) Garden of Delights, (e) Garden of Abode, (f) the Eternal Gardens, (g) the Abode of Peace, (h) the Abode of Residence, (i) planetary orbit, (j) the interceding path

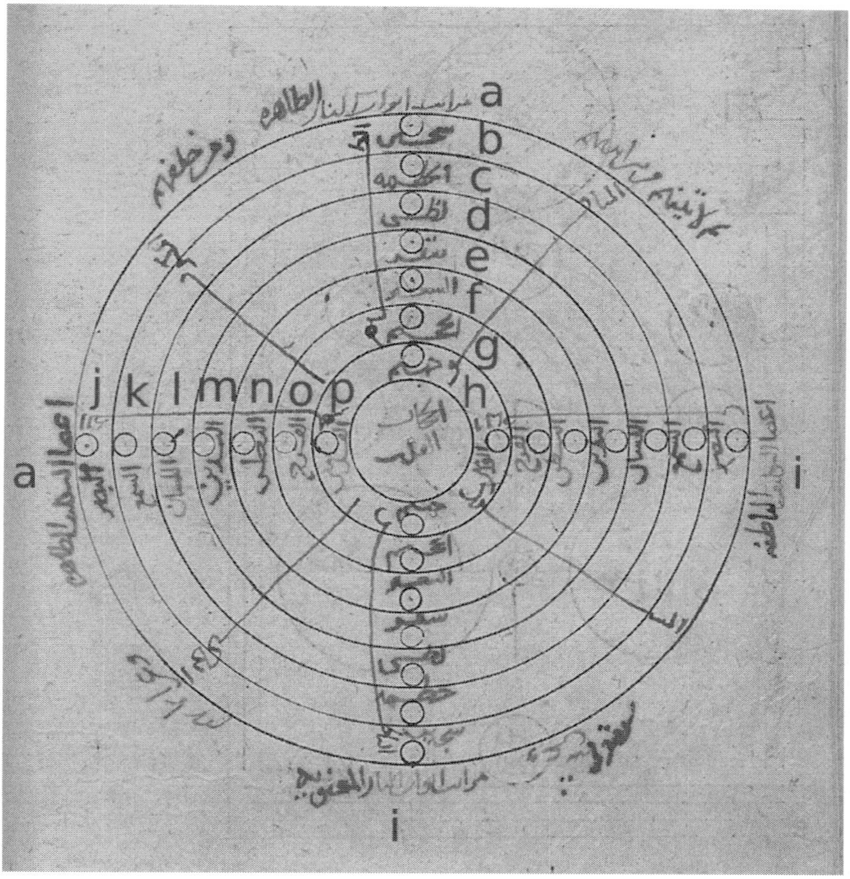

Fig. 50 The seven levels of hell. From top downwards: (a) outward levels of hell, (b) Sijjīn, the vehement hell, (c) al-Huṭama, the abode of crushing fire where hypocrites are punished, (d) Laẓā, where the fierce blaze consumes the bodies of sinners, (e) Saqar, the scorching fire which consumes the bodies but spares the bones of sinners, (f) al-Saʿīr, where the worshippers of fire are punished, (g) al-Jahannam – the deepest level of hell where the idol-worshippers are chained in fire, (h) Ḥamīm, surrounding the veil of the heart, and (i) inward levels of hell. The corresponding human faculties, from top downwards, were identified as: (j) seeing, (k) hearing, (l) speaking, (m) hands, (n) stomach, (o) private parts, (p) feet.

In another diagram, however, Ibn ʿArabī identifies sins and virtues that correspond to the highest degrees of paradise and the lowest degrees of hell (Fig. 51).

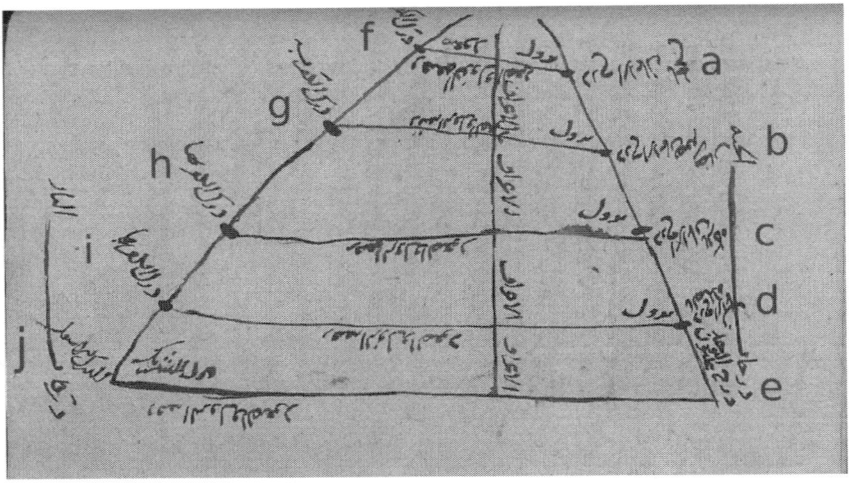

Fig. 51 The highest of virtues and the lowest of sins

Virtues, from top downwards: *(a) the rank of belief in pilgrimage, (b) the rank of belief in fasting, c(c) the rank of belief in alms, (d) the rank of belief in prayer, (e) the rank of belief in monotheism.*

Cardinal sins, from top downwards: *(f) the rank of disbelief in pilgrimage, (g) the rank of disbelief in Ramadan, (h) the rank of disbelief in alms, (i) the rank of disbelief in prayer, (j) polytheism, which leads to the lowest abode of hell.*

The Sphere of the Fixed Stars is the dwelling place of Riḍwān, the guardian of paradise, whose symbol is the letter *shīn* (ش). This sphere was thought to be static in its form and essence. This was due to the fact that there are no movements of celestial bodies to be detected on its surface. In this aspect, it resembles the Starless Sphere and the heavenly Throne and its Pedestal. In his commentary on the *Bezels of Wisdom*, Bosnevi referred to the Sphere of the Fixed Stars as the Throne of Life.[268] Ibn ʿArabī, however, perceived this sphere as the furthermost border of the corporeal world. In Ibn ʿArabī's works, invisibility equals transcendence. Spheres, which are invisible on their own, can only be detected due to the celestial bodies they contain. For this reason, Ibn ʿArabī occasionally compared the heavenly spheres to the letter *nūn*. This was due to the fact that the orthographic form of *nūn* is circular in shape. While one part of the circumference of *nūn*

268 Bosnevi, *Sharḥ Fuṣūṣ* vol.2, pp. 264–9.

is invisible, the other, visible part, stands for the material domain of existence. In this aspect, *nūn* resembles the heavenly spheres, which are only partially visible (i.e. we can detect the movement of the celestial bodies they contain). Apart from the celestial bodies, all other parts of the heavenly spheres are, without exception, invisible. In his *Book of Mīm*, Ibn ʿArabī observed that this can be compared to our immersion in the world of nature, where the darkness of the gross matter prevents us from detecting the world of spirits that corresponds to the upper, invisible part of the heavenly spheres and the orthographic form of *nūn*. In general, only traces of the ultimate reality can be seen by the naked eye. In *The Meccan Revelations,* the fixed stars are identified as the most distant objects the human eye can grasp. The Starless Sphere and the Throne and its Pedestal – all that is above the Sphere of the Fixed Stars – belong to the realm of transcendence due to the fact that they cannot be seen. In contrast, the Sphere of the Fixed Stars stands for immanence and the universe of composed things (*ʿalam al-tarkib*). As such, it was believed to be divided into twenty-eight mansions. Each of these mansions stands for a single day of the lunar phase cycle and one of the twenty-eight letters of the Arabic alphabet.

> He who is Exalted said: *As for the Moon, We have decreed for it mansions. This is the decree of the Inaccessible, the Knowing* (Q.36:38–9). The mansions cover the divisions which belong to the orbit of the zodiac, which the True, Exalted One, appointed for us, since the [naked] eye cannot distinguish these mansions. He made them twenty-eight degrees on the account of the letters of the Breath of the All-Merciful. We only mention this because people believe that there are twenty-eight letters because of these mansions, which determine the number of letters. However, according to us, it is the other way around: the number of mansions is determined by the number of letters.[269]

As the Moon travels through the twenty-eight mansions, it imbues the letters with its power. In return, the letters determine the properties of the zodiac constellations. Although Ibn ʿArabī taught that the lunar mansions are invisible to the naked eye, one of these mansions, the one associated with the letter *wāw*, is depicted on the margins of *The Meccan Revelations* (Fig. 52).

269 *Fut.*IV:103; al-Manṣūb, 6/283-4, *FM.*II:440.

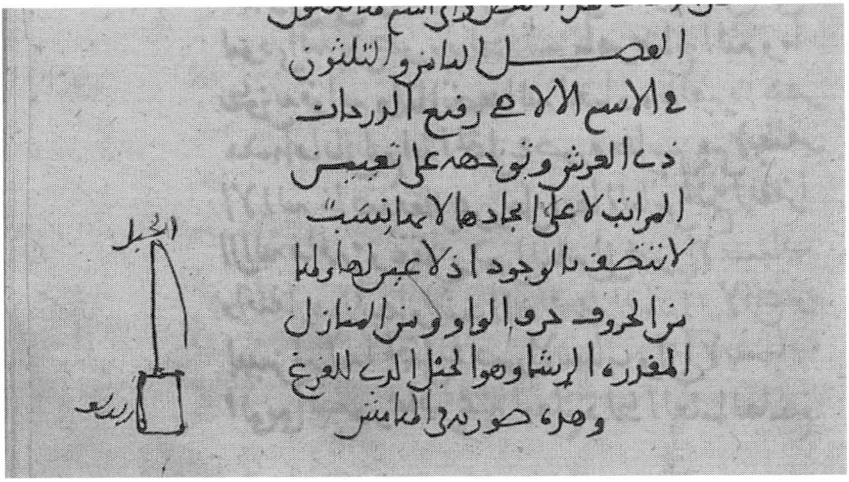

Fig. 52 The lunar mansion of the letter wāw

The lunar mansions divide the Sphere of the Fixed Stars into twenty-eight segments, each of which occupies 12° 51' degrees of the ecliptic circle. As such, they serve to document stages of the Moon's waxing and waning. 'The Moon has a mansion for each day [of the lunar phase cycle]. Thus it cuts across the ecliptic in twenty-eight days. (…). Its mansions are twenty-eight degrees because the letters of His Breath are twenty-eight.'[270] According to legend, Bedouins were able to pinpoint the position of the Moon by observing the stars around it. As the Moon rotates along its axis, its light conceals the nearby stars. The disappearance of different stars in the night sky was then used as a criterion to determine the position of the Moon along the ecliptic and estimate the size of its mansions. Since the Moon's path is within 5° of the ecliptic, the stars that were used to determine the position of the lunar mansions mostly belong to the zodiac constellations. *Sharaṭayn*, the first mansion, thus extends between 0° and 12° 11' 26" of the ecliptic circle. Its position is determined by bg Arietis, which belongs to the first segment of the Aries constellation. Al-Ṣūfī (d. 376/986), an eminent Shirazi astronomer, noted that Sharaṭayn came to be identified as the first lunar mansion due to its associations with Aries, the vernal equinox and the beginning of the solar year. This led Varisco to the conclusion that the two systems, the lunar mansions and zodiac constellations, were once seen as part of a larger cosmological

270 *Fut.*IV:112; al-Manṣūb, 6/297–8; *FM.*II:446–447.

whole.[271] Emilie Savage-Smith believed that notions of the lunar mansions in the pre-Islamic calendars and poetry have been chiefly inspired by the works of Indian astronomers and the *nákṣatra* system they established. However, other scholars linked these teachings to *hsiu*, the lunar mansions of the Chinese tradition, and the ancient Babylonian astronomy which might have served as an inspiration for the Chinese, Hindu and Bedouin narratives alike.[272] *Anwāʾ*, a popular ninth-century genre of literature, speculated that Bedouin tribes relied on lunar mansions to predict weather and mark the passage of time. However, Savage-Smith questioned the accuracy of this system by pointing out that there is actually little similarity between the visual representations of lunar mansions in medieval Islam and the actual positions of stars that determine their position.[273] As a matter of fact, lunar mansions were rarely represented on Islamic celestial globes and astrolabes. When they were, they were usually marked by small dashes intersecting the ecliptic (Fig. 53). On celestial maps, however, the lunar mansions are typically depicted above the zodiac constellations (Fig. 54).

However, two major obstacles make it difficult to ascertain the actual position of the lunar mansions and their correspondences with the zodiac constellations. The first of these obstacle springs from the fact that even when depicted, lunar mansions were primarily used as decorations. When documenting the position of the lunar mansions, astronomers rarely strived for precision. The second obstacle is the result of the fact that the stellar nomenclature that was used in pre-Islamic Arabia was different from the medieval works which were based on Ptolemy's *Almagest*. Even when they shared the same name, Bedouin star groupings did not necessarily correspond to the Ptolemaic constellations we know today. For example, as King pointed out, the constellation that was known among the Bedouins as Aquarius (*al-dalw*) covers large parts of the presently-recognized Aquarius constellation, Pegasus and Pisces.[274] In addition, on the celestial globes

271 al-Ṣūfī, *Kitāb ṣuwar al-kawākib*, p. 142.

272 See Savage-Smith, *Celestial Mapping*, pp. 31, 53 and King, *In Synchrony with the Heavens*, p. 119. Babylonian origins of the lunar mansions were, however, heavily disputed by Varisco. He asserted that there is no clear evidence in support of Savage-Smith's theory on the references of the lunar mansions in pre-Islamic poetry. Varisco, *Illuminating the Lunar Mansions*, pp. 493–4.

273 Savage-Smith, *Celestial Mapping*, p. 54.

274 King, *In Synchrony with the Heavens*, pp. 114–7. See also Ward, 'The Inscription on the Astrolabe by Abd al-Karim in the British Museum', p. 345.

Fig. 53 A thirteenth-century astrolabe with lunar mansions

and in Sufi manuscripts alike, Bedouin star groupings could overlie Ptolemaic constellations. Although medieval scholars commonly made assumptions about the size of the lunar mansions, these were mostly based on simple mathematical deductions (for example, 360 ÷ 28 =

Fig. 54 Ottoman celestial map with lunar mansions, zodiac constellations and the heavenly spheres

12.8, a common estimation of the size of each mansion in the works of medieval astronomers). Among the Sufis, astronomical observations were atypical. When it comes to Ibn ʿArabī's works, the positions of the lunar mansions were deemed to be as follows:

Ibn ʿArabī associated each of the twenty-eight lunar mansions with one of the Most Beautiful Names of God. These Names can be consulted in Table 14. He believed that each mansion was assigned an angelic spirit to guard it. The names of these angels correspond to the letters of the Arabic alphabet, 'with the first among them being the angel of the letter *hā'*, followed by the angel of the letter *hamza* and the angel of the unpointed letter *ʿayn* etc.'[275] While each of these angels

275 *Fut.*IV:115; al-Manṣūb, 6/304–5; *FM.*II:448.

Table 14 The Lunar Mansions

	Name of Mansion	Letter	Position of Mansion	Divine Name
1	*Sharaṭayn, the Two Signs*	*hamza*	*β γ Arietis*	*al-Badīʿ, the Incomparable*
2	*Buṭayn, the Belly of Aries*	*hāʾ*	*ε δ ρ Arietis*	*al-Bāʿith, the Resurrector*
3	*Thurayyā, the Many Little Ones*	*ʿayn*	*Pleiades*	*al-Bāṭin, the Inward*
4	*Dabarān, the Follower*	*ḥāʾ*	*α Tauri,*	*al-Ākhir, the Last*
5	*Haqʿa, the White Spot*	*ghayn*	*λ φ1 φ2 Orionis*	*al-Ẓāhir, the Outward*
6	*Hanʿa, the Mark*	*khāʾ*	*γ ξ Geminorum,*	*al-Ḥakīm, the Wise*
7	*Dhirāʿ, the Forearm*	*qāf*	*α β Geminorum*	*al-Muḥīṭ, the Encompassing*
8	*Nathra, the Gap of a Crib*	*kāf*	*ε γ δ Cancri, ʻthe star nathrā in the Cancer constellation*	*al-Shakūr, the Thankful*
9	*Ṭarf, the Glance*	*jīm*	*κ Cancri, λ Leonis, the ṭarf star*	*al-Ghaniyy, the Self-Sufficient*
10	*Jabha, the Forehead*	*shīn*	*ζ γ η α Leonis*	*al-Muqaddir, the Determiner*
11	*Zubra, the Mane*	*yāʾ*	*δ θ Leonis*	*al-Rabb, the Lord*
12	*Ṣarfa, the Changer*	*ḍād*	*β Leonis*	*al-ʿAlīm, the Omniscient*
13	*ʿAwwāʾ, the Barker*	*lām*	*β η γ δ ε Virginis, the ʻawwāʾ star*	*al-Qahhar, the Subduer*
14	*Simāk, the Unarmed*	*nūn*	*α Virginis*	*al-Nūr, the Illuminator*
15	*Ghafr, the Cover*	*rāʾ*	*ι κ λ Virginis, the gharfu star*	*al-Muṣawwir, the Fashioner*

	Name of Mansion	**Letter**	**Position of Mansion**	**Divine Name**
16	*Zubānā, the Claws*	*ṭā'*	*α β Librae, the two claws of Scorpio*	*al-Muḥsī, the Appraiser*
17	*Iklīl, Crown of the Forehead*	*dāl*	*β δ π Scorpii*	*al-Mubīn, the Clarifier*
18	*Qalb, the Heart*	*tā'*	*α Scorpii*	*al-Qābiḍ, the Constrictor*
19	*Shawla, the Sting*	*zāy*	*λ υ Scorpii, the stinger of Scorpio*	*al-Ḥayy, the Living*
20	*Na'ā'im, the Ostriches*	*sīn*	*σ φ τ ζ γ δ ε η Sagittarii, the na'ā'īm star*	*al-Muḥyī, the Life-giver*
21	*Balda, the City*	*ṣād*	*vacant space*	*al-Mumīt, the Destroyer*
22	*Sa'd al-dhābiḥ, the Fortune of Slayers*	*ẓā'*	*α β Capricorni*	*al-'Azīz, the Inaccessible*
23	*Sa'd bula'a, the Fortune of the Swallower*	*thā'*	*μ ε Aquarii*	*al-Razzāq, the Sustainer*
24	*Sa'd al-su'ūd, the Fortune of the Fortunate*	*dhāl*	*c1 Capricorni, β ξ Aquarii*	*al-Mudhill, the Abaser*
25	*Sa'd al-akhbiya, the Fortune of the Tents*	*fā'*	η ζ π γ*Aquarii*	*al-Qawī, the Strong*
26	*al-Fargh al-muqaddam, the First Spout*	*bā'*	*α β Pegasi*	*al-Laṭīf, the Subtle*
27	*al-Fargh al-thāni, the Second Spout*	*mīm*	*δ γ Pegasi*	*al-Jāmi', the Combining*
28	*Baṭn al-ḥūt, the Belly of the Fish*	*wāw*	*β Andromedae*	*al-Rāfi', the Exalter*

was entrusted with the protection of a letter whose name it shared, masters of the science of letters were thought to be able to use these letters to bind the angels to their will. Like the Bedouins of pre-Islamic Arabia, Ibn ʿArabī held that familiarity with the lunar mansions and their corresponding letters could also be used to influence weather. In the early seventh century CE, similar beliefs and practices were heavily condemned by the Prophet Muhammad. However, later jurisprudents eventually came to an agreement that while any kind of sorcery is strictly forbidden, it is still permissible to rely on the lunar mansions and fixed stars for time-telling and navigation.[276] In medieval Islam, space was thought to be determined by the boundaries of physical bodies. On his side, Ibn ʿArabī held that God created celestial bodies for human beings to rely on them for time-telling.[277] The movement of planets, elaborated by Bosnevi in his commentary on Ibn ʿArabī's *Bezels of Wisdom*, is akin to roads on earth, signalling directions and time.[278] While spheres turn so that we can determine time, the movement of celestial bodies is determined by the twenty-eight lunar mansions. By dividing the Starless Sphere into watch-towers, God provided human beings with the criteria for measuring time and navigation. From this sphere, Ibn ʿArabī believed, it is possible to speak of space and distance. The rotation of the heavenly spheres is to remain unchanged until Judgement Day, when dark clouds will be summoned to conceal the movements of the celestial bodies and 'a day will be like a month and a day like a week and the rest of his days will be like your days'.[279]

In Ibn ʿArabī's works, the notion of space, directions and orientation in space were also associated with the four jinn letters (*ʿayn, ghayn, sīn* and *shīn*). In his model of the universe, the Sphere of Saturn lies underneath the Sphere of the Fixed Stars. He associated the Sphere of Saturn with the prophet Abraham, Saturday and the Divine name *al-Rabb*, the Lord. In his works, this sphere is usually represented by the letter *yāʾ* (ي). Of this letter, al-Sulamī recorded the following:

> A certain Sufi said that while He made *alif* the first of the letters, *yāʾ* is the last. While *alif* stands for the oneness and singularity of God, *yāʾ* represents one man's poverty, obedience and worship. If you were to join the two letters together, *alif*, which is the first,

276 See Ibn al-Jawzī, *Aḥkām al-nisāʾ*, p. 166, and Ibn Qutayba, *K. al-Anwāʾ*, p. 14.
277 *Fut.*I:187; al-Manṣūb, 1/369; *FM.*I:120.
278 Bosnevi, *Sharḥ Fuṣūṣ* vol.2, p. 264.
279 *Fut.*I:440; al-Manṣūb, 2/130; *FM.*I;292.

and *yā'*, which is the last – but in reverse order, you would get *yā* (ي + ا = يا), an exclamation which is the manifestation of the act of worship the servants do before their Master by calling Him out: 'O God, O Benefactor, O Merciful!'. This is the goal of all sages and mystics, where the needs of sages are fulfilled and the exclamations of mystics are answered.[280]

Those who reach the Sphere of Saturn learn that, apart from jinn, no creature is destined for wretchedness – and that even among jinn, some are intended for salvation as His kindness takes precedence over His wrath. In the Sphere of Saturn, an adept learns to appreciate the beauty of creation and be grateful to God, the Creator of Beauty. Those who reach this sphere are taught what sets mankind apart from other living beings and thus get to acknowledge the excellence of human nature. They are informed how the creation of Adam was different from the creation of Eve and how the creation of Jesus differed from the creation of other children of Adam. In addition, they learn to interpret the act of genesis which involved both hands of God and resulted in the creation of mankind.[281] The Sphere of Saturn was identified as the dwelling place of Azrael, the angel of death and guardian of the gates of hell. Here grows *Sidrat al-muntahā*, the famous Lote tree. In the Qur'an, this tree is referred to as 'the Lote-tree of the Furthest Boundary' (Q.53:14). While its roots belong to the realms of hell, its branches reach to the heavenly gardens. This tree was said to bear two types of fruit: the sweet kind for the just souls of heaven and the bitter ones for the denizens of hell.[282] *Rā'* and *bā'*, the two letters that form the Divine Name *al-Rabb*, the Lord, stand for the sweet fruit and green leaves of this tree. The number of sweet fruits on its branches was said to correspond to the number of good deeds committed by the inhabitants of the heavenly gardens, while the numerous, sweet fruits of the Lote tree are greatly outnumbered by its sour fruits and thorns, which grow for every bad deed committed. In Ibn 'Arabī's works, the bitter fruit and infernal roots of the Lote tree are symbolized by the

280 al-Sulamī, *Sharḥ ma'ānī al-ḥurūf*, pp. 372–5. *Yā'*, the name of the letter, is pronounced the same as the exclamation for the vocative in Arabic (*yā Zayd*, O Zayd).

281 The act of genesis which involved the two hands was interpreted by al-Qashānī as the allegory for the dichotomy of the Divine nature – for He is simultaneously described as Gentle, Vanquisher, Beneficial, Harmful etc. Al-Qashānī also refers to this term as 'the red ruby', i.e. the blending of the soul's luminosity with the darkness of the body (*Glossary of Sufi Technical Terms*, p. 32).

282 Bosnevi, *Sharḥ Fuṣūṣ* vol.2, p. 264.

letters *alif, lām* and *hā'*, which form the Divine Name Allah. One reaps what one sows – and souls, quite literally, feast on the fruits of their deeds in the afterlife. In this model, *alif, lām* and *hā'* also stand for the archangel Gabriel and the light that shines around the Lote tree. On its branches, angels were said to receive records from the Preserved Tablet. As for the fragrance of this tree, it was said to originate from the divine name *al-Raḥmān* and the Breath of the All-Merciful.[283] While Ibn ʿArabī associated the Lote tree with the Sphere of Saturn, Bosnevi maintained that it is actually located between the seventh and eighth spheres. From the branches of this tree, the archangel Gabriel presides over the heavenly spheres and the corporeal world beneath. His true form is pure light, and he was thought to possess authority over the creatures born from the four elements.[284] In this aspect, archangel Gabriel is not an exception. Ibn ʿArabī taught that that what is high rules over what is low – a proposition which is, in this case, to be interpreted literally. Gabriel's residence is the Sphere of Saturn, the First Heaven. All spirits underneath this sphere fall under his dominion – and the same goes for every other spirit. In Ibn ʿArabī's model of the universe, one's place of residence can be taken as a clear indicator of one's rank in the universe.

Following the chapter on the Sphere of Saturn, Ibn ʿArabī's narratives on the heavenly spheres and their properties become noticeably shorter. In contrast to the elaborate discussions on the Starless Sphere, the Sphere of the Fixed Stars and the Sphere of Saturn, only a few paragraphs are dedicated to each of the spheres underneath. The discussion on the Sphere of Jupiter, which is the Second Heaven, opens with the following explanation:

> This discussion addresses the existence of this heaven and the remaining heavens and orbits, just as we did before, except for the fact that I will, from now on, just point out the specific property that is singled out for the heaven in question. As for this heaven [i.e. the Sphere of Jupiter], God inspires its order (amr) into it. Verily, it would be too lengthy to point out the specific order of each heaven and we have already discussed some of this in a substantial section in my book *al-Tanazzulāt al-Mawṣiliyya*.[285]

283 *Fut.*IV:107; al-Manṣūb, 6/290; *FM.*II:442.
284 Bosnevi, *Sharḥ Fuṣūṣ* vol.3, pp. 396, 423.
285 *Fut.*IV:110; al-Manṣūb, 6/296; *FM.*II.444.

Such a claim is a gross overstatement, however, as the section in question is only a few paragraphs long. As a result, little can be ascertained on the Sphere of Jupiter. In Ibn ʿArabī's works, this sphere is associated with knowledge, gentleness and compassion in general. As such, it was perceived as one of the stabilizing forces in the universe and the dwelling place of the angel Muqarrab. In addition, Ibn ʿArabī associated the Second Heaven with the Divine Name *ʿAllām*, the One Who Knows the unseen, and the letter *ḍād* (ض). This letter was thought to conceal 'strange knowledge which only a few know and the vast majority of people should not know at all'.[286] Moses, the prophet who presides over this sphere, entrusts adepts who reach it with the secret of his conversation with God. The conversation in question was recorded in the Sura *Ṭā Ḥā*:[287]

> *'What is in your right hand, O Moses?'*
>
> *He said: 'My staff. I lean upon it and bring down leaves for my sheep and I have no other use for it.'*
>
> *He (i.e. the Creator) said: 'Cast it down, O Moses.'*
>
> *Thus he cast it down and lo and behold, it became a snake, moving swiftly.*

As Ibn ʿArabī pointed out, one normally does not ask self-evident questions. God, the All-Knowing, had no need to ask any questions at all. No one knows what God wanted upon asking Moses what was in his hand – i.e. none except Moses himself and those singled out by God. The secret of *ḍād* is also the secret of perception. In the Qurʾan, Moses' staff turns into a snake. A staff is not a snake, and a snake is not a staff – and yet, one came to be transformed into the other[288]. The secret of perception requires that one comes to terms with this process and figures out how organic matter can transform from one form into another in such a way that it does not stop being either a snake or a staff for a single moment. This is the secret of the letter *ḍād*.[289]

286 Ibid. See also Bosnevi, *Sharḥ Fuṣūṣ* vol.2, p. 264.
287 Q.20:17–20.
288 *Fut.*III:418; al-Manṣūb, 5/491–2; *FM.*II:277–8.
289 Ibid.

Underneath the Sphere of Jupiter lies the Sphere of Mars. It was associated with the prophet Aaron and the Divine name *Qahhār*, the Subduer. Ibn ʿArabī taught that this is the sphere of awe, intensity, fear and problems. It is the place of the manifestation of strong, active forces and the Divine name *al-Qādir*, the Powerful One. In Ibn ʿArabī's works, the Sphere of Mars is associated with spilled blood, rage and the spoken letter *lām* (ل). As such, it was ruled by the angel al-Khāshi.[290]

In contrast, the Sphere of Sun was perceived as the sphere of life and fragrances. It was associated with the Divine Name *al-Muḥyī*, the Creator of Life, the prophet Idris and the letter *nūn* (ن). Of this letter and its sphere, Ibn ʿArabī recorded the following:

> It is from the realm of breaths and perfumes so it has a [special] way in the nasal passages which no other letters can use. It is a most noble letter.[291]

Like the letter *bā', nūn* was identified as the letter which stands for the act of coming together and the uniting of opposites since, when *nūn* is pronounced, the tongue and the upper palate come together.[292] This letter was compared by Jaʿfar ibn al-Ṣādiq to the light that was bestowed upon the Prophet Muhammad. From this light, all living beings were created.[293] In his commentary on *Bezels of Wisdom*, Bosnevi maintains that the Sphere of the Sun is the most supreme of all spheres (*falak al-aflāk*). Due to the fact that it occupies the central position in Ibn ʿArabī's model of the universe, with three planetary spheres above and below, the Sphere of the Sun also came to be identified as the heart of the world (*qalb al-ʿalām*) and the spiritual heart of the heavenly spheres.[294] As such, it was commonly compared to the heavenly Throne. The Sphere of the Sun was thought to conceal the secret of sexual union and the alternations of day and night. However, this sphere also stands for the living and the dead, love and kindness and all things seen and unseen. Ibn ʿArabī taught that this is the sphere of the *quṭb*, the Pole.[295] In his commentary on Ibn ʿArabī's *Bezels of Wisdom*, al-Qashānī identified the Pole Star as 'the locus of God's sight

290 See Bosnevi, *Sharḥ Fuṣūṣ* vol.2, p. 263, and *Fut.*IV:111; al-Manṣūb, 6/297; *FM.*II:445.

291 Ibn ʿArabī, *K. al-Bā'*, p. 13.

292 Ibid, p. 14.

293 al-Sulamī, *Ḥaqā'iq al-tafsir*, p. 167.

294 Bosnevi, *Sharḥ Fuṣūṣ* vol.2, pp. 263, 275.

295 *Fut.*IV:111; al-Manṣūb, 6/297–8; *FM.*II:445. Elmore, *Islamic Sainthood*, p. 454.

throughout the world and throughout all time'.[296] In Ibn ʿArabī's works, the *quṭb* is chiefly perceived as the symbol of stability. As such, it was occasionally identified with *alif.* Ibn ʿArabī's science of letters speaks of the twenty-eight letters and *alif.* In a similar way, his model of the universe has twenty-eight lunar mansions and the *quṭb*. This accounts for the total number of twenty-nine. Just as *alif*, the letter that is not a letter, enables the pronunciation of all other letters, the *quṭb*, which is no mansion, secures the stability of the twenty-eight mansions and the universe in general. Although invisible and, for the most part, unknown in terms of properties, its influence spreads throughout the world and supports it with divine energy (*himma*).

Underneath the Sphere of the Sun lies the Sphere of Venus, whose symbol is the letter *rāʾ* (ر). In Ibn ʿArabī's works, this sphere was associated with two Divine Names: *al-Laṭīf,* the Form-Giver, and *al-Wadūd*, the One who Loves Dearly. It was perceived as the domain of air, ruled by the prophet Joseph and angel by the name of *al-Jamīl.*[297] This heaven provides assistance to poets, craftsmen and composers. Those who reach it learn what it takes to produce a true piece of art and how beauty and attention to detail, once united, give birth to wisdom. From this sphere, the four humours (yellow bile, blood, phlegm and black bile) are orchestrated as they merge to form the human body and personality. Joseph, the prophet who presides over this sphere, holds the knowledge of imaginal forms. He teaches adepts how archetypes cross from imaginal to physical, from *Jabarūt* to *Mulk*, in order to be transformed into corporeal forms of existence. According to Ibn ʿArabī, this knowledge is transferred by means of symbols that 'show the years through the image of a bull; their abundant pasture in fatness, knowledge through the image of the milk and stability in religion through the image of a binding rope'.[298]

As for the Sphere of Mercury, underneath the Sphere of Venus, it came to be associated with the letter *ṭāʾ* (ط) and the Divine Names *al-Bāriʾ* (the Shaper), *al-Muḥṣī* (the Reckoner), *al-Ḥakīm* (the Wise) and *Sarīʿ al-ḥisāb* (Swift in Reckoning).[299] Here dwell *al-Nāshitat*, the class of angels whose main duty is to gently separate the soul from the body at the moment of death. In his commentary on *Bezels of Wisdom*, Bosnevi recorded that the commander of these angels is the angel by

296 al-Qashānī, *Glossary of Sufi Technical Terms*, p. 97.
297 Bosnevi, *Sharḥ Fuṣūṣ* vol.2, p. 270.
298 *Fut.*III:412. Akkach, *Cosmology and Architecture*, p. 35.
299 Bosnevi, *Sharḥ Fuṣūṣ* vol.2, p. 270.

the name of Rūḥ.[300] The Sphere of Mercury is the realm of Jesus, the prophet entrusted with the secret of breath, and John (Yahyā), who was entrusted with the secret of life. In Ibn ʿArabī's works, the breath – be it human or the Breath of the All-Merciful – is always associated with life. If it were not for the Breath, no life could exist. In a similar way, the two prophets, Jesus and Yahya (John), share the same heaven – for the secret of breath is also the secret of life.[301] In this heaven, adepts are able to determine their current step-level of spiritual development and compare it to the step-level of the Divine presence. Those who reach this sphere also learn how one idea can take many different forms. They are instructed in the mysteries of way-stations, spiritual stations and the secret of oneness. In Ibn ʿArabī's works, the Sixth Heaven is also associated with familiarity with *sīmīyāʾ*, whose primary medium, he maintained, are nouns and letters – and not, as some falsely believe, human blood and other occult instruments. However, the main lesson of the Sphere of Mercury is the secret of the creative word *kun.* In this place, adepts come to learn how Jesus the prophet used this word to revive the dead and breathe life into birds made of clay.[302] The secret of *kun* is the secret of creation. *The Tree of Being*, an apocryphal text misattributed to Ibn ʿArabī, contains the following passage on the creative word *kun*:

> The K of *kun* was the K of the treasure (*kanziyya*): 'I was a hidden treasure; I was unknown but I wanted to be known', and he saw the secret of the N, that it was the N of 'Yea, verily' (*anāniyya*): *Verily I am Allah, there is no deity save Me* (Q.20:14). Then when he was sure of the form of the letter and had become quite sure of the hope, there appeared to him from the K of the treasure the K of honouring (*takrīm*): *Verily We have honoured the children of Adam* (Q.27:70–72), and the K of 'I was' (*kuntu*): 'I was his hearing and his seeing and his hand.' Also from the N there was drawn forth for him the N of 'Yea, verily' (*anāniyya*) and the N of light (*nūr*): *And We appointed for him light* (Q.6:122), by which is attained the N of bounty (*niʿma*): *Would ye number the bounties of Allah ye would not be able to count them* (Q.14:34, 16:18). Iblis, on the other hand, may Allah curse him, spent 40,000 years in the School of

300 Ibid.

301 *Fut.*III:412; al-Manṣūb, 5/481; *FM.*II:274.

302 Ibid.

> Instruction examining the letters of *kun*. The Teacher left him to himself, letting him depend on his own strength and ability, so he used to look at the similitude of *kun* to see in its similitude the K of his own unbelief (*kufr*), so that *he exalted himself and disdainfully refused and became proud* (Q.2:34–32). Also he saw in it the N of his own fiery nature (*nār*): *Thou didst create me of fire* (Q.7:11–12, 37:76–77), by which are attained the K of his unbelief and the N of his fiery nature: *so that they are hurled down into it* (i.e. into Hell Fire, Q.26:94).[303]

In his *Book of Mīm*, Ibn ʿArabī recorded that *Kun* is the essence which gives birth to existence (*kawn*).[304] All things in existence emerge from *kāf*, *damma* and *nūn*, the three letters that form the word *kun*. In light of the fact that God used three letters to create the world, Ibn ʿArabī warned those who have plundered the secrets of the Sphere of Mercury that, theoretically speaking, it would be strictly forbidden to use only one letter in similar endeavours. An explanation why this is the case was provided in his *Book of Mīm*:

> The Divine command [*kun*] is expressed by three letters since every creative manifestation implies the intervention of three elements: syllogism, corporal engendering and, in principle, the manifestation of particular essences.[305]

The creative word *kun* contains two consonants and a vowel. The consonants, *kāf* and *nūn*, stand for the Creator and the created. The vowel, *ḍamma*, is what lies in between. Together, these letters stand for the Divine presence in general. Ibn ʿArabī taught that the Divine presence consists of the Divine Essence, Divine Acts and Divine attributes. In this model, *alif*, the Divine Essence, is represented by the letter *kāf*. Its creation is *nūn*, the material world. As for *ḍamma*, the 'moving' vowel of the creative word *kun*, it stands for Divine attributes and the notion of the *barzakh*. This term, Ibn ʿArabī cautioned, is notoriously hard to comprehend. In his works, it covers every border and every line of separation. The *barzakh* is the threshold between life and death, positive and negative, unknown and known. It is something that separates two things and, at the same time, combines the attributes

303 Jeffrey, *Ibn al-Arabi's Shajarat al-Kawn*, pp. 65–6.

304 Ibn ʿArabī, *K. al-Mīm*, fol.18.

305 Ibn ʿArabī, *K. al-Mīm*, fol.15.

of both. Ibn ʿArabī thus compared it to a form in the mirror that both is and is not the observer.[306] As such, the *barzakh* is rarely visible. 'We know that some separator exists, but the eye cannot perceive it. However, the mind feels its presence even if one cannot grasp what the *barzakh* really is.'[307] Between light and darkness, the *barzakh* is the shadow. In other words, *kāf*, the Creator, is the essence whose shadow is the existence (*kawn*). In this model, the symbol of that shadow is the letter *wāw*. Ibn ʿArabī associated the letter *wāw* in *kawn* with the Divine Name *Huwa*, 'He' (Fig. 55). In *The Meccan Revelations*, this letter emerges as one of the main symbols of the *barzakh*. In the *Book of Mīm*, however, Ibn ʿArabī recorded that 'between us and God the most High lies a shadow. This shadow is the veil of *kun*.'[308] The symbolism of both *wāw* and *ḍamma* thus came to be attributed to the word *kun* in general. In Ibn ʿArabī's works, this vowel also stands for the Perfect Human, the ultimate symbol of the *barzakh*, 'who is the link between the Truth and the creation by the virtue of his affinity to both'.[309] This insight eventually came to be depicted in the margins of *The Meccan Revelations*:

Fig. 55 The Divine Name Huwa, He

> During the night when I was writing this section [on the sphere of Mercury], on the fourth night of the month Rabiʿ al-ākhir in the year 627H, Wednesday night on the twentieth of February (Shubāṭ), I saw in a spiritual revelation the outward form of [the word] the Divine 'He-ness' (*huwiyya*) and its inwardness, in a vision I verified for myself. Never have I seen such a vision in any revelation of mine. From the vision there came to me knowledge, pleasure and delight such as cannot be conveyed to those who have not tasted it. How beautiful a spiritual event

306 *Fut.*I:459, 461; al-Manṣūb, 2/459; *FM.*I:304.

307 *Fut.*II:422, al-Manṣūb.IV: 15; *FM.*I:667.

308 Ibn ʿArabī, *K. al-Mīm*, fol.18.

309 Al-Qashānī, *Glossary of Sufi Technical Terms*, p. 19. Ibn 'Arabī's notion of the Perfect Man, as the mirror of the Creator and the synthesis of all divine names, will be examined in detail in the chapter on the isolated letter *wāw*.

> it was! Such a vision has no falsehood in it, it cannot be made lower or higher. I have drawn its image in the margin just as it is and whoever depicts it cannot alter it. Its shape was a white light on a red carpet.[310]

Underneath the Sphere of Mercury, which holds the secret of *kun*, lies the Sphere of the Moon. Due to its proximity to the Earth, Ibn ʿArabī also referred to this sphere as 'the closest heaven'. In his works, this sphere is associated with the letter *dāl* (د) and the Divine Name *al-Khāliq*, the Creator. Here lives the soul of Adam, the first man, from the time of his death. However, the Sphere of the Moon is also the domain of the angel known as *al-Mujtabā*, the Chosen One, who serves as the deputy of the archangel Gabriel. In his commentary on the *Bezels of Wisdom*, Bosnevi also refers to this angel as Ismāʿīl, the Creating Mind. It is however important to take into account that, in Ibn ʿArabī's works, the Sphere of the Moon was primarily associated with the prophet Adam. Although they share the same name, the angelic spirit by the name of Ismāʿīl was thought to be completely unrelated to the prophet Ismāʿīl. His was the dominion over Earth, the world of creation and confusion. Like any other spirit, Ismāʿīl is powerless to exercise his authority above his place of residence – and his sphere was deemed to be the most insignificant of all heavenly spheres. Due to its insignificance, the Sphere of the Moon rotates with great speed around its axis. In another place, however, Bosnevi asserts that the Sphere of the Moon is cold and wet in nature. As it borders the Orbit of Fire, the interaction between the two induces it to rotate as fast as it does.[311]

Below the Sphere of the Moon extends the Orbit of Fire. The orbits of Air, Water and Earth lie beneath it. None of these orbits is, however, to be mistaken for one of the elements which form organic matter – for Ibn ʿArabī believed that the existence of the four elements precedes the creation of orbits that came to be named after them.[312] He taught that the Sphere of the Moon is directly connected to the Orbit of Fire. In his works, this orbit is commonly referred to as the sea filled with fire (*al-baḥr al-masjūr*). In contrast, the Sphere of Moon was perceived as the place of utmost coldness. Through the interplay between this sphere and the fiery orbit underneath, animals, minerals

310 *Fut.*IV:118; al-Manṣūb, 6/ 309; *FM.*II:449.

311 Bosnevi, *Sharḥ Fuṣūṣ* vol.3, p. 369. See also Bosnevi, *Sharḥ Fuṣūṣ* vol.2, p. 270.

312 *Fut.*IV:118; al-Manṣūb, 6/309-10; *FM.*II:449.

and plants thrive on Earth.[313] In Ibn ʿArabī's works, the Orbit of Fire is associated with the Divine Name *al-Qābiḍ*, the Restricting, and the letter *tāʾ* (ت). In his commentary on the *Bezels of Wisdom*, al-Qashānī noted that this letter stands for the divine Essence – 'as seen from the viewpoint of specific individuations and multiplicity'.[314] The Orbit of Fire is the home of *al-Sābiqāt*, the class of angels named for their tendency to 'fulfil their orders in a hurry'. Ibn ʿArabī claimed to have seen how jinn sneak up to the Orbit of Fire to spy on *al-Sābiqāt* angels in order to learn some of the secrets they received by means of revelations. However, they are quickly banished by comets.[315] In Bosnevi's commentary on the *Bezels of Wisdom*, fire came to be described as the strongest of all elements. For according to Bosnevi, while fire has impact on every single element, there is no element that can influence fire.[316]This was, however, far from the truth. Writing on the Orbit of Air, Ibn ʿArabī recorded the following *ḥadīth qudsī*:

> When God created the Earth, it started shaking. Thus He created mountains and set them down on Earth. God's angels, full of awe at the strength of these mountains, asked if there is anything stronger than the mountains. He said: 'Yes, iron.' Then they asked if there is anything stronger than iron. He said: 'Yes, fire.' Then they asked if there is anything stronger than fire. He said: 'Yes, water.' And they asked Him if there is anything stronger than water. And He said: 'Yes, air.'[317]

Apart from human beings, Ibn ʿArabī believed, there is not a single force in the universe that is more powerful than air. In his works, this Orbit was described as the root of all life. For this reason, it came to be associated with the Divine Name *al-Ḥayy*, Living, and the letter *zāy* (ز). Its secret is the secret of receptivity and comparison. Due to the fact that air was believed to be warm and moist in nature, the Orbit of Air was believed to be unconnected to any of its neighbouring orbits. For while moistness does not allow it to merge with the orbit of Fire, the warmth of its nature keeps it away from the Orbit of

313 *Fut.*IV:97; al-Manṣūb, 6/271; *FM.*II:436.

314 al-Qashānī, *Glossary of Sufi Technical Terms*, p. 106.

315 For this and other classes of angels, see Q 79:1–5. For jinn and the comets, see Q 72:6–8. See also *Fut.*IV:118–9; al-Manṣūb, 6/309-10; *FM.*II:450.

316 Bosnevi, *Sharḥ Fuṣūṣ* vol.2, p. 271–2.

317 *Fut.*IV:119; al-Manṣūb, 6/313; *FM.*II:450. See also Ibn ʿArabī, *Divine Sayings,* p. 26.

Water. From this orbit, *al-Ra'd*, the angel of thunder, coordinates the efforts of angels who are in charge of protecting the people from sin.[318] Underneath his domain is the Orbit of Water. Ibn ʿArabī associated this orbit with life and purity in general. His teachings were primarily based on the Qurʾan, where it was recorded how the rain, heaven sent, fortifies the hearts and purifies mankind from the defilements of Satan. In the eighth verse of the Sura *al-Anfāl*, it is also said that God sent down heavy rains to drench the desert sand before the battle of Badr so that the Muslim soldiers could advance. Based on these narratives, Ibn ʿArabī recorded the following:

> When impurity based on doubts is banished by water that was sent down by God, the foulness based on ignorance perishes and the gauzy veil is lifted from the heart. You will come to see with your own eyes the angelic realms in heaven and earth, and your essence will be fortified by knowledge and you will know the significance of each breath and movement. You will make use of knowledge, heavenly sent, the knowledge that cleansed you in the water which He made descend outwardly as a sign of its impact on the inward.[319]

In the same way as he provided footholds for soldiers during the battle of Badr, God fortifies hearts that are pure. As a result, water came to be identified as the remover of doubts, impurity and ignorance. In Ibn ʿArabī's works, it was associated with the Divine Name *al-Muḥyī*, the Life-Giver and the letter *sīn* (س).[320] In his *Bezels of Wisdom*, Ibn ʿArabī describes *sīn* as 'one of the extra letters (*zawāʾid*)', based on its grammatical function which he reads into a Qurʾanic verse of the Pharaoh to Moses:

> '*If you take any god other than me, we shall put you among the imprisoned* (*masjūnīn*)' (Q.26:29). The letter 's' in the word *sijn* is one of the extra letters, so in other words: 'we shall cause you to be concealed, for by what you affirmed about me, you have forced me to say to you what I have said to you.'[321]

---

318 Bosnevi, *Sharḥ Fuṣūṣ* vol.2, p. 273.
319 *Fut.*IV:122; al-Manṣūb, 6/316; *FM.*II:453.
320 *Fut.*IV:123–124; al-Manṣūb, 6/316; *FM.*II:453.
321 *Fuṣūṣ*, p. 196.

The Orbit of Water was thought to be inhabited by *al-Tāliyāt*, angels whose main duty is to help mankind to refrain from sin. They are ruled by al-Zājir ('the One who restrains from sin'), an angel whose dominion extends to the domain of Earth.[322] Ibn 'Arabī believed that God created the Earth in two days and designated it to serve as a nourisher for the human beings, animals, plants and minerals. Although it occupies the lowest position in the hierarchy of heavenly spheres, the creation of the Earth was thought to precede the emergence of the Orbit of Water, Air and Fire:

> Of the four pillars, the Earth was the first to be created. Air was next, followed by fire and the seven heavens. The reports of God, the Exalted One, concerning the Earth necessarily imply that the Earth is intelligent – for He describes it as speaking and refusing. He addresses the Earth and it speaks back to Him and He describes it as obeying, taking and enveloping in order to point out its knowledge and intelligence.[323]

In the works of Ibn 'Arabī, the Earth is associated with the Divine Name *al-Mumīt*, the Destroyer, and the letter *ṣād* (ص). The letter *ṣād*, which is also the title of the thirty-eighth sura of the Qur'an, describes the circularity of trial, retribution and ultimate forgiveness within the all-embracing Compassion. In other places, *ṣād* is linked to the divine Pen and Protected Tablet (*al-lawḥ al-maḥfūẓ*) and the heart of the Perfect Human. Ibn 'Arabī came to learn of the secrets of this letter in a dream (Fig. 56). The dream in question was however received by Abū Yaḥyā Babkar al-Hashmī al-Tuwaytimī, who was one of Ibn 'Arabī's followers who confided in him:

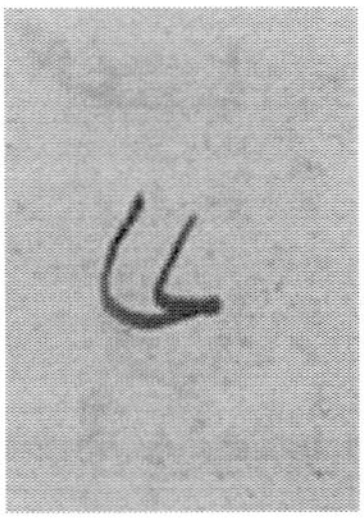

Fig. 56 The state of sleep, as depicted in the margin of The Meccan Revelations

322 Bosnevi, *Sharḥ Fuṣūṣ* vol.2, p. 274.
323 *Fut.*IV:124; al-Manṣūb, 6/320; *FM.*II:453.

Last night, I had a dream. While I was sitting, you were lying on your back in front of me and speaking of the *ṣād*. I recited an improvised poem to you:

Ṣād is the letter overlooking all – and the *ṣād* in the *ṣād* is more truthful still.
In my dream, you said to me: 'what proof of it do you have?'
I said: 'The *ṣād* has a circular shape and nothing takes precedence over the circle.'[324]

Having heard 'the good news', Ibn ʿArabī rejoiced. For while the revelation was received by his student, not for one moment did he doubt that it was actually intended for him. In al-Tuwaytimī's dream, he was lying on his back. This is the posture of relaxation one would normally assume after a day of hard work and 'the position of the prophet, ready to receive whatever Heaven grants him'. Thus he interpreted that the revelation was intended for him, as a blessing of the prophets.[325] Ibn ʿArabī taught that *ṣād* is the letter of truth (*ṣidq*), well-formed and guarded. In his works, *ṣād* is described as 'the great noble letter'. He believed that this letter is referred to in the Qurʾanic revelation: *We forgave him that and he had access to Our Nearness and a fine journey's end* (Q.38:25). According to Ibn ʿArabī, the letter *ṣād*, and the sura in question, speak of the prophets, mysteries of the world and hidden, strange signs and wonders.[326] The complete, full circles of the letters *ṣād* and *ḍād* take us even deeper into the secret of timelessness than *nūn* – alas, the secret of this orthography is forbidden to be disclosed in writing. This secret is only for the ears of a gnostic (*ʿārif*), whose submission is beyond question – even the *nūn* and its secret, once verified 'will appear strange wonders which will bewilder the intellect with the splendour of their beauty'.[327] In his commentary on the *Bezels of Wisdom*, Bosnevi recorded that all elements and kingdoms of the universe are subjected to Earth. According to Bosnevi, God carefully watches over the Earth – for this is the home of the four species of the universe: humans, animals, plants and minerals.[328]

324 *Fut.*I:114; al-Manṣūb, 1/220; *FM.*I:71.
325 Ibid.
326 Ibid.
327 *Fut.*I:89; al-Manṣūb, 1/181; *FM.*I:54.
328 Bosnevi, *Sharḥ Fuṣūṣ* vol.2, p. 274.

2.6. *Ẓā', Thā', Dhāl, Fā', Bā' and Mīm: the Six Kingdoms*

Ibn 'Arabī held that there are six species in the universe: angels, jinn, humans, plants, animals and minerals. In his works, these are commonly referred to as the six kingdoms. Out of the six kingdoms of the universe, four were thought to be located on Earth. These are the human, animal, plant and mineral kingdoms. As their kingdoms belong to Earth, the bodies of the aforementioned species are built of fire, water, air and earth. 'These kingdoms,' Ibn 'Arabī recorded, 'receive their nourishment from the four elements and there is mutual sharing between them. If something in the creation would seek out nourishments for its body, which is composed of the four elements, from something other than these elements, it would not be able to receive it.'[323] Apart from human beings, the minerals, plants and animals are also among the servants of God. Ibn 'Arabī taught that all creatures of the Earth, down to the lowest of worms, live to celebrate the Creator. For this reason, each kingdom of the Earth has received divine messengers and a letter of the alphabet as its symbol. In this regard, minerals are not an exception, in spite of the fact that their nature was thought to be inert.

> Compulsion is inducement of the created to do something that is within its power to resist. However, a mineral is never compelled to obedience. There is no need for it since it would be unimaginable that a mineral could stir to action on its own. This is evident even to the rational mind.[324]

While the inert nature of minerals makes it unlikely that they could turn to sin, they are also among the species the divine messengers were sent to.[325] In Ibn 'Arabī's works, minerals are represented by the letter *ẓā'* (ظ) and the Divine Name *al-'Azīz*, the Inaccessible. Ibn 'Arabī described minerals as 'masters of the Divine protocol and teachers of good manners'.[326] By their nature, minerals are somewhat akin to God, as they are (mostly) immune to the passage of time. However, Ibn 'Arabī taught that the nature of minerals is also prone to sickness. He taught that sicknesses in both human beings and

323 *Fut.*I:148; al-Manṣūb, 1/308; *FM.*I:96.

324 *Fut.*I:70; al-Manṣūb, 1/150; *FM.*I:42.

325 *Fut.*I:225; al-Manṣūb, 1/420; *FM.*II:147.

326 *Fut.*IV:132; al-Manṣūb, 6/337; *FM.*II:460.

minerals are to be attributed to deficiencies and imbalances of the four elements that form their bodies. He also believed that brass, iron and lead are especially prone to sicknesses which manifest on their surface in the form of rust. Just as a doctor would seek to balance the four elements with remedies in order to secure the health of a human body, each mineral seeks to balance its structure in order to be transmuted into gold. This is the ultimate goal of every specimen of the mineral kingdom. While some minerals are known to have been transmuted in a split second, as if by chance, others have spent aeons attempting to reach this goal. In this aspect, the transmutation process is akin to the spark of divine revelation. Sometimes however, humans were thought to be able to play a hand in this process:

> Everything that comes into being as a mineral seeks to evolve into perfect completion – and this is gold. (...) A wise man (*ḥakīm*) provides knowledge of remedies and medicines to remove an illness when it occurs, depending on the personality of a patient and the degree of perfection [of a mineral] – and when it comes to minerals, this is gold. This is how he removes the sickness and rectifies and adjusts a mineral until it reaches perfection.[327]

While the inert nature of minerals has been commonly compared to plants, Ibn ʿArabī noted that the major difference between the two is reflected in the fact that plants are in a state of constant growth. Growth, he observed, can be identified as a steady movement of plants, with their branches constantly reaching upwards as their roots dig downwards, deeper into the soil. While gold was perceived as the most noble of minerals, among plants, this status belongs to the date palm. For, according to legend, when God created Adam in his own form, some clay remained after the process was completed. God used this clay to create the date palm. 'For this reason,' Ibn ʿArabī believed, 'the date palm is a sister to Adam, peace be upon him, and it is our aunt. The Law refers to the date palm as "aunt", links it to the believer and to it belong the mysteries that do not belong to other plants.'[328] Having created the date palm, God realized that some more clay still remained, 'hardly visible, like the measure of a sesame seed'.[329] Thus He extended

327 *Fut.*I:233; al-Manṣūb, 1/433; *FM.*I:152.
328 *Fut.*I:195; al-Manṣūb, 1/379; *FM.*I:126.
329 Ibid.

the remaining clay to create one of the seven earths that ʿAbd Allāh b. ʿAbbās was referring to.[330] This earth was a place unlike any other. If the heavenly Throne, Pedestal, heaven and hell were to be placed next to it, they would be like 'a ring tossed in a desert of this earth. Hers are the strange things and wonders that cannot be measured, and its station overwhelms the intellect'.[331] Ibn ʿArabī described his visit to God's Great Earth in the first chapter of *The Meccan Revelations*, where he states that plants, animals and minerals he encountered in God's Great Earth are unlike anything anyone has seen before. Among its greatest wonders are the ocean of dust with its stone ships, which eventually came to be depicted in the margins of *The Meccan Revelations*:

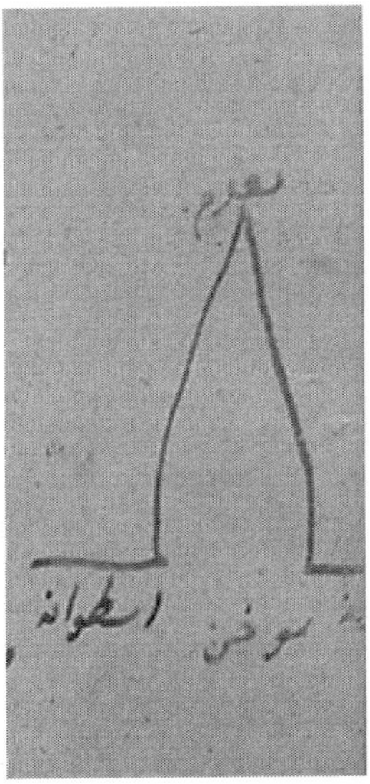

Fig. 57 Stone ship of God's Great Earth

> In that world I saw an ocean of sand, flowing like water, and I saw stones small and large flowing towards one another, like iron flows towards a magnet. When they came together, they could not come apart without someone intervening, just as when one takes the iron away from the magnet without the magnet being able to hold on. But if one fails to separate them, these stones continue to stick to one another at a set distance; when they are all joined, they have the form of a ship. I myself saw a small vessel with two hulls. When a boat is thus constructed, its

330 See the previous chapter for the discussions on ʿAbd Allah b. ʿAbbās and the seven heavens and earths of the Islamic normative tradition.

331 *Fut.*I:195; al-Manṣūb, 1/379; *FM.*II:126.

> passengers jump into the sea, and then they embark for wherever they wish. The deck of the vessel is made of grains of sand or of dust, soldered together in a special way. I have never seen anything so marvellous as these stone vessels floating on an ocean of sand![332]

In Ibn 'Arabī's works, plants are commonly compared to the letter *thā'* (ث) and the jewellery adorning the Earth.

> The Earth is adorned with the finery of its flowers and the vestments of her plants and her abundant blessing comes forth; and the eyes of the creation are blessed with her splendid sight, and their noses with her breezes and their throats with her pure food.[333]

While some animals thrive on plants that would prove to be poisonous for other species, some plants grow where others could not. For this reason, the kingdom of plants came to be associated with the Divine Name *al-Razzāq*, the Sustainer of all living beings.[334] While minerals are distinguishable by their simple corporeal form, plants require nourishment to thrive. However, both plants and minerals are devoid of senses. As such, they were thought to be deaf, blind, unintelligent and mute. Once a corporeal form has been endowed with the five senses and a need for nourishment, the created being is referred to as an 'animal'. In Ibn 'Arabī's works, animals are represented by the letter *dhāl* (ذ) and the Divine Name *al-Mudhill*, the Abaser. He attributed this name to two verses: one from the Sura *Yā Sīn*, and the other from the Sura *al-Jāthiyah*. In *The Meccan Revelations*, these verses are quoted as a single line of verse which reads: *We tamed them for them [i.e. We tamed animals for humans], and thus some of them they ride on and some of them they eat and We have subjected to you whatever is in heavens and earth – all from Him! Verily, these are the signs for those who know.*[335] In accordance with the Islamic normative tradition, Ibn 'Arabī held that all species of the universe are subjected to the authority of human beings. In this aspect, angels

332 *Fut.*I:198–199; al-Manṣūb, 1/384; *FM.*II:129. See also Addas, 'The Ship of Stone', Journal of the Muhyiddin Ibn 'Arabi Society, 1996. Accessed online 26 January 2021.
333 *Fut.*I:18; al-Manṣūb, 1/74; *FM.*I:4.
334 *Fut.*IV:136; al-Manṣūb, 6/341; *FM.*II:462.
335 For the original references, see Q.36:72 and 45:13.

are not an exception. Although they do not lack in intelligence, angels were created to be obedient. They have no need of messengers since their obedience to God is unwavering. For this reason, the spiritual ascension of angels is possible only through the increase of knowledge and not through the accumulation of good deeds and virtues. However, although the increase of knowledge is not forbidden to angels, their learning capacity appears to be limited. Diligent and obedient, they are familiar with a few Divine Names only – those they can use to praise God. Other Divine Names, more terrifying, are unknown to them and they seem to be incapable of learning.[336]

In Ibn ʿArabī's works, angels are associated with the letter *fāʾ* (ف) and the Divine Name *al-Qawī*, the Strong. They are the creatures of light that see that God's will is being done. According to legend, while seven angels are required to ensure the growth of a single leaf, one angel accompanies every drop of rain. The most powerful among the angels were thought to be created from the breath of women, 'as this is the most powerful of all breaths'.[337] Out of the twenty-eight letters of the Arabic alphabet, eighteen were thought to belong to angels. The Arabic word for angel, *malak*, means a messenger – and Ibn ʿArabī taught that the number of angelic letters implies that the main duty of angels is to serve as intermediaries between God and the world. To prove his point, he specified that the world was created in six days. When six is multiplied by three, the number which stands for the three worlds of *Mulk*, *Malakūt* and *Jabarūt*, the result is eighteen – which is the number of angelic letters (3 x 6 = 18). In his works, Ibn ʿArabī speaks of three human and three divine letters. When the number of divine letters is multiplied by three, the result is nine. This is the so-called *aflāq iqlāʾ*, the knowledge God grants to men. In Ibn ʿArabī's works, the number 9 can also stand for *aflāq al-talaqqī*, i.e. for man's receptiveness towards God. In this model, angels are the subtle connection (*raqāʾiq*) between the two - 'and wherever the human world meets the Divine, an angel is their meeting point. It is at this point that each angel comes to existence.'[338] By their upward, downward and horizontal movements between men and God, angels set the universe in motion (Fig. 58). For this reason, Ibn ʿArabī compared them to the Breath of the All-Merciful and the short vowels that 'move' the consonants in sentences.

336 *Fut.*I:392; al-Manṣūb, 2/56; *FM.*I:259

337 *Fut.*IV:142–3; al-Manṣūb, 6/353; *FM.*II:466.

338 Ibn ʿArabī, *Meccan Revelations* vol.2, p.156.

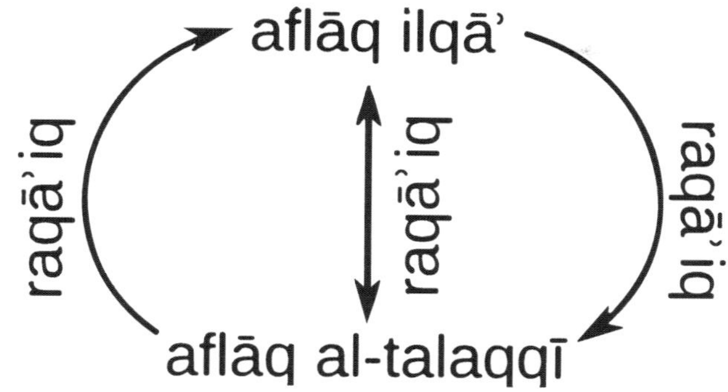

Fig. 58 Angels as raqā‘iq: the subtle connection between God and men

Ibn ‘Arabī taught that the angelic nature is somewhat akin to the nature of jinn. He believed that jinn were created 60,000 years before the creation of Adam took place. In his works, the isolated letter *bā’* is used as a recurring symbol for the kingdom of jinn. According to Chodkiewicz, Sufis maintained that this letter stands for ‘the world of secrets’, ‘the world of light’ and ‘the medial position between the setting and the rising Sun’ – and its colour was thought to be between brown and yellow.[339] While angels were created from light, jinn were the creatures of fire. Although their fiery bodies resemble the light of the angelic nature, jinn need organic food to survive. For this reason, they are commonly referred to as ‘the heavy ones’. Except when warned by God and the prophets, human beings are mostly unaware of the presence of jinn. This is how they came to be associated with the Divine Name *Laṭīf*, the Subtle. When revealed, jinn appear to the naked eye as a smoking blaze of fire. This is due to the fact that, in order to create jinn, God mixed fire with air. Created by means of air, jinn were thought to reproduce by casting air into the wombs of female jinn. Since other elements mingle with fire in the constitution of jinn, their nature draws them to the corporeal world. Jinn tend to meddle in the affairs of people – and sometimes, evil jinn nest in the hearts of men and compel them to sin. The fiery nature of jinn often makes them arrogant and destructive. As a dominant element of jinn nature, fire seeks to grow, subdue and burn bright – for it is the most elevated in rank among the elements. As a result, fire becomes the source of

339 Chodkiewicz, *An Ocean Without Shore*, p. 69.

their downfall – for in the Qur'an, the Sura *al-Dhāriyāt* reads how God created jinn only to worship Him.[340]

What jinn fail to notice is that the water and clay that were mixed to create Adam are more powerful than fire due to the stability of earth and the cold nature of water. Since Adam had power and stability on his side, God ordered jinn to prostrate themselves in front of him.[341] Of the six species of the universe, humans were the last to be created. In spite of this fact, their spiritual rank was thought to be the highest. Just as the sequence of the letters of the Arabic alphabet goes on until it reaches the letter *mīm*, the creation of humans was perceived as the ultimate goal to which the universe was heading from the beginning, when the First Intellect (*hamza*) appeared in the world.

> Between the two arcs of the circle stands the entirety of what God has created – that is, the species of the world, between the First Intellect, which is the Pen, and the human being, which is the last thing to be created.[342]

Ibn ʿArabī taught that human beings were created in order to bring together all truths of the universe.[343] In his *Commentary on the Most Beautiful Names of God* (*Sḥarh asmāʾ Allāh al-ḥusnā*) al-Qushayrī (d. 465/1074) recorded that that the following legend was circulating among the Sufis:

> It has been narrated in the tradition and lore how God created 600 wings for the archangel Gabriel, prayers and peace be upon him, and had them inlaid with sapphires, pearls and golden bells and suffused them with musk. Each bell has a sublime sound and tone to it, unlike any other. When the archangel Israfil sings his praises to God, he interrupts angelic choirs due to the sublime sound of his voice. In a similar fashion, the light of the heavenly Throne, were it to appear in front of us, would outshine the light of the Sun to the same degree as the Sun would outshine a lamp. There are other examples of created things, yet God, may He be praised, never said of any other thing that they were in the best of forms, nor did he say to any of them: '*Indeed, I created you*

340 Elmore, *Islamic Sainthood*, p. 365. The original reference can be found at Q 51:56.
341 *Fut.*I:202; al-Manṣūb, 1/388–9; *FM.*I:131; Q 18:50.
342 *Fut.*I:193–194; al-Manṣūb, 1/376; *FM.*I:125.
343 *Fut.*III:226; al-Manṣūb, 5/116–7; *FM.*II:150.

> *in the best of forms!*' (Q 95: 4). However, He said all of this to human beings He created from clay. But enough of the things in nature. Let us move on the words of the Exalted One: '*He loves them and they love Him*' (Q 5: 54). Did He ever say something like this to one of the angels or to any other beautiful thing? No, never! He said that only of the children of Adam. It was a blessing bestowed upon them above all others by the grace of God in His kindness and mercy.[344]

Ibn ʿArabī described human beings as vessels and veils of light. Apart from jinn, humans are the only species that can learn, develop and, to a degree, dictate its fate. While the nature of jinn is fire, the primary constituents of the human nature are light, water and fire that came to be moulded into clay. Ibn ʿArabī taught that clay is the major component of the human body. As such, it anchors us to the material domain of existence. Behind it, however, is the promise of divine light. Humans, he believed, are 'the most complete configuration of all beings created (…) in the form of the twenty-eight letters'.[345] Ibn ʿArabī's analogies between the human body and the letters of the Arabic alphabet are not unique in Sufi literature. For example, Faḍl Allāh Astarābādī taught that the letters of the alphabet are engraved into human bodies – a fact that was thought to be the most evident in the human facial features.[346] In his research on *Jawāhir al-sirr al-munīr*, a Sufi treatise attributed to Ibn Sabʿīn, Akkach documented Sufi tendencies to rely on complex tables of correspondences between the microcosm and the letters of the Arabic alphabet. While the outward forms of letters were usually associated with the body, their meanings were compared to the human spirit. 'The letters', Ibn Sabʿīn recorded, 'are formed in the image of a human figure, as a person standing upright, whose creation is perfect, that is, composed of two parts: spirit and body.'[347] (Fig. 59)

---

344 al-Qushayrī, *Sharḥ asmā' Allāh al-ḥusnā*, pp. 130–131.

345 *Fut.*III:184; al-Manṣūb, 5/36–7; *FM.*II: 123.

346 Faḍl Allāh Astarābādī's work *Jāvidān-nāma* distinguishes between seven major lines on the human face. Their position is indicated by the hairline, two eyebrows and four eyelashes. These are the so-called 'maternal' lines, which constitute the most basic divine writing on the human face. Multiplied by four natural elements (earth, water, air and fire), they produce twenty-eight lines.

347 Ibn Sabʿīn, *Jawāhir al-sirr al-munīr*, 10/6; Akkach, *Cosmology and Architecture*, p. 99.

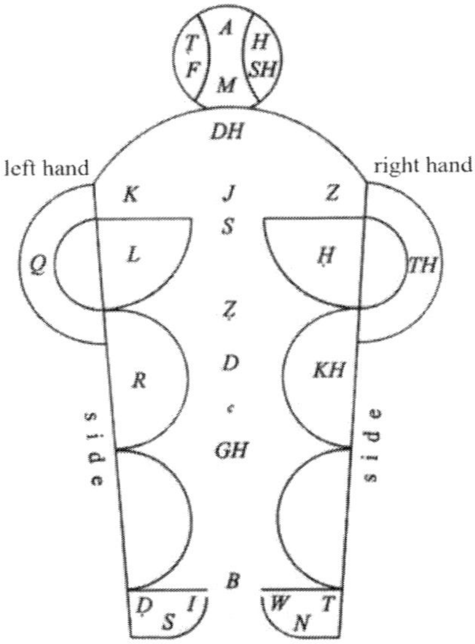

Fig. 59 Ibn Sabʿīn's table of correspondences between the microcosm and the letters of the Arabic alphabet

In the introductory chapter of the present study, we have seen how different parts of the universe were thought to have retained the properties of letters that brought them into existence. Human beings, Ibn ʿArabī believed, are the only species whose constitution reflects all realities of the universe. Each human is a master copy of the universe, and 'the condensed summary of the great cosmos'.[348] Everything that can be found in the greater existence (*al-kawn al-akbar*), which is the universe, can also to be found in the lesser, human existence (*al-ʿayn al-aṣghar*). Similar notions can be traced in Islamic culture from the mid-eighth century. In his *Book of Animals* (*Kitāb al-Ḥayawān*), al-Jāḥiẓ (d. 255/868) recorded the following description of human nature:

> He is the microcosm, son of the great cosmos, because they found in him all forms that are contained in the world (…) They called him the microcosm because they found him capable of depicting all things with his hand and imitating all sounds with his mouth and because his limbs are apportioned according to the twelve signs of the zodiac and the seven planets. In him, likewise, are yellow bile, which is the product of fire; black bile,

348 *Fut.*III:184; al-Manṣūb, 5/36; *FM.*II.124.

> the product of earth, blood, the product of air; and phlegm, the product of water; and in harmony with his four humours were tuned the four strings [of the lute]. Therefore, they perceive him as the world in small (*'ālam ṣaghīr*) - for within him are all of the world's parts, mixtures and natures.[349]

A similar paragraph was also preserved in *The Meccan Revelations*:

> Adam, the human being, is an allegorical expression of the whole world. He is just a small human and, at the same time, the condensed summary of the macrocosm. However, when it comes to the universe, it is not within the power of any human being to comprehend it due to its great size and magnitude.[350]

Ibn 'Arabī identified the microcosm, *al-'ālam al-saghīr*, as the summary of all human traits and faculties. However, in contrast to Ibn Sab'īn's diagram, he established his own table of correspondences between the human body and the universe (Table 15).

In Ibn 'Arabī's works, the macrocosm is commonly referred to as the Greater Kingdom (*al-mulk al-akbar*). It consists of the unseen world and the seen, their inhabitants and the laws that govern them. Bosnevi later proposed that the second consonant of the word Allah, *lām*, could be used as a symbol of the relationship between God (*alif*) and the world (*nūn*).[351] Omnipotent, God was the hidden treasure that loved to be known. Although omniscient, He found Himself dissatisfied – for according to Ibn 'Arabī, abstract knowledge, even when absolute, does not equal perception, i.e. seeing yourself in relation to someone else, in the eyes of someone else. For this reason, God created the world to serve as His mirror. It was an unpolished mirror, 'like a well-prepared, yet lifeless ghost'.[352] The reflection it provided proved to be twisted: for how could He, who is Omnipotent and Eternal, be reflected in something that is limited and ethereal? Unable to live up to its task, the nature of the world becomes chaotic, trapped in the state of perpetual change. Ibn 'Arabī taught that the act of genesis is not a process that took place in a distant past. The universe, he recorded, 'is written in

349 al-Jāḥiẓ, *Kitāb al-Ḥayawān*, pp. 212–214.
350 *Fut.*III:184; al-Manṣūb, 5/36; *FM.*II:124.
351 Bosnevi, *Sharḥ Fuṣūṣ* vol.1, pp. 136–137.
352 *Fut.*I:49. See also Akkach, *Cosmology and Architecture*, p. 106.

Table 15 Correspondences between the microcosm and the macrocosm according to Ibn ʿArabī

Microcosm	**Macrocosm**
Spirit	*Muhammadian Reality, the orbit of Life*
Body	*Throne*
Soul	*Pedestal*
Heart	*Populated House*
Strength	*Angelic realm*
Cognitive faculties and breath	*Sphere of Saturn*
Back of the head and memory	*Sphere of Jupiter*
Crown of the head and intellect	*Sphere of Mars*
Reflective faculties and the middle of the brain	*Sphere of the Sun*
Estimative faculties and instincts	*Sphere of Venus*
Faculty of Imagination	*Sphere of Mercury*
Sensory organs	*Sphere of the Moon*
Yellow bile, digestion	*Orbit of Fire*
Attracting faculties and blood	*Orbit of Air*
Repelling faculties and phlegm	*Orbit of Water*
Grasping faculties and black bile	*Earth in general*
Skin	*Black earth*
Body fat	*Dust-coloured earth*
Flesh	*Red earth*
Veins	*Yellow earth*
Nerves	*White earth*
Muscles	*Blue earth*
Bones	*Green earth*
Perceiving faculties	*Spirit-being entities*
All that is sensory in humans	*Animals*
All that is subject to growth	*Plants*
All that is void of senses in humans	*Minerals*

letters on the spread-out parchment of existence and the writing on it continues, forever, without end'.[353] Ultimately, the creative word *kun* in the imperative has neither future nor past tense. The Breath of the All-Merciful thus keeps blowing, annihilating and (re)creating inanimate objects and living beings.

Ibn ʿArabī maintained that the chaotic nature of the world can be compared to attempts to engage in Qur'anic studies. On the surface, the Holy Qur'an looks like any other book. However, what it contains is the speech of God. Ibn ʿArabī held that each word of God has countless meanings. In the Qur'an, he believed, everyone finds what he desires 'since the Qur'an has the quality of gathering together the Whole'.[354] The speech of God that is recorded in the Qur'an is the same as the creative word dictated to the Highest Pen. Ultimately, there is little or no difference between the Qur'an and the world. If one were to return to a Qur'anic verse and interpret it the same way as yesterday or the day before yesterday, Ibn ʿArabī would take this as a sound proof of his ignorance. Just as the meaning of the Qur'an constantly shifts and transforms in the mind of the reader, living beings and inanimate objects emerge and perish before the eyes of a beholder. Ultimately, no linguistic form and no single surface are spatially big enough to serve as a mirror for His introspection. When the burden of this task was offered to the heaven, the earth and the mountains, they shrank in fear and refused to carry it. However, man accepted the burden. Having accepted what the heaven, earth and mountains have refused, a small man becomes the spirit in the body of the world.[355] While heaven and earth are spatially bigger than a human being, the human heart is the only form that can embrace the Creator.[356] In the end, the heaven is only heaven and the earth is earth. However, man is a little bit of both, 'the child of two' and 'the copy of entirety'.[357] For this reason, human beings came to be associated with the Divine name *al-Jāmiʿ*, the All-Inclusive. Ibn ʿArabī compared the human heart to

---

353 *Fut.*I:158; al-Manṣūb, 1/323; *FM.*I:101.

354 *Fut.*III:259; al-Manṣūb, 5/178; *FM.*II:172. Interestingly enough, Chittick made the same observations about Ibn ʿArabī's works, which were also a product of divine revelations. Chittick. *The Self-Disclosure of God*, p. 9.

355 Elmore, *Islamic Sainthood*, p 386. See also Bosnevi, *Sharḥ Fuṣūṣ* vol.1, p. 38. The original reference to the 'trust' (*amāna*) that the human took on can be consulted at Q 33:72.

356 'My earth and heaven embrace Me not, but the heart of my servant does embrace Me,' reads the *ḥadīth qudsī*. This hadith had a strong impact on the teachings of Ibn ʿArabī.

357 *Fut.*I:328; al-Manṣūb, 1/614; *FM.*I:216.

spring, when everything blooms anew, new beginnings and the beauty of the world of nature. In his work, the heart is also associated with the circular form of the letter *ṣād*, the Sura *Yā Sīn* and the Kaʿba.[358] As the most sacred site in Islam, throughout the centuries, the Kaʿba has been known as the House of God and the heart of the universe. During the hajj, pilgrims make seven circles around the Kaʿba: one circle for each of the seven heavens, seven earths and the seven heavenly spheres. In addition, the seven circles that pilgrims are required to make have been compared to the human body and the angels around the heavenly Throne.

> My Kaʿba is the heart of existence. My Throne belonging to the heart is a bounded body. But neither of these encompasses Me and what is reported of them isn't reported of Me… The circles of the Kaʿba correspond to the circles of your heart (a) since both the Kaʿba and your heart have in common the fact that they are hearts (Fig. 60). The circles of your body are like the circles of the Throne since both share the common attribute of being all-encompassing… You are the ones circling the heart of the existence of the universe – these are the mysteries of the ones who truly know.[359]

Fig. 60 The circles of the heart, the Great City

358 Elmore, *Islamic Sainthood*, p. 270.
359 *Fut.*I:84; al-Manṣūb, 1/173; *FM.*I:50.

During the hajj, pilgrims circle around the Kaʿba, deep in prayer, in order to get closer to God. However, a *ḥadīth qudsī* points out another option: for 'he who knows himself knows his Lord'. While Ibn Taymiyya dismissed this hadith as a Sufi fabrication, Ibn ʿArabī had no doubt of its authenticity, 'for can't you see the embrace of *lām-alif* and how, in pronunciation, *lām* comes before *alif*? This is a proof for the one who looks.'[360] Man was created in God's form. 'Absolute being, *alif*, inclines in this presence to the creative process of bringing into being. The limited being, *lām*, inclines towards being brought into being at the moment of creation. This is why *lām* [i.e. Adam] emerges in the form of *alif* [i.e. the Creator].'[361] A recurrent symbol of this premise is *nūn*, the last consonant of the divine name *al-Raḥmān*. This letter signifies that we cannot know Him – except through ourselves. By knowing ourselves, we come to know God – and by seeing us, God sees Himself.

On the authority of the Qur'an, Ibn ʿArabī maintained that man was created in God's form. In his works, this form is primarily associated with the inner state or being. Ibn ʿArabī's reasoning was based on the fact that, in the Qur'an, God described Himself as the eyesight and the sense of hearing of a believer rather than saying that He is someone's eyes and ears. In order to get closer God, a man must live up to his full potential. The only things standing in his way are his personal fallacies and imperfections – however, in spite of the fact that man was created in God's form, it would be mistaken to focus on physical constitution in order to lift the veil between the Creator and the created. *We created humanity from the finest stature*, reads the fourth verse of the Sura *at-Tīn*, *and then We returned Him to the lowest of the low* (Q.95:4–5). Ibn ʿArabī referred to this process as the long descent of the letter *mīm*.[362] In the *ḥadīth qudsī*, the Prophet Muhammad is reported to have said, 'I am Aḥmad without *mīm*.' In the human constitution, the letter *mīm* stands for the physical body, a mortal shell destined to wither and die. Once *mīm* has been obliterated, Aḥmad becomes *Aḥad* – the One. This is the spiritual ascent of the letter *wāw* and the process of transformation into the Perfect Human. In his works, Ibn ʿArabī referred to this process as 'the conquest of the great city'.[363]

360 *Fut.*I:163; al-Manṣūb, 1/332; *FM.*I:105.
361 *Fut.*I:119; al-Manṣūb, 1/228; *FM.*I:75–6.
362 *Fut.*I:99; al-Manṣūb, 1/196; *FM.*I:61.
363 Elmore, *Islamic Sainthood*, pp. 498–500.

2.7. Conquest of the Great City: the Letter Wāw and the Step-levels of Spiritual Development

Beyond *wāw*, there are neither levels of existence nor letters to follow. In Ibn ʿArabī's works, this letter stands for the step-levels of spiritual development, i.e. for 'any place in which God descends towards you or in which you descend upon Him'. These step-levels have no spatial existence in Ibn ʿArabī's model of the universe, and there is no diagram to depict them. However, all diagrams in Ibn ʿArabī's hand aim at helping those who visualize them to ascend through the step-levels of spiritual development. In his *Glossary*, al-Qashānī recorded that the presence of Divinity is the ultimate goal of the heart and the final stage of the spirit. Arrival (*waṣl*) is 'an ascent after descent' and 'the return [of the mystic] to the state of union by following the path to God and in God by praising His qualities and losing themselves in them until they reached true reunion in Eternity without end – just as they were originally in Eternity without beginning.'[364] This is the knowledge of a man who has realized that there is nothing in existence apart from God and himself.

In Ibn ʿArabī's teachings, the symbols of this realization are the letters *wāw* and *alif*, where '*alif* is His and *wāw* means you'.[365] By the letter *wāw*, God links the possessor of this knowledge to Himself. In the Islamic science of letters, *wāw* was thought to be the strongest of all letters. This was due to the fact that air passes through all sixteen points of obstruction in the human articulatory system before the labial *wāw* can be pronounced. As a result, *wāw* amasses the power of all other letters. While *wāw* is the strongest of the letters, *hā'* was deemed to be the weakest since it is pronounced deep in the chest and has no opportunity to grow on the strength of other letters. Ibn ʿArabī compared the difference in strength between *wāw* and *hā'* to a common, 'animal' man and the Perfect Human as the seal of creation.

> In the *wāw* is the capacity of all the letters… In the same way, man is the final goal of the Breath and of the divine words that designate the kinds of things, for within him is the capacity of every existent thing in the cosmos, since he possesses all the levels [of the cosmos]. This is why he alone was singled out for the [Divine] Form. Thereby he brings together in himself

364 al-Qashānī, *Glossary of Sufi Technical Terms,* p. 22.

365 *Fut.*I:93; al-Manṣūb, 1/187; *FM.*I:57.

> the divine realities, which are the names, and the realities of the [entire] cosmos, for he is the last existent thing. The Breath of the All-Merciful did not bring him into existence without placing within him the capacity of all step-levels of the universe. His nature contains things which have not been manifested in any other part of the universe, nor in any Divine Name since, due to the distinctiveness of each Name, it does not bestow what any other Name bestows. For this reason, the human being is the most perfect thing in existence, and *wāw* is the most perfect letter.[366]

In Sufi tradition, human knowledge has been compared to the dot underneath the letter *bā'*. However, apart from the diacritical mark, the orthographic form of *bā'* also contains an archigrapheme. The human perception, broadened through spiritual practices and knowledge, has a potential to comprehend the diacritical mark and the archigrapheme alike. Apart from *wāw*, the isolated letter *bā'* thus appears as a recurrent symbol of the Perfect Human in Sufi literature. Created in God's form, the Perfect Human is the seal of creation and the mirror polished. On the surface of this mirror glitters the form of the Real.

> The heart of the Perfect Human, which became closed to anything other than the truth, is the heart that reached the rank of union, the state of annihilation in the True.[367]

Alif and *wāw*, the first and the final point of the circumference of creation, unite in the heart of the Perfect Human. In the Islamic normative tradition, *alif* is commonly referred to as *Aḥad*, the One. However, in the Arabic language, the same meaning can be conveyed by the word *wāḥīd*. The fact that their morphological forms differ from one another serves as a warning that servanthood (*'ubūdiyya*) is not to be mistaken for lordship (*rubūbiyya*). The same warning echoes from the divine and human letters. We have seen how each of these categories has three letters. But while the equal number of human and divine letters implies that man was created in God's form, the existence of the two categories of letters (divine and human, containing three

366 *Fut.*II:396. See Chittick, 'The Anthropology of Compassion', *JMIAS* 48, 2010. Accessed online 26 January 2021.

367 al-Qashānī, *Glossary of Sufi Technical Terms*, p. 11.

letters each) indicates that the viceregent of Allah is not Allah himself. He is however neither more nor less than 'the all-inclusive Word, the master copy (*nuskha*) of the universe'.[368]

As the letter *wāw* contains the strength and properties of all other letters, the nature of the Perfect Human (a) reflects the properties of spirits (b), imaginal bodies (c) and corporeal forms (d) (Fig. 61). The only thing that is missing is the transcendent, eternal *alif.* The Perfect Human, Ibn 'Arabī observed, is the shadow of God in everything other than God.[369] As the seal of the creation and the mirror of the unseen and the seen, the Perfect Human is also symbolized by *ḍamma*, the last, invisible short vowel from the Divine Name Allah(u). Among men, countless have reached this stage – and among women, Maryam and Āsiya bint Muzāḥim.[370] The hearts of those who obtained this knowledge were said to contain unspeakable treasures, on a par with the one which the Prophet Muhammad found in the Ka'ba and decided not to remove for the sake of the world. In Ibn 'Arabī's works, this treasure was described as God's knowledge of Himself. As such, it has little in common with rational knowledge. By intellect, we can only know what God is not. To find out what God truly is, one has to search within oneself. To do so, it is necessary to purify the heart from the taint that arises from adding others to Him who is One.[371] The main preconditions to ascend from *mīm* to *wāw* are spiritual strivings (*mujāhada*), continuous effort and endurance. Ibn 'Arabī strongly recommended reciting the Shahāda and Takbīr to breach the gate of the great city (Fig. 62).

Both of these phrases, 'there is no God but God' (*lā ilāha illā Llāh*) and 'God is great' (*Allāhu akbar*), were said to invoke the Trustworthy Spirit (*al-rūḥ al-amīn*) to descend to the human heart, thus enabling him to conquer the City.[372] In order to help His viceregent to live up to his potential, God sent down the Qur'an, the last of the revealed books, and the Prophet Muhammad to serve him as a role-model.

368 *Fut.*I:210; al-Manṣūb, 1/399; *FM.*II:136.

369 *Fut.*V:412; Corbin, *Creative Imagination*, p. 191.

370 In spite of this fact, Ibn 'Arabī maintained that 'everything that a man can attain – spiritual stations, levels or qualities – can be attained by women if God wills, just as they can be attained by a man if God wills' (*Fut.*III:89).

371 *Fut.*I:552; al-Manṣūb, 2/342; *FM.*I:366.

372 Elmore, *Islamic Sainthood*, p. 500.

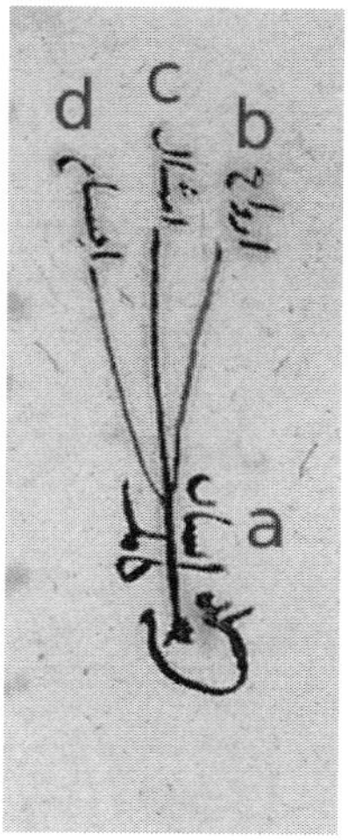

Fig. 61 The nature of the Perfect Human

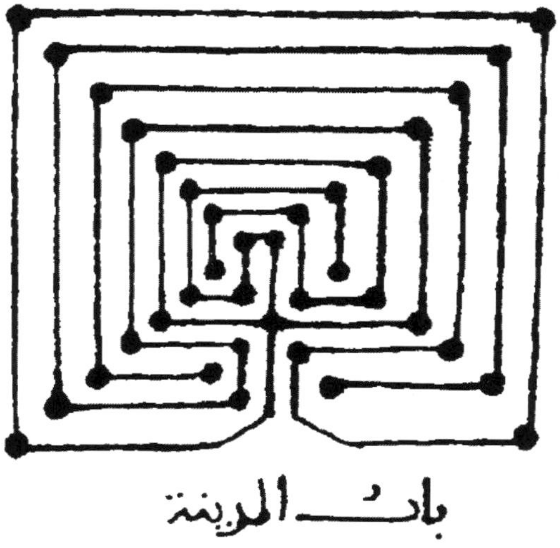

Fig. 62 Gate of the Great City. The centre of the diagram represents the human heart

The Path-beater makes the course of the journey clear for the traveller and the one making this journey so that he may see the wonders, acquire knowledge and the mysteries (…). The Path-beater is the Lawgiver and the path he set down for us is the Law. Whoever takes this path will reach the Truth.[373]

373 *Fut.*IV:19; al-Manṣūb, 6/122; *FM.*II:383

Among the Sufis, it has been said that the Perfect Human glorifies God through all the glorifications in the cosmos. Due to its shape, the letter *lām*, which is the symbol of the power of the divine Essence (*alif*), could not create human beings (*mīm*) directly – and thus it went on to create the world (*nūn*) instead (Fig. 63).[374] In the eyes of Ibn ʿArabī, the world is a symbol (*mithāl*) whose meaning is God. As such, it was represented by the isolated letter *bā'*.

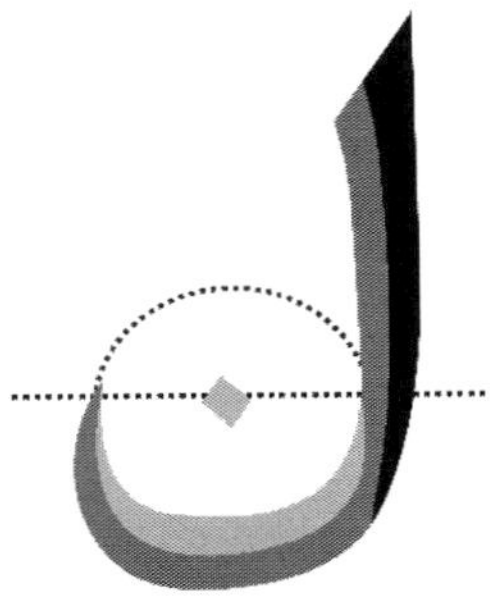

Fig. 63 Alif, lām and nūn as the Divine essence, the (Perfect) human and the world

> Do you not see now how your Lord extended the Shadow? The world is extended from the *bā'* when it met with the Real just as a shadow extends from an object when it meets the Sun. And as the shadow of a thing is according to the form it extends from, so the universe arises according to the form of the *bā'*.[375]

We have seen that the isolated letter *bā'* also appears in Ibn ʿArabī's works as a symbol of the Perfect Human. To study the world is to study the man and by knowing ourselves, we come to know God – and thus we return to the three great books of the Islamic science of letters. Divine revelation, human body and the universe are, ultimately, nothing more than a text, written in the letters of the Arabic alphabet on the parchment of existence. Familiarity with the letters can thus help us come to terms with man, world and the revelation alike. While God created the world to provide a seeker with directions on the path of wisdom, Ibn ʿArabī relied on diagrams and calligraphy. The outward forms of these diagrams and letters are the divine truths made visual. As such, they were intended to help those with reduced understanding (*al-afhām al-qāṣira*) to reach the higher spiritual truths.

374 Ibn ʿArabī, *Meccan Revelations* vol.2, p. 167.
375 Ibn ʿArabī, *Kitāb al-Bā'*, trans., p. 18.

The reason why Ibn ʿArabī focused on diagrams and calligraphy is the same reason that led God to create the world. God wished to be known and the world was created in such a form so that it can direct His creatures towards Him. Ibn ʿArabī's diagrams were intended to serve the same purpose. By visualizing their outward forms, an adept comes to terms with his inner Self – and thus, (in)directly, makes his way towards the Creator.[376] Building on the pioneering works of Pierre Lory, the present study has outlined some of the ways in which Ibn ʿArabī contested, synthesized and extended the dominant intellectual paradigms of his day – as well as the positive and negative receptions with which his efforts were met in the centuries after his death. While Ibn ʿArabī's diagrams and calligraphy are divine truths made visual, the present study is the mystical made rational. As such, it is but a shadow of the shadow. Nevertheless, as Ibn ʿArabī liked to say, when it comes to the divine mysteries, 'the inability to achieve perception is also perception'.[377]

376 *Fut.*III:226–227; al-Manṣūb, 5/116-7; *FM.*II:150-1.

377 In the Islamic normative tradition, this saying was originally attributed to Abū Bakr (d. 13/634), the first Muslim caliph. See *Fut.*I:84; al-Manṣūb, 1/174, 300; *FM.*I:51.

List of Tables

Table 1	The Arabic script in the common *hijā'ī* order	pp. 14-15
Table 2	The disjoined letters	p. 25
Table 3	The Four Natures of the Letters	p. 34
Table 4	The elements and the alphabet	p. 38
Table 5	Ibn Sawdakīn's table of correspondences	p. 38
Table 6	Al-Būnī's table of correspondences	p. 38
Table 7	The cryptographic script	p. 54
Table 8	The archigraphemes and the Arabic letters	p. 74
Table 9	The Act of Genesis and its stages	p. 77
Table 10	Sībawayh's sequence of the letters of the Arabic alphabet	p. 79
Table 11	Al-Laythi's sequence of the letters of the Arabic alphabet	p. 79
Table 12	Sun letters and moon letters	p. 106
Table 13	The roots of all existence	p. 133
Table 14	The Lunar Mansions	pp. 168-9
Table 15	Correspondences between the microcosm and the macrocosm according to Ibn 'Arabī	p. 194

List of Figures

Fig. 1 In the Master's hand: the opening paragraph of Ibn ʿArabī's *Book of the Letter Bā'* .... p. 13
Source: Ibn ʿArabī, *Kitāb al-Bā'*, MS Yusuf Aga 4868, fol. 2

Fig. 2 Ibn ʿArabī's talisman for harnessing the spiritual power of the disjoined letters *alif-lām-mīm* .... p. 33
Source: Ibn ʿArabī, *Kitāb al-Mīm*, MS Veliyuddin 1759, fol. 16. Courtesy of the Muhyiddin Ibn Arabi Society, Oxford

Fig. 3a One goal, two paths and a single starting point: a sketch from the margins of *The Meccan Revelations* .... p. 43
Source: Ibn ʿArabī, *Futūḥāt al-Makkiyya* vol. 26 (MS Evkaf 1870), fol. 84

Fig. 3b The Path of Reflection and the Path of Revelation..... p. 44
Source: Ibn ʿArabī, *Futūḥāt al-Makkiyya* vol. 6, p. 182

Fig. 4 The four categories of Closeness .... p. 46
Source: Ibn ʿArabī, *Futūḥāt al-Makkiyya* vol. 14 (MS Evkaf 1855), fol. 111

Fig. 5 Different ranks of the inhabitants of paradise............ p. 48
Source: Ibn ʿArabī, *Futūḥāt al-Makkiyya* vol. 26 (MS Evkaf 1870), fol. 94.

Fig. 6 Ibn ʿArabī's illustrations of one of the tablets of revelation he received .... p. 53
Source: Ibn ʿArabī, *Futūḥāt al-Makkiyya* vol. 16 (MS Evkaf 1860), fol. 147

Fig. 7 The only surviving piece of writing in cryptographic script in Ibn ʿArabī's hand with translation by G. Elmore p. 55
Source: Ibn ʿArabī, *Kitāb ʿAnqā' mughrib*, MS Berlin 3266, fol. 45. (Ms. or. oct. 3266, f. 45v. © STAATSBIBLIOTHEK ZU BERLIN - Preussischer Kulturbesitz, Orientabteilung)

Fig. 8 Ibn ʿArabī experimenting with the orthographic forms that resemble one another in the margins of the *Book of Mīm* .... p. 63
Source: Ibn ʿArabī, *Kitāb al-Mīm*, MS Veliyuddin 1759, fol. 16. Courtesy of the Muhyiddin Ibn Arabi Society, Oxford

Fig. 9 The archaic vocalization system attributed to Abū al-Aswad al-Du'alī .... p. 70
Source: Qur'an, Metropolitan Museum New York; see Ettinghausen, Richard, 'Islamic Art', Metropolitan Museum of Art Bulletin vol. 33, no. 1 (Spring 1975). ill. p. 14 (b/w).

Fig. 10 Short vowels .... p. 71
Author: Dunja Rašić

Fig. 11 The long vowels in Arabic .... p. 72
Author: Dunja Rašić

Fig. 12 Three Basmalas in Ibn 'Arabī's hand .... p. 72
Source: Ibn 'Arabī, *Futūḥāt al-Makkiyya* vol. 1 (MS Evkaf 1845), fol. 2; *Futūḥāt al-Makkiyya* vol. 3 (MS Evkaf 1845), fol. 141

Fig. 13 The letters of the alphabet and their points of articulation according to Ibn 'Arabī .... p. 81
Author: Dunja Rašić

Fig. 14 The Divine Name Allah .... p. 91
Source: Ibn 'Arabī, *Futūḥāt al-Makkiyya* vol. 3 (MS Evkaf 1845), fol. 141

Fig. 15 Letters and the act of prayer .... p. 92
Author: Dunja Rašić

Fig. 16 Human nature .... p. 93
Author: Dunja Rašić

Fig. 17 Ibn 'Arabī's sequence of letters with *lām-alif* .... p. 96
Source: Ibn 'Arabī, MS Veliyuddin 1759, fol. 80

Fig. 18 The Act of Genesis .... p. 98
Source: Ibn 'Arabī, *Futūḥāt al-Makkiyya* vol. 24 (MS Evkaf 1868), fol. 87.

Fig. 19 *Alif*, the Divine Essence .... p. 99
Author: Dunja Rašić

Fig. 20 The Act of Genesis according to E. Winkel .... p. 99
Author: Dunja Rašić

Fig. 21 The Most Beautiful Names of God and the world.... p. 101
Source: Ibn 'Arabī, *Futūḥāt al-Makkiyya* vol. 26 (MS Evkaf 1870), fol. 93.

Fig. 22 The Divine Name *al-Raḥmān* .... p. 104
Source: Ibn 'Arabī, *Futūḥāt al-Makkiyya* vol. 3 (MS Evkaf 1845), fol. 141

Fig. 23 The universe and the knot of *lām-alif* .... p. 104
Author: Dunja Rašić
Fig. 24a The letter *nūn* and the visible and invisible world.... p. 105
Author: Dunja Rašić
Fig. 24b The circle of *nūn* .... p. 105
Source: Ibn ʿArabī, *Kitāb al-Mīm*, MS Veliyuddin 1759, fol. 20. Courtesy of the Muhyiddin Ibn Arabi Society, Oxford
Fig. 25 Divine Love and the Love of the Servant .... p. 106
Source: Ibn ʿArabī, *Futūḥāt al-Makkiyya* vol. 30 (MS Evkaf 1874), fol. 60.
Fig. 26 The material world as a sign leading towards the knowledge of the invisible world and the Creator .... p. 108
Source: Ibn ʿArabī, *Kitāb al-Jalāla wa huwa kalimāt Allah*, MS Yusuf Aga 4859, fol. 180
Fig. 27 Two bow lengths: considering the Unapparent by means of the apparent .... p. 109
Source: Ibn ʿArabī, *Futūḥāt al-Makkiyya* vol. 18 (MS Evkaf 1862), fol. 126.
Fig. 28 Image of the Primordial Cloud and All It Contains .. p. 120
Source: Ibn ʿArabī, *Futūḥāt al-Makkiyya* vol. 26 (MS Evkaf 1870), fol. 90.
Fig. 29 The thirty stations of the angels filled with love....... p. 122
Author: Dunja Rašić
Fig. 30 *Hamza*, the Highest Pen .... p. 122
Author: Dunja Rašić
Fig. 31 *Hā'*, the Protected Tablet .... p. 122
Author: Dunja Rašić
Fig. 32 Universal Nature .... p. 124
Author: Dunja Rašić
Fig. 33 Universal Body .... p. 126
Author: Dunja Rašić
Fig. 34 The Primordial Cloud as *alif* madda and the world as the dripping of ink from the Higher Pen........................ p. 129
Author: Dunja Rašić
Fig. 35 The Roots of Existence .... p. 132
Source: Ibn ʿArabī, *Futūḥāt al-Makkiyya* vol. 4 (MS Evkaf 1848), fol. 92.

Fig. 36 The Throne and its surroundings .... p. 136
Source: Ibn ʿArabī, *Futūḥāt al-Makkiyya* vol. 26 (MS Evkaf 1870), fol. 91.

Fig. 37 *Bismi* .... p. 138
Source: Ibn ʿArabī, *Futūḥāt al-Makkiyya* vol. 3 (MS Evkaf 1845), fol. 141

Fig. 38 The Throne on the Day of Resurrection .... p. 141
Source: Ibn ʿArabī, *Futūḥāt al-Makkiyya* vol. 26 (MS Evkaf 1870), fol. 48.

Fig. 39 The Divine Name al-Raḥīm .... p. 144
Source: Ibn ʿArabī, *Futūḥāt al-Makkiyya* vol. 3 (MS Evkaf 1845), fol. 141

Fig. 40 The World .... p. 144
Source: Ibn ʿArabī, *Futūḥāt al-Makkiyya* vol. 26 (MS Evkaf 1870), fol. 94

Fig. 41 The letter *ṣād* .... p. 145
Author: Dunja Rašić

Fig. 42 Ephemeral nature of the world and the laws that govern it .... p. 146
Source: Ibn ʿArabī, *Futūḥāt al-Makkiyya* vol. 4 (MS Evkaf 1848), fol. 56

Fig. 43 Circumference of the Circle: We are from God and to Him we return .... p. 148
Author: Dunja Rašić

Fig. 44 The heavenly spheres .... p. 149
Source: Ibn ʿArabī, *Futūḥāt al-Makkiyya* vol. 26 (MS Evkaf 1870), fol. 92.

Fig. 45 Ibn ʿArabī's model of the universe .... p. 151
Author: Dunja Rašić

Fig. 46 *Bayt al-Maʿmūr*, the Kaʿba of the highest heaven.... p. 152
Source: Ibn ʿArabī, *Futūḥāt al-Makkiyya* vol. 16 (MS Evkaf 1860), fol. 111

Fig. 47 The Earth (centre) surrounded by the Spheres of Water, Air and Fire .... p. 153
Source: Ibn ʿArabī, *Kitāb ʿUqlat al-mustawfiz*, MS Yusuf Aga 4690, fol. 11

Fig. 48 Watch-towers of the Starless Sphere and the zodiac constellations of the Sphere of the Fixed Stars......... p. 159
Author: Dunja Rašić

Fig. 49 The heavenly gardens .... p. 160
Source: Ibn ʿArabī, *Futūḥāt al-Makkiyya* vol. 26 (MS Evkaf 1870), fol. 91.

Fig. 50 The seven levels of hell .... p. 161
Source: Ibn ʿArabī, *Futūḥāt al-Makkiyya* vol. 26 (MS Evkaf 1870), fol. 93

Fig. 51 The highest of virtues and the lowest of sins........... p. 162
Source: Ibn ʿArabī, *Futūḥāt al-Makkiyya* vol. 20 (MS Evkaf 1864), fol. 74.

Fig. 52 The lunar mansion of the letter *wāw*......................... p. 164
Source: Ibn ʿArabī, *Futūḥāt al-Makkiyya* vol. 17 (MS Evkaf 1861), fol. 96

Fig. 53 A thirteenth-century astrolabe with the lunar mansions .... p. 166
Source: British Museum 1855, 0709.1

Fig. 54 Ottoman celestial map with the lunar mansions, the zodiac constellations and the heavenly spheres .... p. 167
Source: MS *Zubdat al-tawārikh*. Istanbul: Museum of Turkish and Islamic Arts, 1583

Fig. 55 The Divine Name *Huwa*, He .... p. 178
Source: Ibn ʿArabī, *Futūḥāt al-Makkiyya* vol. 17 (MS Evkaf 1861), fol. 58.

Fig. 56 The state of sleep, as depicted in the margin of *The Meccan Revelations* .... p. 182
Source: Ibn ʿArabī, *Futūḥāt al-Makkiyya* vol. 16 (MS Evkaf 1860), fol. 77

Fig. 57 Stone ship of God's Great Earth .... p. 186
Source: Ibn ʿArabī, *Futūḥāt al-Makkiyya* vol. 2 (MS Evkaf 1846), fol. 92

Fig. 58 Angels as *raqāʾiq*: the subtle connection between God and men .... p. 189
Author: Dunja Rašić

Fig. 59 Ibn Sabʿīn's table of correspondences between the microcosm and the letters of the Arabic alphabet..... p. 192
Source: Akkach, *Cosmology and Architecture in Pre-modern Islam,* p. 99.

Fig. 60 The circles of the heart, the Great City.................... p. 196
Source: Ibn ʿArabī, *Kitāb ʿAnqāʾ mughrib*, MS Esad Efendi, fol. 46

Fig. 61 The nature of the Perfect Human .... p. 201
Source: Ibn ʿArabī, *Futūḥāt al-Makkiyya* vol. 24 (MS Evkaf 1868), fol. 96.
Fig. 62 Gate of the Great City .... p. 201
Source: Ibn ʿArabī, *Kitāb ʿAnqāʾ mughrib*, MS Berlin 3266, fol. 41 (Ms. or. oct. 3266, f. 41v. © STAATSBIBLIOTHEK ZU BERLIN - Preussischer Kulturbesitz, Orientabteilung)
Fig. 63 *Alif*, *lām* and *nūn* as the Divine essence, the (Perfect) human and the world .... p. 202
Author: Dunja Rašić

Bibliography

Abrahamov, Binyamin, *Ibn al-ʿArabī and the Sufis*, Oxford, 2014.

Addas, Claude, *Quest for the Red Sulphur: The Life of Ibn ʿArabī*, Cambridge, 1993.

———, 'The Ship of Stone', *The Journal of the Muhyiddin Ibn ʿArabi Society* 19 (1996).

Affifi, A. E., '*Fihrist al-Mu'allafāt*: The Works of Ibn ʿArabī', *Bulletin of the Faculty of Arts* 8 (1954), pp. 109–117, 193–207.

Agazzi, Evandro, 'The Universe as a Scientific and Philosophic Problem', in *Philosophy and the Origin and Evolution of the Universe*, eds. Evandro Agazzi and Alberto Cordero, pp. 1–53, Dordrecht, 1988.

Akkach, Samer, 'Ibn ʿArabī's Cosmology and the Sufi Concept of Space and Time', in *Constructions of Time in the Late Middle Ages*, ed. Richard J. Utz, pp. 115–143, Evanston, 1997.

———, *Cosmology and Architecture in Pre-modern Islam*, New York, 2005.

Akman, M. Kubilay, and Donna M. Brown, 'Ahmad Al-Buni and His Esoteric Model', *The Esoteric Quarterly* (2018), pp. 51–75.

Albright, William, 'The Supposed Babylonian Derivation of the Logos', *Journal of Biblical Literature* 39 (1920), pp. 143–151.

Alibhai, Shams, *The Shajarat al-Kawn Attributed to Ibn ʿArabi: An Analytical Study*, PhD Thesis, McGill University, 1990.

Alsamaani, Nader Ahmad, *An Analytic Philosophical Approach to Ibn ʿArabi's Concept of Ultimate Reality*, PhD dissertation, University of Birmingham, 2017.

al-ʿĀmilī, Bahā' al-Dīn Muḥammad b. Ḥusayn, *Tashrīḥ al-aflāk*, 1232 AH, Washington, Library of Congress QB23.

Āmulī, Shams al-Dīn Muḥammad, *Nafā'is al-funūn fī ʿara'is al-ʿuyun*, Tehran, 1891.

Aṭṭār, Farīd al-Dīn, *Ushturnāma,* Tehran, 1960.

Ayoub, Mahmud, *Redemptive Suffering in Islam: A Study of the Devotional Aspects of Ashuraʿ in Twelver Shiʿism*, The Hague, 1978.

Bakar, Osman, *Classification of Knowledge in Islam: A Study in Islamic Philosophies of Science*, Cambridge, 1999.

al-Balādhurī, Ahmad b. Yaḥyā, *The Origins of the Islamic State: K.Futūḥ al-buldān*, trans. Francis Murgotten and Philip Hitti, vol. 2, New York, 1968.

Bashir, Shahzad, *Fazlallah Astarabadi and the Hurufis*, Oxford, 2005.

——, *Messianic Hopes and Visions: The Nurbakshiya Between Medieval and Modern Islam*, Berkeley, 2003.
al-Bauniyyah, Aishah, *The Principles of Sufism*, New York, 2014.
Bayraktar, Mehmet, 'Cosmological Relativity of Ibn al-Arabi', *Ankara Üniversitesi İlahiyat Fakültesi Dergisi* 28 (1986), pp. 127–133.
Bernards, Monique, *Establishing a Reputation: The Reception of Sībawayh's Book*, PhD dissertation, Catholic University of Nijmegen, 1992.
al-Bīrūnī, Abū Rayḥān, *The Book of Instruction in the Elements of the Art of Astrology*, trans. Robert Ramsey Wright, Whitefish MT, 2004.
Bosnevi, Abdullah, *Sharḥ Fuṣūṣ al-ḥikam: Tumačenje dragulja poslaničke mudrosti*, vols. 1–4, Sarajevo, 2009.
Böwering, Gerhard, 'Sulamī's Treatise on the Science of the Letters (*'ilm al-ḥurūf*)', in *In the Shadow of Arabic: the Centrality of Language to Arabic Culture*, ed. Bilal Orfali, pp. 339–397, Leiden, 2011.
Burckhardt, Titus, *Mystical Astrology According to Ibn 'Arabi*, Louisville, 1977.
——, *Art of Islam: Language and Meaning*, Bloomington, 2009.
Bursevi, Ismail Hakki, *Fusus al-hikam: Ismail Hakki Bursevi's Translation of And Commentary on Fusus Al-Hikam by Muhyiddin Ibn 'Arabi*, rendered into English by Bulent Rauf, vols. 1–4, Oxford, 1985.
Canteins, Jean, 'The Hidden Sciences in Islam', *Islamic Spirituality: Manifestations*, ed. Seyyed Hossein Nasr, pp. 447–468, New York, 1997.
Carter, Michael, 'Ṣarf et khilāf, contribution à l'histoire de la grammaire arabe', *Arabica 20* (1973), pp. 299–304.
Chittick, William. 'The Anthropology of Compassion'. *Journal of the Muhyiddin Ibn 'Arabi Society* 48 (2010), pp. 1–17.
——, 'Death and the World of Imagination: Ibn al-'Arabī's Eschatology', *The Muslim World* 78 (1988), pp. 51–82.
——, *Ibn 'Arabi, Heir to the Prophets*, Oxford, 2005.
——, *Imaginal Worlds: Ibn al-'Arabī and the Problem of Religious Diversity*, New York, 1994.
——, 'Microcosm, Macrocosm and the Perfect Man in the View of Ibn al-'Arabī', *Islamic Culture. An English Quarterly* 63 (1989), pp. 1-11.
——, *The Self-Disclosure of God: Principles of Ibn 'Arabī's Cosmology*, New York, 1998.
——, *The Sufi Path of Knowledge: Ibn al-'Arabī's Metaphysics of Imagination*, New York, 1989.

Chodkiewicz, Michel, *An Ocean Without Shore: Ibn ʿArabi, The Book and the Law*, New York, 1993.

——, *Seal of the Saints: Prophethood and Sainthood in the Doctrine of Ibn al-ʿArabī*, Cambridge, 1993.

Clark, Jane, and Hirtenstein, Stephen, 'Establishing Ibn ʿArabī's Heritage: First findings from the MIAS Archiving Project', *Journal of the Muhyiddin Ibn ʿArabi Society* 52 (2012), pp. 1–32.

Cole, Juan, 'The World as Text: Cosmologies of Shaykh Ahmad al-Ahsa'i', *Studia Islamica* 80 (1994), pp. 145–163.

Corbin, Henry, *Creative Imagination in the Sufism of Ibn ʿArabi*, Princeton, 1969.

Czapkiewicz, Andrzej, *The Views of the Medieval Arab Philologists on Language and its Origins in the Light of as-Suyūṭī's al-Muẓhir*, Krakow, 1988.

Daftary, Farhad, *Ismaili History and Literary Traditions*, London, 2008.

Danecki, Janusz, 'Early Arabic Phonetic Theory. Phonetics of al-Khalīl b. Aḥmad and Sībawayhi', *Rocznik Orientalistyczny* 39 (1978), pp. 51–66.

De Cillis, Maria, *Free Will and Predestination in Islamic Thought: Theoretical Compromises in the works of Avicenna, al-Ghāzālī and Ibn ʿArabī*, London, 2013.

Durkheim, Emile, *The Elementary Forms of Religious Life*, New York, 1965.

Ebstein, Michael, and Sara Sviri, 'The So-Called *Risālat al-ḥurūf* (Epistle of Letters) Ascribed to Sahl al-Tuṣtāri and the Letter Mysticism in al-Andalus', *Journal Asiatique* 299 (2011), pp. 213–270.

Elmore, Gerald, *Islamic Sainthood in the Fullness of Time*, Leiden, 1999.

Fahd, Toufic, 'Siḥr', *Encyclopaedia of Islam, Second Edition*, eds. P. Bearman et al.

——, 'D̲j̲afr', *Encyclopaedia of Islam, Second Edition*, eds. P. Bearman et al.

——, 'La magie comme 'source' de la sagesse, l'apres l'œuvre d'al-Bunī', *Res Orientales XIV* (2002), pp. 61–108.

Fatoorichi, Pirooz, 'The Problem of the Beginning: Modern Cosmology and Transcendent Ḥikmah Perspectives', *Islamic Studies* 39/4 (2000), pp. 633–656.

Fitzpatrick, Richard, *A Modern Almagest. An Updated Version of Ptolemy's Model of the Solar System*, The University of Texas at Austin, 2010.
Freudenthal, Gad, 'The Problem of Cohesion between Alchemy and Natural Philosophy: from Unctuous Moisture to Phlogiston', *Alchemy Revisited, Proceedings of the International Conference of the History of Alchemy at the University of Groningen,* ed. Z.R.W.M. von Martels, pp. 107–117, Leiden, 1989.
Gacek, Adam, 'Arabic scripts and their characteristics as seen through the eyes of Mameluk authors', *Manuscripts of the Middle East* 4 (1989), pp. 144–149.
Gardiner, Noah Daedalus, *Aḥmad al-Būnī and His Readers through the Mamlūk Period*, PhD dissertation, University of Michigan, 2014.
Garrido, Pilar, 'The Science of Letters in Ibn Masarra', *JMIAS* 47 (2010), pp. 47–61.
Goldziher, Ignaz, 'Mélanges judéo-arabes XXIV: La création des lettres', *Revue des Études Juives* 50 (1905), pp. 188–190.
——, 'Ibn Barrağān', *Zeitschrift der Deutschen Morgenländischen Gesellschaft* 68 (1914), pp. 544–546.
——, 'Aus Literatur der muhamedanischen Mystik', *ZDMG* 26 (1872), pp. 764–785.
Grohmann, Adolf, *Arabische Paläographie II: Das Schriftwesen und die Lapidarschrift*, Vienna, 1971.
Gruendler, Beatrice, *The Development of the Arabic Script*, Atlanta, 1993.
Habīb, Mīrzā Ḥabīb Isfahānī, *Khaṭṭ u khaṭṭāṭān*, Istanbul, 1887
al-Ḥakīm, Su'ad, *al-Mu'jam al-Sūfī: al-ḥikma fī al-ḥudūd al-kalima*, Beirut, 1981.
Hamdan, Abdelhamid Saleh, 'Ghazali and the Science of Ḥurūf', *Oriente Moderno Nuova serie* 65 (1985), pp. 191–193.
Heck, Paul, 'The Hierarchy of Knowledge in Islamic Civilization', *Arabica 49* (2002), pp. 27–54.
Heinen, Anton, *Islamic Cosmology: A study of al-Suyūṭi's al-Hay'a as-sanīya fī l-hay'a as-sunnīya*, Beirut, 1989.
Hirtenstein, Stephen, 'In the Master's Hand: A Preliminary Study of Ibn 'Arabi's Holographs and Autographs', *JMIAS* 60 (2016), pp. 65–106
Houdas, Octave Victor, *Recueil de lettres arabes manuscrites*, Algiers, 1891.

al-Ḥujwīrī, ʿAlī b. ʿUthmān, *Kashf al-maḥjūb: The Oldest Persian Treatise on Sufism*, trans. Reynold A. Nicholson, London, 1976.
Ibn Anas, Mālik, *Al-Muwatta*, vol. 1, Cairo, n.d.
Ibn ʿArabī, Abū ʿAbd Allāh Muḥammad al-Ḥātimī aṭ-Ṭāʾī, *K. al-Alif*, Hyderabad, 1989.
——, *K. ʿAnqāʾ mughrib*, MSS: Berlin, Or. 3266 (597 H) and Istanbul, Esad Efendi 1415; ʿĀlam al-Fikr, 2019.
——, *K.al-Bāʾ*, MS: Konya, Yusuf Aga 4868 (602H), trans. S. Hirtenstein and H. Küçük, *Journal of the Muhyiddin Ibn ʿArabi Society* 65 (2019), pp. 1–27.
——, *K. ʿUqlat al-mustawfiz*, MS: Konya, Yusuf Aga 4690 (617H).
——, *Contemplations of the Holy Mysteries: Mashāhid al-asrār al-qudsiyya*, Oxford, 2001.
——, *Divine Sayings 101 Ḥadīth Qudsī. Mishkāt al-anwār*, Oxford, 2004.
——, *Fuṣūṣ al-ḥikam*, Belgrade, 1999.
——, *al-Futūḥāt al-Makkiyya*, MS: Istanbul, Evkaf Müzesi 1845–81 (636H).
——, *al-Futūḥāt al-Makkiyya* vols. 1–4, Beirut, n.d.
——, *al-Futūḥāt al-Makkiyya* vols. 1–12, ed. ʿAbd al-ʿAzīz Sulṭān al-Manṣūb, Cairo, 2010.
——, *al-Futūḥāt al-Makkiyya* vols. 1–9, Beirut, 2011.
——, *K.Inshāʾ al-dawāʾir wa al-jadāwil*, Leiden, 1919.
——, *K. al-Isfār ʿan nataʾij al-asfar*, trans. A. Jaffray as *The Secrets of Voyaging*, Oxford, 2015.
——, *K. al-Jalāla wa huwa kalimat Allah*, MS: Konya, Yusuf Aga 4859 (615H).
——, *Journey to the Lord of Power: Risālat al-Anwār*, Rochester, 1981.
——, *K. Mashāhid al-asrār al-qudsiyya wa maṭāliʾ al-anwār al-ilāhiyya*, Beirut, 2009.
——, *The Meccan Revelations*, vols. 1–2, New York, 2002.
——, *K. al-Mīm*, MS: Veliyuddin 1759 (617H).
——, *Rasāʾil Ibn ʿArabī*, Tehran, 1997.
——, *The Seven Days of the Heart: Prayers for the Nights and Days of the Week*, Oxford, 2000.
——, *K. al-Tajalliyāt*, MS: Veliyuddin 1759 (620H).
——, *Tarjumān al-ashwāq: A Collection of Mystical Odes*, London, 1911.

——, *The Universal Tree and the Four Birds: al-Ittiḥād al-kawnī*, Oxford, 2006.
Ibn Durustawayh, ʿAbd Allāh, *Taṣḥīḥ al-faṣīḥ,* Baghdad, 1975.
Ibn al-Jawzī, ʿAbd al-Raḥmān, *Aḥkām al-nisā'*, Cairo, 1997.
Ibn Jinnī, Abū al-Fatḥ, *Sirr ṣināʿat al-iʿrāb* vol. 1. Cairo, 1954.
Ibn Khaldūn, Abū Zayd ʿAbd al-Raḥmān, *al-Muqaddima*, vol. 3, New Jersey, 1980.
Ibn Manẓūr, Muḥammad b. Mukarram, *Lisān al-ʿAra*b vol. 1, Beirut, 1997.
Ibn Nadīm, Muḥammad, *al-Fihrist*, vol. 1, London, 1970.
Ibn Qutayba, Abū Muḥammad ʿAbd Allāh, *K. al-Anwā'*, Hyderabad, 1956.
Ibn al-Sarrāj, *K. al-Uṣūl fī al-naḥw*, vol. 1, Beirut, 1987.
Ibn Taymiyya, Taqī al-Dīn Aḥmad, *Majmū' fatāwā Shaykh al-Islām Aḥmad ibn Taymiyya*, vol. 11, Riyadh, 1922.
Idel, Moshe, 'Kabbalah and Elites in Thirteenth-Century Spain', *Mediterranean Historical Review* 9 (1994), pp. 5–19.
Izutsu, Toshihiko, 'The Basic Structure of Metaphysical Thinking in Islam', in *Collected Papers on Islamic Theology and Mysticism*, ed. Hermann Landolt, pp. 97–132, Tehran, 1971.
——, *Sufism and Taoism: A Comparative Study of Key Philosophical Concepts*, Los Angeles, 1983.
al-Jāḥiẓ, Abū ʿUthman ʿAmr, *K. al-Ḥayawān*, vol. 1, Cairo, 1939.
Jeffrey, Arthur, 'Ibn al-ʿArabī's Shajarat al-Kawn', *Studia Islamica* 10 (1959), pp. 43–77.
Johns, Anthony, 'Daḳā'iḳ al-ḥurūf by Abdul al-Rauf of Singkel', *Journal of Royal Asiatic Society* (1955), pp. 139–158.
Kabbani, Hisham, *Angels Unveiled, Sufi Perspective*, Fenton, 2009.
Karamustafa, Ahmad, 'Cosmographical diagrams', *Cartography in the Traditional Islamic and South Asian Societies* (1992), pp. 71–89.
King, David A., *In Synchrony with the Heavens: Studies in Astronomical Timekeeping and Instrumentation in Medieval Islamic Civilization*, vol. 1, Leiden, 2005.
Knysh, Alexander, *Ibn ʿArabi in the Later Islamic Tradition: The Making of a Polemic Image in Medieval Islam*, New York, 1999.
Kramer, Samuel Noah, *From the Poetry of Sumer: Creation, Glorification, Adoration*, Berkeley, 1970.
Lambton, Ann, *State and Government in Medieval Islam*, London, 1981.
Landau, Rom, *The Philosophy of Ibn ʿArabi*, London, 2008.

Lane, Andrew, *Abd al-Ghani al-Nabulusi's Commentary on Ibn Arabi's Fusus al hikam*, Oxford, 2001.
Langermann, Tzvi, 'Arabic cosmology', *Early Science and Medicine* 2 (1997), pp. 185–213.
Levy, Ruben, *The Maʿālim al-qurba fī aḥkām al-ḥisba of Ḍiyā' al-Dīn Muḥammad ibn Muḥammad al-Qurashī al-Shāfiʿī, known as Ibn al-Ukhuwwa*, London, 1938.
Lings, Martin, *A Sufi Saint of the Twentieth Century: Shaikh Ahmad Al-ʿAlawi*, New York, 1971.
López-Anguita, Gracia. 'Ibn ʿArabī's Metaphysics in the Context of Andalusian Mysticism: Some Akbarian Concepts in the Light of Ibn Masarra and Ibn Barrajān', *Religions* (2021), pp. 1–19.
Lory, Pierre, 'The Symbolism of Letters and Language in the Work of Ibn ʿArabī', *Eye of the Heart: A Journal of Traditional Wisdom* (2008), pp. 141–150.
——, *La science des lettres en Islam*, Paris, 2004.
Marlowe, Christopher, *The Tragical History of Doctor Faustus*, London, 1905.
Martin, John, *Theurgy in the Medieval Islamic World: Conceptions of Cosmology in Ibn al-Būnī's Doctrine of Divine Names*, Cairo, 2011.
Massignon, Louis, 'La Philosophie Orientale', *Memorial Avicenna IV* (1954), pp. 1–18.
——, *The Passion of al-Hallāj*, vol. 3, New Jersey, 1982.
McAuley, Denis, *Ibn ʿArabi's Mystical Poems*, Oxford, 2012.
——, 'An A to Z of Sufi Metaphysics: Ibn ʿArabi's Muʿashsharāt', in *The Meeting Place of British Middle East Studies*, eds. Amanda Phillips and Refqa Abu-Remaileh, pp. 60–77, Newcastle upon Tyne, 2009.
Melvin-Koushki, Matthew, 'Astrology, Lettrism, Geomancy: The Occult-Scientific Methods of Post-Mongol Islamicate Imperialism', *The Medieval History Journal* 19 (2016), pp. 142–150.
——, 'Early Modern Islamicate Empire: New Forms of Religiopolitical Legitimacy', *The Wiley Blackwell History of Islam*, ed. Armando Salvatore, pp. 353–376, Hoboken, 2018.
——, 'Imperial Talismanic Love: Ibn Turka's Debate of Feast and Fight (1426) as Philosophical Romance and Letterist Mirror for Timurid Princes', *Der Islam* 96 (2019), pp. 42–86.
——, 'Introduction: De-orienting the Study of Islamicate Occultism', *Arabica* 64 (2017), pp. 287–295.

———, *The Occult Philosophy of Ṣā'in al-Dīn Turka Isfahanī and the Intellectual Millenarianism in Early Timurid Iran*, PhD dissertation, Yale University, 2012.
———, *The Occult Science of Empire in Aqquyunlu-Safavid Iran: Two Shirazi Lettrists and Their Manuals of Magic*, Leiden, 2018.
Milo, Thomas, 'Authentic Arabic: A Case Study: Right-to-Left Font Structure, Font Design and Typography', *Manuscripta Orientalia* 8 (2002), pp. 49–61.
Mir-Kasimov, Orkhan, 'The Ḥurūfī Moses: An Example of Late Medieval 'Heterodox' Interpretation of the Qur'an and Bible', *Journal of Qur'anic Studies* 10 (2008), pp. 21–49.
———, *Christian Apocalyptic Texts in Islamic Messianic Discourse The 'Christian Chapter' of the Jāvidān-nāma-yi kabīr by Faḍl Allāh Astarābādī (d. 796/1394)*, Leiden, 2017.
———, *Words of Power: Hurufi Teachings between Shi'ism and Sufism in Medieval Islam According to His Jawidan-nama-yi kabir Astarabadi*, London, 2017.
Modarressi, Hossein, *Tradition and Survival: A Bibliographical Survey of Early Shi'ite Literature*, vol. 1, Oxford, 2003.
Moin, Ahmad, *Islam and the Millennium: Sacred Kingship and Popular Imagination in Early Modern Iran*, PhD dissertation, University of Michigan, 2010.
Murata, Sachiko, 'Angels', *Islamic Spirituality: Foundations*, ed. S. H. Nasr, pp. 324–344, New York, 1987.
al-Nābulusī, ʿAbd al-Ghanī, *Sharḥ Jawāhir al-nuṣūṣ fī ḥall kālimat al-Fuṣūṣ al-ḥikam*, vol. 1, Cairo, 1887.
Nallino, Carlo Alfonso, 'Il poema mistico arabo d'Ibn al-Fārid in una recente traduzione italiana', *Rivista degli studi orientali* 9 (1919), pp. 1–106.
Nasr, Seyyed Hossein, *Cosmography in pre-Islamic and Islamic Persia*, Tehran, 1971.
al-Nassir, Abdulmunim, *Sībawayh the Phonologist: A critical Study of the Phonetic and Phonological Theory of Sībawayh as Presented in his Treatise al-Kitāb*, London, 1993.
Nettler, L. Ronald, *Sufi Metaphysics and Qur'ānic Prophets: Ibn 'Arabī's Thought and Method in the Fuṣūṣ al-ḥikam*, Cambridge, 2003.
Netton, Richard Ian, *Allāh Transcendent: Studies in the Structure and Semiotics of Islamic Philology, Theology and Cosmology*, London, 1989.
Nwiya, Paul, *Exégèse coranique et langage mystique*, Beirut, 1970.

Osborn, J.R., *Letters of Light: Arabic Script in Calligraphy, Print, and Digital Design*, Cambridge, 2017.
Petersen, Kristian, *Interpreting Islam in China: Pilgrimage, Scripture and Language in the Han Kitab*, Oxford, 2018.
Porter, Venetia, 'The use of the Arabic script in magic', *Proceedings of the Seminar for Arabian Studies* vol. 40 (2010), pp. 131–140.
———, 'Stones to bring Rain? Magical Inscriptions in Linear Kufic on Rock Crystal Amulet-Seals', in *Rivers of Paradise: Water in Islamic Art and Culture*, eds. S.S. Blair and J. Bloom, pp. 131–151, New Haven, 2009.
al-Qashānī, 'Abd al-Razzāq, *A Glossary of Sufi Technical Terms*, London, 1984.
al-Qayṣarī, Dā'ūd, *Foundations of Islamic Mysticism, Qayṣarī's Introduction to Ibn 'Arabī's Fuṣūṣ al-ḥikam: A Parallel English-Arabic Text*, London and New York, 2012.
al-Qushayrī, 'Abd al-Karīm, *Sharḥ asmā' Allāh al-ḥusnā*, Cairo, 1969.
Rappaport, Roy, *Ecology, Meaning, and Religion*, Richmond, 1979.
Redfield, Robert, *The Folk Culture of Yucatan*, Chicago, 1941.
———, *The Little Community and Peasant Society and Culture*, Chicago, 1960.
———, *The Primitive World and Its Transformation*, Ithaca, 1968.
Ritter, Helmut, *The Ocean of the Soul: Man, the World and God in the Stories of Farīd al-Dīn 'Aṭṭar*, Leiden, 2003.
Ryding, Karin Christina, 'Alchemy and Linguistics: Connections in Early Islam', *Alchemy Revisited. Proceedings of the International Conference on the History of Alchemy at the University of Groningen*, ed. Z.R.W.M. von Martels, pp. 117–120, Leiden, 1989.
Saleh, Yasmine, '"Licit Magic": The Touch And Sight Of Islamic Talismanic Scrolls', PhD dissertation, Harvard University, 2014.
al-Sarrāj, Abū Naṣr, *K. al-Luma' fī l-taṣawwuf*, Leiden, 1914.
Savage-Smith, Emilie, 'Celestial Mapping', *The History of Cartography*, vol. 2, eds. Harley and Woodward (1992).
———, *Islamicate Celestial Globes: Their History, Construction and Use*, Washington, 1985.
Schimmel, Annemarie, *Calligraphy and Islamic Culture*, New York, 1990.
———, *Mystical Dimensions of Islam*, Chapel Hill, 1975.
Schoeler, Gregor, *The Oral and the Written in Early Islam*, London, 2006.

Sells, Michael, *Stations of Desire: Love Elegies from Ibn ʿArabi and New Poems*, Jerusalem, 2000.
———, *The Mystical Language of Unsaying*, Chicago, 1994.
al-Shādhilī, Abū al-Mawāhib, *Illumination in Islamic Mysticism: A Translation, with Introduction and Notes, Based Upon a Critical Edition of al-Šādilī's Qawānīn Ḥikam al-ishrāq*, Lahore, 1939.
Shaikh, Saʿdiyya, *Sufi Narratives of Intimacy: Ibn ʿArabī, Gender, and Sexuality*, Chapel Hill, 2011.
Sībawayh, Abū Bishr ʿAmr, *al-Kitāb*, vols. 1–3, Cairo, 1976.
al-Sirāfī, Ḥasan b. ʿAbd Allāh, *Sharḥ Kitāb Sībawayh*, vols. 1–4, Cairo, 1990.
Starcky, Jean, 'Pétra et la Nabatène', *Dictionnaire de la Bible* 7 (1966), pp. 886–1071.
Stearns, Justin, 'Writing the History of the Natural Sciences in the Pre-modern Muslim World: Historiography, Religion, and the Importance of the Early Modern Period,' *History Compass* 9/12 (2011), pp. 923–51.
Stewart, Devin, 'The Mysterious Letters and Other Formal Features of the Qurʾān in Light of Greek and Babylonian Oracular Texts', in *New Perspectives on the Qur'an, The Qur'an in its Historical Context* vol. 2, ed. Gabriel Said Reynold, pp. 323–348, London, 2011.
al-Ṣūfī, ʿAbd al-Raḥmān, *K. Ṣuwar al-kawākib*, Hyderabad, 1954.
al-Sulamī, Abū ʿAbd al-Raḥmān, 'Ḥaqāʾiq al-tafsir', *Mélanges de l'Université Saint Joseph* 43 (1968), pp. 179–230.
———, 'Sharḥ maʿānī al-ḥurūf', in *The Spirit and the Letter*, ed. A. Keeler, pp. 87–142, Oxford, 2011.
Sviri, Sara, 'KUN – the Existence-Bestowing Word in Islamic Mysticism: A Survey of Texts on the Creative Power of Language', *The Poetics of Grammar and the Metaphysics of Language Conference* (2013), pp. 35–67.
Takeshita, Masataka, *Ibn ʿArabī's Theory of the Perfect Man and Its Place in the History of Islamic Thought*, Tokyo, 1987.
Taylor, Christopher, *In the Vicinity of the Righteous: Ziyara and the Veneration of Muslim Saints in Late Medieval Egypt*, Leiden, 1999.
al-Tirmidhi, Abū ʿĪsā Muḥammad, *The Concept of Sainthood in Early Islamic Mysticism. Two works by al-Ḥakīm al-Tirmidhī*, annotated translation by John O'Kane and Bernd Radtke, Surrey, 1996.
Tucker, William, 'Rebels and Gnostics: al-Mugīra Ibn Saʿīd and the Mugīriyya', *Arabica* 22 (1975), pp. 33–47.

Van den Boogert, Nico, 'Some Notes on Maghribi Scripts', *Manuscripts of the Middle East* 4 (1989), pp. 30–43.
Varisco, Daniel Martin, 'Illuminating the Lunar Mansions (*manāzil al-qamar*) in *Šams al-ma'ārif*', *Arabica* 64 (2017), pp. 487–530.
———, 'The Origin of the *anwā'* in Arab Tradition', *Studia Islamica* 74 (1991), pp. 5–28.
Ward, Rachel, 'The Inscription on the Astrolabe by Abd al-Karim in the British Museum', *Muqarnas: An Annual on the Visual Culture of the Islamic World XXI* (2004), pp. 345–358.
Wasserstrom, Steven, 'The Moving Finger Writes', *History of Religions* 25 (1985), pp. 1–29.
Winkel, Eric, *Youth: The Figurative Made Literal*, Oxford, 2016.
———, *The Interactions*, Books 13–16 of the *Futūḥāṭ al-Makkiyyah*, 2 vols. preprint, 2016.
Wright, William, *Lectures on the Comparative Grammar of Semitic Languages*, Cambridge, 1890.
Yazaki, Saeko, *Islamic Mysticism and Abū Ṭālib al-Makkī*, London, 2012.
Yousef, Mohamed Haj, *Ibn 'Arabī: Time and Cosmology*, London, 2001.
Zildzic, Ahmad, *Friend and Foe: The early Ottoman reception of Ibn 'Arabī*, Berkeley, 2012.

Index

Aaron (prophet) – 174
Abraham (prophet) – 170
Abrahamov, Binyamin – 30
Adam – 4, 6, 40–1, 49, 56, 69 n.12, 80, 93 n.27, 120, 155, 171, 176, 179, 185, 189, 190–1, 193, 197
Akkach, Samer – 52, 125, 136, 191
Akman, Kubilay – 26
ʿAlī – 23, 138
alif (isolated) – 7, 11, 14, 23–4, 34–5, 62, 69, 75, 79, 82 n.38, 84–9, 90–9, 102–3, 105–7, 110–19, 123, 130, 137, 139, 152, 170, 175, 177, 193, 198, 199, 200, 202
– *alif* and the Basmala 137, 138
– *alif* as the first of the disjoined letters *alif-lām-mīm* 12, 32–4, 87–8
– *alif madda* 128–9
– *alif* of the Name *al-Raḥīm* 143
– *alif* of the Name *al-Raḥmān* 103–4
– *alif* of the Name Allah 87, 91, 172
– *alif* with *hamza* 75, 117–8
alphabet (Arabic) – 5–6, 8–12, 18, 21–4, 26–7, 29, 30–1, 34, 35 n.50, 36–8, 40, 61–3, 69, 73–4, 77, 78–9, 81–2, 87–90 93 n.27, 95–7, 99–102, 105, 111–3, 117, 124–5, 130, 153, 163, 167, 184, 188, 190–2, 202
al-ʿĀmilī, Bahāʾ al-Dīn – 156
ʿĀmulī, Ḥaydar – 102
angels – 3, 11, 34–5, 40, 49, 54, 56, 71, 77, 78, 80–2, 109, 120–4, 128, 130, p.136 n.58, 137, 140–1, 151, 155–8, 167, 170–5, 179–82, 184, 187–91, 194, 196
Āsiya bint Muzāḥim – 200
Astarābādī, Faḍl Allāh – 6 n.11, 22, 69, 112, 191
ʿAṭṭar, Farīd al-Dīn – 90-1
ʿayn (isolated) – 11, 15 n.1, 22, 32, 34–5, 69, 71, 75, 77, 81, 82 n.38, 124–5, 127–8, 167–8, 170, 192

bāʾ (isolated) – 7, 10–14, 24, 34–5, 51, 62, 69, 73, 77–8, 81–2, 91–2, 93 n.27, 169, 174, 184, 189, 199, 202
bāʾ of the Basmala – 137–40
bāʾ of the Name *al-Rabb* – 171
barzakh (the intermediate world, border between two things) – 8, 91, 101, 177–8

bāṭin (deeper, allusive meaning, hidden aspects of things) – 24, 116, 168
Basmala – 72, 137–40
al-Bīrūnī, Abū al-Rayḥān – 150
al-Bisṭāmī, Abū Yazīd – 50, 56
Bosnevi (al-Būsnawī, ʿAbd Allāh) – 6, 34 n.49, 112, 115, 118–9, 158, 162, 170, 172, 174, 175, 179–80, 183, 193
Breath of the All-Merciful (*al-nafas al-raḥmānī*) – 10–11, 67–9, 70 n.14, 73, 76–7, 80, 90, 96, 103, 116–7, 121–2, 127, 133, 135, 155, 163–4, 172, 176, 188, 195, 198, 199
Brown, Donna – 26
al-Būnī, Aḥmad b. ʿAlī – 22, 26, 28–9, 36, 38, 39
Burkhardt, Titus – 9, 156

Chittick, William – 9, 30, 195 n.32
Chodkiewicz, Michel – 51, 189
Clark, Jane – 10
Cloud (*al-ʿamāʾ*) – 75, 79, 114–9, 120–5, 129, 131, 135, 143
Cole, Juan – 13 n.28
Corbin, Henry – 67
cosmology – 9, 18, 23, 26, 28, 52, 56, 69, 83, 99, 113, 125, 136, 148, 150–1, 153, 175
cryptographs – 15, 53, 54

ḍād – 4, 11, 14, 15 n.1, 22, 34–5, 69, 75, 77, 81–2, 93, 168, 173, 183
Dajjāl – 112
dāl – 11, 14, 34–5, 57, 62, 69, 75, 77, 81–2, 90, 112, 169, 179
ḍamma – 70–1, 177–8, 200
David (prophet) – 112
De Cillis, Maria – 67–8
dhāl – 11, 14, 34–5, 69, 78, 81–2, 169, 187
dhikr (spiritual practice, the act of "remembrance" of God) – 50–1, 58
disjoined letters (*al-ḥurūf al-muqaṭṭaʿāt*) – 12, 24–6, 31–4, 97
divination from Qurʾanic verses (*khawaṣṣ al-Qurʾān*) – 26
Divinity (*ulūhiyya*) – 93, 95
Dot (*nuqṭa*) – 97–9
al-Duʾalī, Abū al-Aswad – 4, 70
Dust (*habāʾ*) – 11, 75, 122–6, 129, 131–2

Ebstein, Michael – 29–30

Elmore, Gerald – 54–6
essence (*dhāt*) – 33, 67, 75, 82, 87–9, 91, 93, 98–100, 102–3, 105, 108, 110–1, 115–16, 118–19, 128, 140, 168, 177, 178, 180, 202

fā' – 11, 15, 34–5, 70–1, 78, 81, 82 n.39, 88, 112, 169, 188
al-Fārisī, Abū 'Alī – 4
fatḥa 70–1, 104
fawātiḥ see disjoined letters
Fifth Heaven *see* Sphere of Venus
First Heaven *see* Sphere of Saturn
First Intellect (*al-'aql al-awwal*) – 40, 51, 75, 77, 82, 88, 120–2, 124, 129, 130–2, 139, 140, 142, 190
Fourth Heaven *see* Sphere of the Sun

gematria (*ḥisāb al-jummal*) – 26
ghayn – 11, 15 n.1, 22, 34–5, 69, 75, 77, 81, 126–8, 168
al-Ghazālī, Abū Ḥāmid – 28
Goldziher, Ignaz – 83
grace (*'ināya*) – 106
Gruendler, Beatrice – 21

hā' – 10–1, 15, 22, 32, 34–6, 69, 75, 77, 80–2, 87, 91–2, 122, 167–8, 172, 198
ḥā' – 11, 14, 34–5, 69, 75, 77, 80–1, 90, 103–4, 123–4, 168
al-Ḥallāj, Manṣūr – 5, 28, 30, 33, 87, 97
hamza – 11, 34–6, 75, 77, 78, 81–2, 84, 113, 115, 117–19, 121–2, 137–9, 167, 190
ḥarf (pl. *ḥurūf*) (particles, letters) – 21, 83 n.42, 107
Heinen, Anton – 151
Hirtenstein, Stephen – 57, 73
Houdas, Octave – 57

Ibn 'Abbās, 'Abd Allāh – 152, 186
Ibn Abī Jumhūr, Muḥammad – 143
Ibn Aḥmad, Khalīl – 70, 79 n.29, 117
Ibn Anas, Mālik – 22 n.6, 113
Ibn Barrajān, Abū al-Ḥakam – 31
Ibn Jinnī, Abū al-Fatḥ – 117
Ibn Khaldūn, Abū Zayd 'Abd al-Raḥmān – 22, 26–8, 31, 39 n.63
Ibn Masarra, Abū 'Abd Allāh – 28–30, 37, 124, 142

Ibn Sabʿīn, ʿAbd al-Ḥaqq – 122, 191–3
Ibn al-Sarrāj, Abū Bakr b. Sahl – 21 n.5, 61
Ibn Sawdakīn, Shams al-Dīn Ismāʿīl – 32, 36, 38, 95, 139
Ibn Taymiyya, Taqī al-Dīn Aḥmad – 58, 197
Ibn ʿUdd, ʿAdnān – 21
Idris (prophet) – 184
ʿilm, pl. *ʿulūm* as science and/or knowledge of:
– *ʿilm al-awfāq* (the divination method) – 26
– *ʿilm al-faʾl* (bibliomancy) – 27
– *ʿilm al-ḥurūf* (science of letters) – 3, 5–7, 9–12, 16–18, 21–24, 26–31, 36, 39, 41, 51, 56, 61, 82, 111–2, 151, 153, 170, 175, 198, 202
– *ʿilm al-kīmiyāʾ* (alchemy) – 27
– *al-ʿilm al-kullī* (the universal science), *see ʿilm al-ḥurūf*
– *ʿilm al-nujūm* (astrology) – 27
– *ʿilm al-ruqā* (Qurʾanic spell magic) – 27
– *al-ʿilm al-ṭabīʿī* (natural philosophy) –
–*ʿilm al-ṭalāsim* (the art of making talismans) – 32
– occult sciences (*al-ʿulūm al-gharība*) – 26-8, 31, 39, 50, 57, 176
Iṣfahānī, Ibn Turka – 22
Izutsu, Toshihiko – 102

Jabarūt (the intermediate world, *ʿālam al-jabarūt*) – 30, 33, 69–70, 81–2, 92, 105, 138, 152, 175, 188
Jābir b. Ḥayyān – 32
jafr – 23
Jeffrey, Arthur – 68, 177 n.156
Jesus (prophet) – 31, 47, 54, 56, 70 n.14, 171, 176
al-Jīlī, ʿAbd al-Karīm – 32, 93 n.26
jīm – 11, 14, 34–5, 69, 75, 77, 81–2, 156, 168
Joseph (prophet) – 175
al-Junayd, Muḥammad – 50

kāf – 11, 15, 34–5, 62, 69, 75, 81–2, 112, 142, 168, 177–8
karb (the state of absolute abundance of the Divine Being) – 67
kasra – 70–1, 138
khāʾ – 11, 14, 31 n.38, 34–5, 69, 75, 77, 80–1, 133, 142, 168
al-Kharrāz, Abū Saʿīd – 11, 28, 111
khuluq (physiognomy, moral disposition) – 47–9
al-Kirmānī, Ḥamīd al-Dīn – 29
Kramer, Samuel – 68

Kuzminac, Jovan – 103

lām – 11, 15, 34–5, 62, 69, 75, 77, 81–2, 90–2, 95, 103–4, 142, 193, 197, 201
lām-alif – 12, 14, 75, 87, 93, 95–7, 99, 100, 102–4, 131, 197
al-Laythi, Naṣr – 79
Lory, Pierre – 29, 203

al-Mahdawī, Abū al-ʿAbbās – 57
al-Makkī, Abū Ṭālib – 30, 155
Malakūt (the angelic realm, *ʿālam al-malakūt*) – 30, 33, 56, 69, 70, 81–2, 82 n.39, 92, 105 n.67, 138, 142, 152, 188
Marlowe, Christopher – 20
Massignon, Louis – 5, 93
Melvin-Koushki, Matthew – 22, 27
Milo, Thomas – 72–3
mīm 11, 12, 15, 22, 34–5, 59, 60, 62–3, 69, 77, 78, 81–2, 90, 103–5, 111 n.91, 140, 147–8, 169, 190, 197, 200
- *mīm* as the third of the disjoined letters *alif–lām–mīm* 12, 25, 32–4
- *mīm* of the Name *al-Raḥīm* 143
Mir-Kasimov, Orkhan – 6 n.11
Mist (*bukhār*) *see* Cloud
miʿrāj (the ascension of the prophet Muhammad) – 155
Moses (prophet) – 64, 173, 181
al-Mughīra b. Saʿīd – 22–3, 31
Muhammad (prophet) – 22, 24, 34, 40, 45, 58, 81, 96, 109, 121, 135, 141, 156, 170, 174, 197, 200
Mulk (the corporeal world, *ʿālam al-mulk*) – 30, 33, 56, 62, 69, 70, 81–2, 92, 105, 138, 142, 152, 172, 188
Murata, Sachiko – 39

al-Nābulusī, ʿAbd al-Ghanī – 10, 107
Nallino, Carlo Alfonso – 27
Names of God (*asmāʾ Allāh*) – 4, 6, 21, 26, 40, 69 n.12, 70 n.14, 87, 100–1, 112, 115, 119, 135, 137, 144, 153–4, 167, 175, 178 n.162, 188, 190
al-Nasafī, Aḥmad – 29
Neoplatonism – 13 n.28, 29
Netton, Richard – 52

nūn 11, 15, 25, 34–5, 62–3, 69, 75, 77, 81, 91, 103–5, 110, 147, 162–3, 168, 174, 177, 183, 193, 197, 202

ontology – 4, 6, 28, 41, 52, 69, 113, 155
Orbit (air, fire, water) – 77–8, 150, 152, 179–82, 194

Pedestal (*kursī*) – 11, 75, 77, 135–6, 142–3, 150–1, 156–7, 162–3, 186, 194
Pen (*al-qalam*) *see* First Intellect
Perfect Human (*al-insān al-kāmil*) – 31, 34 n.48, 51, 149, 178, 182, 197–9, 200–2
Pole (*quṭb*) – 174–5
Porter, Venetia 32, 57, 79
Primordial Matter (*hayūlā*) 76–7, *see* Dust
Protected Tablet (*al-lawḥ al-maḥfūẓ*) – 88, 120–2, 124, 130, 143, 182
Ptolemy – 148–9, 150, 159, 165

qāf – 11, 13, 15, 34–6, 62, 69, 75, 77, 81–2, 133, 136–7, 168
al-Qāshānī, ʿAbd al-Razzāq – 6, 83, 84, 87, 102, 110, 111, 119, 121, 122, 171 n.15, 174–5, 180, 198
al-Qayṣarī, Dāwūd – 6, 44, 118 n.17, 130

rāʾ – 11, 14, 24, 35, 62, 69, 75, 77, 81–2, 91, 103–4, 112, 143, 168, 171, 175
rational mind (*ʿaql*) – 16, 18, 43–4, 47, 59, 93, 101, 118, 123, 178, 184, 195
Rāzī, Fakhr al-Dīn – 150
resurrection (*qiyāma*) – 56, 101, 141
Rudavsky, Tamar – 150

ṣād – 11, 14–5, 22, 31, 34–6, 69, 77–8, 81–2, 100, 145, 147, 169, 182–3, 196
ṣamt (silence) – 91
Savage-Smith, Emilie – 165
Schimmel, Annemarie – 5, 52, 95, 130
Second Heaven *see* Sphere of Jupiter
sensation (*al-ḥiss*) – 17
Seventh Heaven *see* Sphere of the Moon
al-Shāfiʿī, Abū ʿAbd Allāh – 83
Shariʿa – 44, 60, 61

shīn – 11, 14, 34–5, 69, 75, 77, 81–2, 162, 168, 170
Shiʿi – 23–4, 26, 28
Sībawayh, Abū Bishr ʿAmr – 78–9, 82, 117
siḥr (sorcery) – 26–7
sīmiyāʾ (letter magic) – 26–7, 176
sīn – 11, 14, 22, 34–5, 69, 77–8, 81–2, 137–8, 140, 169–170, 181
al-Sirāfī, Abū Saʿīd – 4 n.5
Sixth Heaven *see* Sphere of Mercury
Sphere of Jupiter 11, 75, 148–150, 152, 172–4, 194
Sphere of Mars 11, 75, 148– 150, 152, 174, 194
Sphere of Mercury 11, 75, 80, 148–150, 152, 175–9
Sphere of Saturn 11, 75, 80–1, 148–152, 170–1, 194
Sphere of the Fixed Stars (*falak al-burūj*) 11, 75, 77, 149, 150, 152, 154, 156–60, 162, 164, 170, 172
Sphere of the Moon 11, 75, 148–50, 152, 155, 179, 194
Sphere of the Sun 11, 75, 148–50, 152, 174–5, 194
Sphere of Venus 11, 75, 148–50, 152, 175, 194
spirits of the letters 8, 19, 42–3
spiritual concentration (*ḥimma*) – 8,
Starcky, Jean – 21
Starless Sphere (*al-falak al-aṭlas*) 11, 75, 77, 150, 153–4, 156–9, 162–3, 170, 172
Straight Path (*al-ṣīrāṭ al-mustaqīm*) – 34, 45
Sufism (*taṣawwuf*) – 28, 30–1, 47, 67, 109
al-Sulamī, Abū ʿAbd al-Raḥmān – 24, 32–3, 46–7, 87, 170–1
sura (chapter of the Qur'an) – 24–5, 31–4, 40, 49, 52, 69, 89, 95–7, 103, 108-10, 138-40, 142, 154, 173, 181–3, 187, 190, 196–7
al-Suyūṭī, Jalāl al-Dīn – 4, 151

tāʾ – 11, 14, 34–6, 62, 69, 73, 75, 77, 82, 169, 180
ṭāʾ 11, 14, 15 n.1, 34–6, 62, 69, 73, 75, 77, 81–2, 100, 169, 175
Takeshita, Masataka – 30
talisman – 10, 26, 31–4, 39, 57
Taṣnīf al-ʿulūm (*The Classification of Sciences*) –27
thāʾ – 11, 14, 31, 34–5, 62, 69, 77–8, 81–2, 169, 187
Thaʿlab, Aḥmad b. Yaḥyā – 5 n.9
Throne (*ʿarsh*) – 11, 75, 77, 133, 135–7, 140–3, 145, 150–1, 155–6, 162–3, 174, 186, 190, 194, 196
al-Tirmidhī, al-Ḥakīm – 5-6
Torah – 22, 54, 109, 139

Tree of Being (*Shajarat al-kawn*) – 68–9, 177
Tūṣī, Naṣīr al-Dīn – 150
al-Tustarī, Sahl – 28–30, 124
al-Tuwaytimī, Abū Yaḥyā Babkar al-Hashmī – 182

Universal Body (*al-jism al-kullī*) – 11, 75, 77, 120, 126–7, 129, 131, 135–6
Universal Nature (*al-tabiʿa al-kulliya*) – 11, 75, 77, 120, 124–6, 129, 131
Universal Soul (*al-nafs al-kulliya*) *see* Protected Tablet
ʿUzayr (prophet) – 45

wāw – 11, 15, 34–5, 37, 62–3, 69, 71, 77–8, 81–4, 90, 112, 147–8, 163, 169, 178, 197–200
Winkel, Eric – 98–9
Wolff, Christian – 150

yāʾ – 11, 15, 32, 34–5, 62, 69, 71, 75, 77, 81–2, 96, 143, 168, 170–1
Yazdī, Sharaf al-Dīn ʿAlī – 22

zāy – 11, 14, 34–5, 62, 69, 77–8, 81–2, 152, 169